Citadel to City-State

The Transformation of Greece, 1200–700 B.C.E.

Citadel to
City-State

by Carol G. Thomas
and Craig Conant

Indiana University Press

BLOOMINGTON *&* INDIANAPOLIS

This book is a publication of

Indiana University Press

601 North Morton Street
Bloomington, IN 47404-3797 USA

http://iupress.indiana.edu

Telephone orders 800-842-6796
Fax orders 812-855-7931
Orders by e-mail iuporder@indiana.edu

MANUFACTURED IN THE UNITED STATES OF AMERICA

Library of Congress Cataloging-in-Publication Data

Thomas, Carol G., date
Citadel to city-state : the transformation of Greece, 1200–700 B.C.E. /
by Carol G. Thomas and Craig Conant.
p.   cm.
Includes bibliographical references and index.
ISBN 0-253-33496-9 (cloth : alk. paper)
1. Greece—Civilization—To 146 B.C. 2. Greece—History—Geometric period, ca.
900–700 B.C. 3. City-states—Greece—History. I. Conant, Craig, date. II. Title.
DF221.5.T46 1999
938'.01—dc21   98-48994
ISBN 978-0-253-33496-1 (cloth : alk. paper)
ISBN 978-0-253-21602-1 (pbk.)

4 5 6 7 8   15 14 13 12 11 10

For my husband, Richard Johnson;
you do persuade my heart (*Odyssey* 23.230).

—CGT

For my mother and father, Vivian and Cyril Conant,
who inspired and supported this work;
and for my wife, Sandy, and my son, Nathaniel,
who helped carry it out.

—CC

For now

truly is a race of iron, and

men never rest from labor and sorrow by

day, and from perishing by night; and the gods lay

sore troubles upon them. But, notwithstanding,

even these shall have some good

mingled with their evils.

Hesiod, *Works and Days* 176–179

CONTENTS

LIST OF ILLUSTRATIONS

PREFACE

In the vast reach of ancient Greek history, a period dubbed "the Dark Age" has modest appeal. By comparison with the time of golden Mycenae, the classical world of Periclean Athens, or the conquest of Persia by Alexander, centuries of poverty and isolation serve only to throw the other periods into greater relief. Or so it would seem until recently. In fact, a 1995 manuscript treating the ancient world simply omitted these four and a half centuries. Yet they deserve mention not merely in the name of historical thoroughness but for their significance in linking two more complex cultures, the Bronze and Classical Ages. More than a link, these four centuries may be studied for their own intrinsic worth. Poverty and silence may be more representative of the human condition than wealth and brilliance in any age, whether it be Classical Greece, Eighteenth Dynasty Egypt, or Ch'in Dynasty China. This book is intended to validate the claims of the Greek Dark Age in the eyes of a broad readership interested in the processes of change, particularly in antiquity.

It rests on the earliest studies of Dark Age Greece and is meant as an introduction to and complement of such seminal, but highly technical works as V. R. d'A. Desborough's *The Last Mycenaeans and Their Successors* (1964), Anthony Snodgrass' *The Dark Age of Greece* (1971), and Nicholas Coldstream's *Geometric Greece* (1977). This study depends, too, on more recent excavation reports and journal literature, on the one hand, and on analyses of the historical framework of the Homeric poems, on the other. Although work in these areas must and will continue, it is now possible to develop a larger and longer view of the entire period by blending the main categories of particular evidence that have been produced. Though the Dark Age may be less dark, it contains many murky, and thus uncertain, points. Of course, this work carries the personal reflections of its authors.

The nature of change can be provocative; it can also be dull. Many readers soon tire of abstract analyses of development and demand to know "*Who* was making these changes?" Unfortunately, this sensible question cannot be answered without written evidence from the very subjects of inquiry. The Dark Age is dark, in large part, because it has left no written records. However, archaeology provides an alternative means of breathing life into process: each century of the Dark Age is marked by basic characteristics and each can be studied concretely through a particular, well-excavated site. We have ventured to create the life of real, but nameless people in six quite different communities—a Plutarch's Lives of Places, not individuals, as it were.

We are indebted to many: those in whose tracks we have followed; friends and colleagues who have offered counsel as our research and writing moved forward. We are grateful to the anonymous reader of the first version of the manuscript submitted to Indiana University Press. Comments from that person called our attention to a number of problems that required remedy. The editorial eye of Richard von Kleinsmid is keen and keenly appreciated. And it has been a pleasure to work again under the guidance of Robert Sloan at Indiana University Press. We also thank Michael Lundell, Assistant Managing Editor at Indiana University Press, for turning his editorial skills to all matters great and small.

A remarkable network of assistants emerged in arranging illustrations for the book. To Alice Alden's skilled draftsmanship we owe the majority of our maps, while Anne Lou Robkin's artistic ability, coupled with a capacity to recreate the past, produced many of the artistic reconstructions. Additionally, for granting permission to reproduce illustrations of various items, we gratefully thank the following: the American School of Classical Studies at Athens; the managing committee of the British School at Athens; the Detroit Institute of Arts Founders Society; the Deutsches Archäologisches Institut, Athens; John M. Fossey, editor and copyright holder of the Boeotia Antigua series, who retains all copyright even after the permission to reproduce figure 2.2 in G. Gauvin and J. Marin "Le Site d'Askra et ses carrières," *Boeotia Antigua* 2 (1992) 7–15 and fig. 15 in P. W. Wallace, "The Tomb of Hesiod and the Treasury of Minyas at Orkhomenos," *Proceedings of the Third International Conference on Boiotian Antiquities* (Amsterdam 1985) 165–179; the Hellenic Geographical Service; Indiana University Press; William A. McDonald; University of Minnesota Press; Oxford University Press; Princeton University Press; Random House; Keith Stanley, editor of *Greek, Roman, and Byzantine Studies*. Without the prompt response to calls for help by friends from Athens to Leiden and London to Durham, North Carolina, and St. Paul, Minnesota, these pages would be far less illuminated by representations. Frances and Howard Keller, who have established a Keller Fund in the Department of History at the University of Washington to assist faculty with research expenses, have substantially subsidized the reproduction of these materials.

We would also like to express our gratitude for the support and assistance of our families and friends. In particular we wish to recognize the assistance of Sandra Conant in putting together the index and of Nathaniel Conant who typed a number of the chapters. To the skill and patience of Ed Kamai we owe migration of electronic text between IBM and Mac platforms, then from electronic bytes to printed manuscript.

INTRODUCTION

The Classical Greeks knew that generation upon generation separated them from their most distant ancestors. According to their earliest known chronological scheme, the past stretched backward from the present Age of Iron to an Age of Heroes, which was preceded by a Bronze Age, a Silver Age, and earliest of all, an Age of Gold. Until recently, modern students of ancient Greece found such an image colorful but worthy of little credence: it was supposed that the Greeks fabricated a past in order to compare more favorably with such venerable contemporaries as Egypt and Babylon.

From the last third of the nineteenth century of the present era, however, believers in the Greeks' view of their past drew confirmation from the soil itself. Several sites demonstrated that civilization had flourished in the Aegean area while the Pharaohs were reaching the pinnacle of power in Egypt and the Hittites were creating an extensive empire reaching out from Anatolia. The cultures of the Greek mainland and neighboring islands had become increasingly complex during the third and second millennia, reaching a high point of power and wealth between 1600 and 1200 B.C.E. Named for its most famous location, this first civilization of Greece has been dubbed the Mycenaean Age.

Unlike Egypt and Babylonia, however, monuments of this Golden Age did not endure. The late thirteenth and twelfth centuries witnessed massive destructions accompanied by vast movements of people throughout the eastern Mediterranean. Damage in the Aegean was particularly severe, tumbling palaces and small villages alike, bringing an end to specialized crafts, causing the loss of literacy, and resulting in enormous depopulation. Yet the decline of population and the forgetfulness of skills were not complete: some people survived to carve out an existence in grim conditions. The collapse of the

Bronze Age civilization and the painfully slow transformation of life over the next five centuries combined to create Classical Greece.

> Greek civilization could never have arisen if . . . disruption had not occurred and had not shaken the old conventions. In the dull, repetitive cases of Mycenaean pottery which can be seen in modern museums, in the palace tablets which now show the centralizing drive of royal masters, we can sense that the Mycenaean world was far too attached to outside models ever to develop an independent outlook of its own. These links were broken. . . . and so men were set free to create new political and intellectual views, once the worst of the chaos was over. (Starr 1961b, 74)

These comments, written over thirty years ago by Chester Starr, represent the once accepted view of the relationship between the first civilization of Greece and its successor, Classical Greece: the two periods and their cultures were thought to be virtually unconnected. According to this view, the chaotic transition from the Bronze to the Iron Age wiped out most traces of Mycenaean culture and caused a clean break which enabled—even forced—a fresh start. Experiments with ways of maintaining individual and communal life in the harsh conditions of the early first millennium produced cultural patterns very different from those of the second millennium and led directly to the institutions and values of Classical Greece. In place of citadels with their kings, massive fortifications, and intricate systems of accounting stood city-states whose citizens governed themselves and whose very records reveal in their purpose, script, and content the immense differences of life.

However, before accepting the argument of a complete break, we would do well to examine its implications. That modern Western society owes an enormous debt to the Classical world has been stated so often that it has become a cliché. Many of our ideas and prejudices regarding politics, the arts, the sciences, and the individual's place in society find echoes in that world. Greek artists, politicians, and philosophers of the sixth, fifth, and fourth centuries were themselves heavily influenced by the works of Homer and Hesiod, works now dated to the late eighth and early seventh centuries. But who or what influenced Homer and Hesiod? According to the view that elements of Bronze Age civilization were virtually erased, the culture of the second millennium could have had no major influence. Thus the

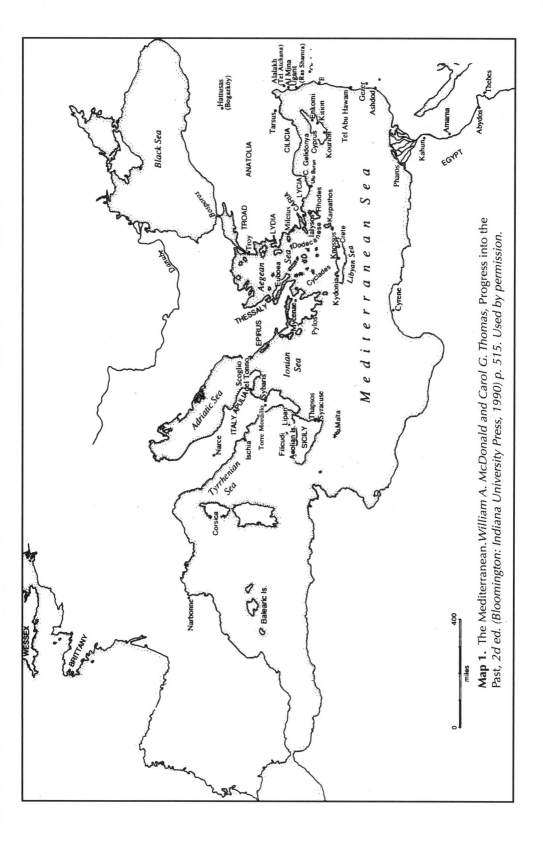

Map 1. The Mediterranean. William A. McDonald and Carol G. Thomas, *Progress into the Past, 2d ed.* (Bloomington: Indiana University Press, 1990) p. 515. Used by permission.

Iliad, while retelling a tale set in the Bronze Age, is describing the world of the Dark Age—an age that effected a clean break with the past. It must be asked whether it is fair to deny to the Bronze Age any reflection or reverberation in subsequent periods. And it is equally necessary to recognize the force of the Dark Age in shaping the features of Classical Greece.

Archaeological evidence has suggested a number of links between the Mycenaean and Classical Ages. The Bronze Age palace site of Athens, for example, was continuously inhabited from the Bronze Age into the Classical period, and other sites have revealed similar continuity. Continuous development marks the language of the inhabitants of Greece; the basic form of the temple can be detected in the large central room, or *megaron*, of the Bronze Age palace; pottery design shows constant evolution across the five centuries; and the tombs of Mycenaean "heroes" were the locations of renewed cult activity in the eighth century. In sum, an increasing body of evidence suggests a different interpretation of the historical path of early Greece, one that sees the Dark Age as a bridge joining the Mycenaean and Classical worlds. To be sure, the two cultures have very distinctive characteristics. However, that very distinction is a result of the Dark Age, which provided not only a bridge but a long period of transition. Five hundred years is, after all, a long time in a culture's history.

We have been speaking confidently of an age with fixed dates, from the end of the thirteenth to the close of the eighth century B.C.E. but it must be stated at the outset that the concept of a dark age—a lengthy, severe, and widespread cultural recession—is a recent product, essentially a twentieth-century creation. Nor is it unanimously accepted even today. The existence of such an epoch has been challenged by some; others argue for a greatly reduced duration. Let us begin with the ancient view.

With the possible exception of Hesiod, no one in antiquity describes a dark age following the Age of Heroes. While Herodotus (1.5.4) had a historical concept of the rise and fall of individual states within the Greek world, he did not extend this idea to encompass a generalized decline in Greek civilization at the end of the Heroic Age. Thucydides was even more positive in his view of the general trend of Greek history. Aside from a lengthy period of political turmoil and movement from north to south (1.12.3–4), he knows of nothing matching our idea of a dark age. His description of earlier times when people were migratory, engaged in no commerce with one another, barely cultivated the land, and had no accumulations of wealth might be a memory of the Dark Age, but it also might be a traditional tale of all very ancient times. In his account of the aftermath of the Trojan war, Thucydides tells of civil strife and movements of people that forced others into exile and forced cities to move to new locations, but nothing in his account serves as evidence for the widespread destruction and decline in population we associate with the Dark Age.

One would think that the poet of the *Iliad* and *Odyssey*, living at the end of the eighth century, would have more to say about the dark time which immediately preceded his own. He does not. Except for a passing unfavorable comparison between the strength of the men of his own day and that of the heroes in his poetry, there is no overt indication that the poet lived in a society just emerging from one of the darkest periods of history.

Thus the lone exception to the apparent forgetfulness of the ancients is Hesiod. In a famous passage in *Works and Days* (109–201), the poet sets forth an inexorably descending order of world ages: Gold, Silver, Bronze, Heroes, and finally, his own age, a cruel Age of Iron. The naming of the last three ages seems, to the casual observer, an uncanny coincidence. The age preceding the Dark age was indeed an age of bronze, and since Hesiod includes the heroes of the Trojan War in his Age of Heroes he is again recalling what is probably memory of an historical event. The Bronze Age and Trojan War were followed by an age when the use of iron grew more prevalent and, at least in its earlier phases, this age was indeed poor, hard, and cruel.

However, in spite of these coincidences, Hesiod's concept of unrelieved decline from "the Beginning" may be a religious or philosophical idea, or perhaps it is a literary device. It is not a genuine idea of history, for it is not so much Hesiod's intention to retell a sequence of past events as it is to show the downward trajectory of those events. Moreover, the picture of his own age casts doubt on the validity of the account as historical since that world had reclaimed a share of political stability, possessed a burgeoning population which had to be relieved by means of colonization, and was beginning to employ an art of writing distinct from the script employed in the Bronze Age citadels. Difficult as it is for people to put their own times or even the recent past into perspective, one would think that Hesiod, a likely witness to the renaissance of the eighth century, would have realized that things were getting better. Perhaps it is only natural to glorify the past at the expense of the present and thus Hesiod was simply following the dictates of human nature rather than those governing sober historical inquiry. Whatever the explanation may be, Hesiod recalls the past following the Trojan War with no more accuracy than the other ancient sources.

Since no one before the twentieth century C.E. thought to make a serious exploration of the Greek Dark Age, the preceding can hardly serve as a fair criticism of Hesiod or any other Greek writer of antiquity.[1] Just as the Greeks knew about the Age of Heroes and of events in their own times, all the while ignoring or glossing over the intervening years of which they knew little or nothing, so modern scholars since Schliemann have had a tendency to choose for their areas of study either the Bronze Age or the literate Greek world after ca. 750, while ignoring the awkward gap in between, characterized by neither palaces nor poetry. Even the archaeological rediscovery of Bronze Age Greece did not encourage recognition of a Dark Age.[2] Schliemann's claims to have uncovered the site of the Trojan War and the homes of the Greek warriors were often greeted with merciless ridicule, especially in his native Germany. For the Germans, trained in the textual analytical school, Schliemann's excavations at Troy and Mycenae were at best an inconvenience, and at worst, an act of grave robbery. Thus, those of this conviction could not acknowledge the existence of a Greek Dark Age because such acknowledgment would lend authority to Schliemann and his ridiculous notions. Some classical scholars reacted positively to Schliemann's discoveries but even enthusiasts were not led to investigate the Mycenaean collapse and its aftermath. In their zeal to link Schliemann's discoveries with passages from the *Iliad*, his supporters were for a time convinced that Homer must have been a contemporary of the Trojan War. If this were so, there could be no dark age separating Homer from the heroic setting of his poems.

Perhaps the chief impetus to define the awkward gap was tied to the means used to record the epics—the Greek alphabet. Only when the Greek development of the alphabet was fixed in time did scholars begin to take seriously the concept of a dark age: at the same time that evidence seemed to point to an eighth-century date for the return of literacy, Schliemann's successors at Mycenae and Troy were becoming more secure in dating their finds to the second half of the second millennium. Between the latest Mycenaean material and the adoption of the alphabet lay a four-century-long hiatus—a chronological and cultural blank. It is this hiatus which is now known as the Greek Dark Age. To this day, it is a matter of some debate whether the term "dark age" refers to the conditions prevailing during those centuries or our own ignorance of them.

Initially, this "new" era was described only in comparison with the high cultures which had preceded and followed it.[3] The Dark Age was a trough into which the brilliant Mycenaean civilization had somehow fallen and from which the miracle of Classical Greece was somehow to emerge. However, as evidence continued to accumulate for the cultures on either side of the Dark Age divide, it became increasingly apparent that great differences separated the Mycenaean Age from the Classical period, and scholars began to ask how the one gave rise to the other. With this question, the period between the two ages achieved a new significance.[4]

As we have seen, some deny any direct link between Mycenaean and Classical Greece. On the view that there was complete, or nearly complete, discontinuity between the two periods, the importance of the Dark Age was as fallow ground from which sprang the glory of Classical Greece. The reconstruction of British scholar Vincent Desborough sets forth the essential features of this position. The Mycenaean citadels were destroyed one by one toward the end of the thirteenth century or early in the twelfth by unknown agents. Some sites were subsequently reoccupied and, as in the case of Mycenae, even regained a modicum of their former prosperity before disaster struck again. New invaders accomplished a second destruction and remained in the affected areas long enough to pillage, but they did not settle there. Later still, during the late twelfth or early eleventh century, a new population came into the destroyed world from the north—this was the Dorian Invasion. Encountering a lingering but weak Mycenaean inheritance, the Dorians submerged it in customs of their own. With the exception of the potter's craft, these northerners retained little of Mycenaean culture. Certain religious beliefs and practices may have continued, but in Desborough's estimation (1964, 243–44), archaeology does not supply good evidence. We will examine the pros and cons of this argument in subsequent chapters. For now we will only state that for each "invasion" Desborough found no instance in which the "invaders" actually settled down to enjoy their ill-gotten gains. In every case of destruction, either Mycenaeans reoccupied the site or it was abandoned. As for the intruders, they seem to have vanished into thin air leaving Desborough at a loss to explain their actions.

This view has been modified considerably in the last twenty-five years. Invaders and new populations figure far less prominently and, at the same time, evidence of continuity in artifact types and cult practices is growing steadily. Additionally, new directions in the field of archaeology are proving especially beneficial to the study of this little-documented period of Greek antiquity. Slow but constant change can be detected even in cultures with such meager records as that of the "hiatus" in early Greece.

The Nature of the Evidence

Even the very limited written evidence that exists for Late Bronze Age Greece vanishes for the Dark Age. Its centuries were apparently a time of non-literacy, at least from our perspective: while it is possible that some Dark Age Greeks could read and write, no evidence survives for the benefit of the historian.

Consequently, physical remains must be our primary source; in fact, the standard accounts are largely presentations of the material evidence. As J. N. Coldstream put it in his treatment of Greek civilization from circa 900 to 700 B.C.E., "Until the rise of archaeological research, very little could be known about this long and obscure period" (1977, 17). As a result of its reliance on physical remains, the resulting picture bears the characteristic marks of archaeological data. The dates that emerge are relative rather than absolute; when a way of life can be defined, it describes groups of people not individuals; types of objects and patterns, not specifics, form the thrust of the story. But there are several kinds of archaeological evidence: settlements, sanctuaries, tombs and even whole cemeteries, and specific objects are sufficient to recreate a narrative of the five dark centuries.

Settlement sites fell off dramatically in the twelfth-century time of troubles; however, some important settlements continued, and these are well-known as a consequence of their earlier (and sometimes later) importance. Continuing excavation provides an increasingly clear picture of such major centers as Mycenae, Tiryns, Argos, Athens, and Knossos. Less prominent Bronze Age sites were also continuously occupied—or almost so. Excavations at such sites are revealing the kinds of settlement that succeeded when the Mycenaean centers collapsed. Among the most thoroughly explored are Nichoria in the southwest Peloponnese; Lefkandi, Chalcis, and Eretria on the island of Euboea; Koukounaries on Paros; Zagora on Andros; Emporio on Chios; several locations on the southern coast of Cyprus; Kato Syme Biannou, Dreros, Kavousi, Vronda, and Kastro on Crete; Smyrna in Asia Minor; and, particularly for the late Dark Age, new settlements in Sicily and southern Italy. Sanctuaries have received the attention of archaeologists for similar reasons: their role in Classical Greece naturally has created interest in their origin.

Not only homes of the living but burials for the dead reveal patterns of communal organization—even when, as in the case of Perati in Attica and Vronda on Crete, they are cemeteries without apparent settlements. In a recent, innovative use of burial patterns, some archaeologists have found a way to discern developments within the social structure in Dark Age Greece (I. Morris 1987; Whitley 1991b).

Excavations of both burials and settlements uncover objects, and for the Dark Age, pottery is the most abundant category of remaining evidence. Its development provides the main dating scheme of the age: Submycenaean, Protogeometric, and Geometric all refer to shape, ceramic technique, and design of pottery forms as they changed over time. Metal objects reveal technology, indicate types of items in use, and in a more general way, provide a dating scheme: as iron technology spread, the Bronze Age yielded to the Iron Age. Rarer materials, such as ivory and gemstones, form a part of the physical record that is especially important in judging links with the larger Mediterranean world since often their provenance is foreign.

When remains are as limited as they are for Dark Age Greece, the picture is extremely sketchy. Consequently, recent developments that turn the discipline of archaeology in new directions have been especially useful. The "new archaeology," which uses the environment as a larger context for its investigation and relies on methods other than those employed in excavation, is well suited to study of the Greek Dark Age. Through "survey archaeology" a specific region is examined by teams of people walking at fixed intervals and advancing in a line. Their purpose is to note and record features of the terrain and artifacts on the land's surface. Clusters of artifacts and unusual features of the land are signs of earlier sites, and identification of sites is the objective of these surveys, whose goal is to detect the changing relationship between the environment and human activity. While special attention is often directed to a specific period of time, the net of survey archaeology is usually cast widely.

The University of Minnesota Messenia Expedition, one of the first large efforts, carried the subtitle *Reconstructing a Bronze Age Regional Environment* (McDonald and Rapp, 1972). Although special attention was given to the Bronze Age, the interdisciplinary team studied the habitation pattern in a region of 1400 square miles for all periods from the Neolithic to the Roman era. Subsequent surveys tend to have a similarly wide chronological range. An on-going series of articles in the *American Journal of Archaeology* is reviewing the extent and character of archaeological evidence in various periods and regions of Greece.[5] The published articles treating Aegean prehistory focus on the Bronze Age, but since it is the very nature of archaeology to examine the evidence over time, the discussions are extremely helpful to students of the Dark Age.

The archaeological record can also be used in a very different way: evaluation of items missing from the record will suggest at least a cultural level of society even if it will not provide a full picture of life. The Greek Dark Age deserves its name, in large measure, because of the limited evidence it furnishes to modern-day students. By comparison with the preceding Bronze Age, the physical remains are simpler as well as fewer. Palace centers fell into ruins and were not rebuilt; with them disappeared both the administrative records and the road systems that had linked parts of a territory with one another. Large works projects of every sort are no longer in evidence, and great stores of wealth are not to be found. Earlier indications of variety quickly dwindled: while some eighty pottery shapes were known from Bronze Age Pylos alone, only ten shapes are defined for the Submycenaean period. Foreign objects too are minimal in the Dark Age while they were in clear evidence during the Late Bronze Age. The universality of cultural features intensifying in Greece during the fourteenth and thirteenth centuries separated into regionalism in succeeding centuries

The absences, considered together, offer up the outlines of a description: while Bronze Age society was based on centers of power that were in contact with one another and with other parts of the Aegean and Mediterranean in ways that generated impressive wealth, the refugee communities particularly characteristic of the early Dark Age existed in relative isolation. Rather than the complex, hierarchical stratification indicated by Bronze Age remains, Dark Age evidence speaks to homogeneity and simplicity of social organization.

Although some would contest it, the prevailing view is that the Dark Age was totally non-literate. The limited literacy of the Mycenaean Linear B tablets employed for accounting purposes appears to have disappeared in the early twelfth century with the collapse of the administrative systems that had called it forth. A new form of writing—alphabetic—made its earliest attested appearance during the eighth century. Thus, no written records exist for most of the period. However, collective memory was necessary to survival even in these hard times—probably especially in such hard times. Greeks of the Dark Age relied on memory and oral tradition to pass essential information from one generation to the next. We possess a final product of that tradition in the Homeric poems, captured in more durable form toward the end of the Dark Age itself.

Finally, the Dark Age gains some advantage from its position between the better known Bronze Age and Classical civilizations. The nature of both is attested in some detail, and those natures vary in many ways. In the century prior to the beginning of our period, the Mycenaean world remains still largely intact. Although the palace center at Thebes was destroyed earlier in the thirteenth century (or perhaps at the end of the fourteenth) the landscape of coastal Thessaly, central Greece, and the Peloponnese continued to be dominated by such monumental centers as Iolkos in Thessaly, Gla and

Orchomenus in Boeotia, Mycenae and Tiryns in the Argolid, and Pylos in Messenia. By the end of our period in the eighth century, however, all of the palaces and citadels have been swept away, and Greece is well on its way toward a new political, social, and economic dispensation, which is reflected in the rise of the *polis*.

The differences between the two types of political structure could hardly be more pronounced. Judging from the evidence of the Linear B tablets, the Mycenaean states, like their contemporaries in Egypt, Anatolia, and the Near East, appear to have been highly centralized. The forces of production would have been directed largely inwards toward the citadel, which maintained, by means of a large administrative system, contact with and control over the population and the economic activities in the countryside.

Just as the citadel dominated the political, economic, and perhaps the religious life of the Mycenaean state, so the king, the *wanax*, dominated the citadel. As Klaus Kilian (1988) has shown, the palace was the administrative, political, military, and religious center of the state, and within the palace, the great hall or *megaron*—the throne room of the *wanax*—was the center and power apex of the citadel. By the mid-fourteenth century (if not earlier) the *wanax* of many citadels appears to have gathered into his hands the reins of power of all aspects of Mycenaean government.

During the following century, palace architecture and adornment bears out the elevated status achieved by the *wanax*. He has become associated with such beings as griffins, two of which flank the throne at Knossos. At Tiryns, the *megaron* looks through an intervening "vestibule" onto an altar. There has evolved a separation of the *wanax* from the mundane, a separation reflected in the religious and supermundane qualities associated with the later Greek use of the word *anax*. In this level of control, it is difficult to avoid drawing parallels with the authority enjoyed by Hittite or Mesopotamian kings and Egyptian pharaohs. In this respect, as in many others, Mycenaean political organization appears to be best understood within the context of the great civilizations of the eastern Mediterranean Late Bronze Age.

Nowhere, on the other hand, will one find a parallel to the Mycenaean citadel or to the *wanax* in the *polis* of the Archaic and Classical periods. In place of the citadel and the palace is the *agora*, or common meeting place; an assembly (*ekklesia*), council (*boule*), and the people (*demos*) have replaced the *wanax*. The reality behind the symbolism of the citadel structure and the position of the *wanax* is that of the enormous accumulation and concentration of power. By contrast, the reality symbolized by the *agora* and the assembly is the dispersal of power. Even in those states, such as Sparta, that retained kingship in some form, the power exercised by the kings was severely circumscribed. The authority of the Mycenaean *wanaktes* was increasingly great, while the few kingships surviving into the Archaic period were much more limited.

The power concentrated in the edifice of the Mycenaean citadel and in the person of the *wanax* emanated outwards to affect the countryside and periphery. In the *polis*, power resided in the periphery and came together—through *synoikismos*—to become temporarily concentrated in the *agora* for the purpose of making decisions and taking action. From a top-down command structure evidenced in the Mycenaean states, we arrive at an architecture of command in the eighth century which, if not bottom-up, is nevertheless a dispersed command, distributed among the members of the *aristoi*—those members of the community deemed worthy by blood and the accumulation of material wealth to speak and act for the whole community.

The nature of command and the distribution of power within the Mycenaean citadel and the Archaic *polis* can be explained and predicted by what we know or suspect about the origins of the two polities. The Mycenaean citadel began its life at least partly as a redistribution center, a sort of warehouse for the gathering and redistribution of agricultural surpluses. An unforeseen consequence of the foundation of such a center may have been its transformation into a bastion of political as well as economic power.

When Mycenaean power was collapsing at the end of the thirteenth century and during the twelfth, these centers were broken up, as were the kingdoms themselves, and the concentrated power residing in those centers was dispersed to the periphery. The remnants of political authority and control passed to the villages which survived the collapse. Gradually, as conditions in the tenth and ninth centuries became more settled, neighboring villages came together in a process known as *synoikismos*. We are no more certain of the motives behind this process than we are of the institution of the redistributive centers earlier, but it is probably safe to assume that they included economic and political security. The difference between this process and its Bronze Age counterpart is that power remained dispersed, most likely among the leading men of the various villages. Thus we see in embryonic form the dispersal and exercise of power through a process of synoecism and consensus, which characterize political action in the later *poleis* of the Archaic and Classical periods.

Chronology

Precision of dating in this story is, admittedly, impossible. However, in the long view, our interest must rest in just such broad patterns. Its length is, in fact, one of the most striking features of the Greek Dark Age. The four centuries from ca. 1150–750 B.C.E. seem well-nigh interminable, especially when we consider the relative poverty of archaeological material gleaned from this period. The bulk of our evidence is pottery, and even the potter's art seems nearly static. Anthony Snodgrass, author of one of the few standard surveys of the era, describes the "very slow rate of development in the potter's art in Greece" (1971, 112–13). The basic divisions are few, and the time-spans they represent are long (Hurwit 1985, 36 ff.). Differences are often nearly undetectable, especially to the untrained eye. Consider, for example, the distinction between Early and Middle Geometric: in the first, "ornament has nowhere to go but up and down, but it is almost infinitely expandable, and in the Middle Geometric period (850–760) it gradually and rigorously begins to spread" (Hurwit 1985, 62).

It is perhaps not surprising that some scholars have sought ways to shorten the period. As recently as 1991, a group of British scholars argued that the length of the Dark Age should be halved.[6] They maintained that the absolute chronology, derived ultimately from Pharaonic Egypt, was flawed and in need of radical revision. As it was pointed out at the time, however, such schemes intended to ameliorate the "awkward gap" of the Dark Age have instead created as many problems as they solve. While a shortened Dark Age might resolve chronological discrepancies at some sites, it would cause confusion at others. At Assiros in Toumba in central Macedonia, for example, there is continuity from the Late Bronze Age to the very end

Table 1: Chronology of Greek Dark Age Pottery Styles

Submycenaean	1125–1050 B.C.E.
Protogeometric	1050–900 B.C.E.
Geometric	900–700 B.C.E.
Early	900–850 B.C.E.
Middle	850–760 B.C.E.
Late	760–700 B.C.E.

of the Dark Age. Its origins are demonstrably linked to the Bronze Age, while later settlements are shown to be separated by destruction debris indicative of local disruptions. In other words, a single settlement has not been defined erroneously as two or more. The nine phases of the site are dated between ca. 1300 and 700 B.C.E., allowing fifty years for every phase, with the exception of the two latest, which are each accorded a full century (Wardle 1980). Other sites show a similar richness that could be compressed only with difficulty.

Furthermore, it bears pointing out that the Dark Age is not unique. Other periods and other regions have experienced declines which, though not so severe, were just as long. The Middle Bronze Age on the Greek mainland (or the Middle Helladic period ca. 2100/2000–1600 B.C.E.) is, like the Dark Age, a time of material decline from the Early Bronze Age. The period is at least as long as the usual dates for the Dark Age, and like the latter epoch, coincides with similar, though less lengthy, disruptions in Egypt. The Middle Bronze Age ends with the same suddenness that closes the Dark Age: the wealth of the Shaft Graves at Mycenae, with similar expressions elsewhere on the Greek mainland, finds an echo in the flurry of change at the end of the eighth century. The pattern of Greek development may lie in the alternation between substantial periods featuring simplicity of social organization and accommodation to natural conditions and periods of growth in population and social complexity. In this view, the Dark Age is neither so unique nor so peculiar as it has seemed.

One thing is certain: the Dark Age was ushered in by the dramatic collapse of the Mycenaean civilization. While a full understanding of the widespread difficulties of the thirteenth and twelfth centuries may never be possible, one broad explanation is that of system collapse—a sudden and severe economic, political, and social dislocation affecting most of the Eastern Mediterranean civilization of the Late Bronze Age. Specific situations varied according to local conditions and reactions. A single "cause" explaining the collapse has yet to be isolated and defined, and indeed there may be no single cause: invaders, natural disasters, local uprisings, civil war, disruption of essential trade routes—all seem to have played a part in the drama. Every aspect of life was affected during the time of troubles, with each undergoing a forced transformation (Renfrew 1972, 1979, 1987).

The following chapters describe this forced transformation, serving as a kind of bridge connecting the Bronze Age world of palaces and kings to the world of the Archaic *polis*. The current state of our knowledge permits some chronological division—though it may have moved at a snail's pace, the Dark Age did show changes over time. This account will use the division of centuries, which bears some resemblance to reality while serving as a convenient tool. Each hundred-year block is marked by basic characteristics, and each can be studied concretely through a particular, well-excavated site.

The twelfth century was a time of collapse of the old civilization. After a brief consideration of the nature of the difficulties and theories explaining them, the discussion will turn to consequent developments, especially population decline and dispersal, collapse of administrative centers together with tools of social management, and the nature of the surviving "Submycenaean" communities. Since Mycenae itself was one of the survivors, it will be the concrete illustration of the first dark century.

Even the poor descendants of the great citadels disappeared in the eleventh century, so our primary concern turns to the communities that replaced them at that time. It would seem that certain of the "communities" were migratory groups, some of whom were already in Greece, while others took advantage of the collapse to wander in from other regions. The site of Nichoria, once part of a Mycenaean kingdom but now quite independent, reveals all of these features during what was probably the "darkest" century of the Dark Age.

In the tenth century, parts of Greece experienced an up-turn. Much of the improvement came from Athens, both the home of a

Map 2. Sites showing the Dark Age transformation of Greece. *Drawing © Anne Lou Robkin. Used by permission.*

new pottery style and the source of the movement of small groups across the Aegean to Asia Minor. Inasmuch as Athens was a Mycenaean center, it is well suited to show continuity with the past as well as transformation into a new form of society.

A neighbor to Athens, Lefkandi, on the island of Euboea, represents the ninth century. This tiny community of people became a conduit to the more advanced cultures of the eastern Mediterranean, offered "heroic" burial to two of its members, and took the time and effort to erect a building some 30 feet wide and 150 feet long. The "heroic" tradition is so prominent in Euboean evidence that the island has been proposed as the home of the adaptation of the alphabet for the purpose of rendering more permanent the epic songs of Homer.

Speed of change is clearly evident in developments of the eighth century, which is acclaimed an age of revolution, a period of renaissance. Population growth, colonization, intensifying contacts with other cultures, and wave after wave of influence from them signal the end of darkness. By the close of the century, the autonomous *polis* had become the accepted way of life throughout Greece, the Homeric pantheon of gods was fully formed, and the seeds of the Classical Greek material culture had been planted. Corinth exemplifies the far end of the bridge.

By way of conclusion, we will return to Hesiod, the one Greek who seemed to appreciate the difference between his world and that of much earlier heroes. It was through the widespread dissemination of his poetry and that of Homer that the Greek pantheon of gods was fully formed. The results of the Dark Age transformation stand out strikingly in Hesiod's poetry and in his community, Ascra. This small, but tightly knit community reveals the material, political, and intellectual foundations of Classical Greece.

Citadel to
City-State

1

Mycenae

The End of the
Bronze Age

The most notable feature of twelfth-century Greece is its antithesis to the prominent character of the thirteenth century: collapse of
kingdoms and the individual sites contained within them replaced
the consolidation evident in much of southern and east-central
Greece during the preceding three hundred years. Kingdoms centered on Pylos, Mycenae, Tiryns, Athens, Iolkos, Orchomenus, and
Thebes were rocked by troubles, internal and external, brought on
by nature as well as human agency. By the close of the century, small
impoverished settlements defined the way of life for those who had
survived the "time of troubles."[1] Moreover, the number of sites of
any sort fell off sharply. The visual picture changes from a map dotted with settlements to one containing about thirty-five settlements
in the post-palatial period, including sites in Asia Minor, Crete, and
the Cyclades as well as on the mainland.[2] The changes occurred rap-
idly: only a century separated the earliest destructions, in the last

quarter of the thirteenth century, from the final signs of collapse. Along with physical destruction came institutional change: the increasingly complex administrative structures that had accompanied the growth of territorial states faded as those states disintegrated.

In spite of the enormity of the difficulties, certain settlements were not destroyed. Some Mycenaeans escaped destruction and retained institutions, technologies, and beliefs from the past. Thus, as we have argued in the introduction, the elements for rebuilding a culture following the devastations were at hand. They would be reshaped, certainly, but they were not newly minted. Reshaping would take different forms, inasmuch as isolation of the twelfth-century settlements bred regional distinctions. We have selected Mycenae to represent the first century of the Dark Age. Because Mycenae had become one of the preeminent powers in Hellas, it represents well the nature of Bronze Age civilization, the starting point of our story. And since it retained a position of some importance in the diminished conditions of the twelfth century, it also reflects the altered situation created by the collapse. It is, in other words, a bridge connecting Bronze Age life to the ensuing Dark Age.

This bridge stretches from the late thirteenth century to the last quarter of the twelfth century, roughly a hundred years. Because of the nature of the evidence, dates will be approximate. When pottery provides the frame of reference, we will employ the generally accepted scheme based on pottery sequences. For the thirteenth and twelfth centuries, the correlation between the mainland sequence and absolute chronology consists of two main periods: that before the massive disruptions (1330–1200) is called Late Helladic IIIB, while that following the onset of difficulties (1200–1100) is known as Late Helladic IIIC.

The Site

The ancient citadel of Mycenae is situated on a rocky, roughly triangular hill that rises some 280 meters above sea level and 100 meters above the plain—a last, unpretentious foothill of Mount Zara to the east, thrust out into the Argive Plain.[3] Even without fortifications, the hill is highly defensible. To the north the land drops away precipitously, and while the south slope is gentler, it is by no means easy.

1. Aerial view of Mycenae. *Courtesy of the Hellenic Military Geographical Service, Athens. Used by permission.*

To the southeast is the Chavos Ravine, a sheer drop of sixty meters, and beyond the ravine there are only the final cliffs and spurs of Mount Zara, allowing no room for hostile formations. Only from the southwest can the citadel be approached with ease, but this opening provided by nature has been effectively closed by Mycenae's military engineers.

The hill is both low enough and high enough to provide easy access to, and a wide prospect of, the plain below, which Mycenae shared with three other important sites—Tiryns, Argos, and Midea. The site is strategically placed to control both the overland route from the Argolid north to Corinthia and the isthmus beyond, and to the northwest, the mountain passes to Arcadia.

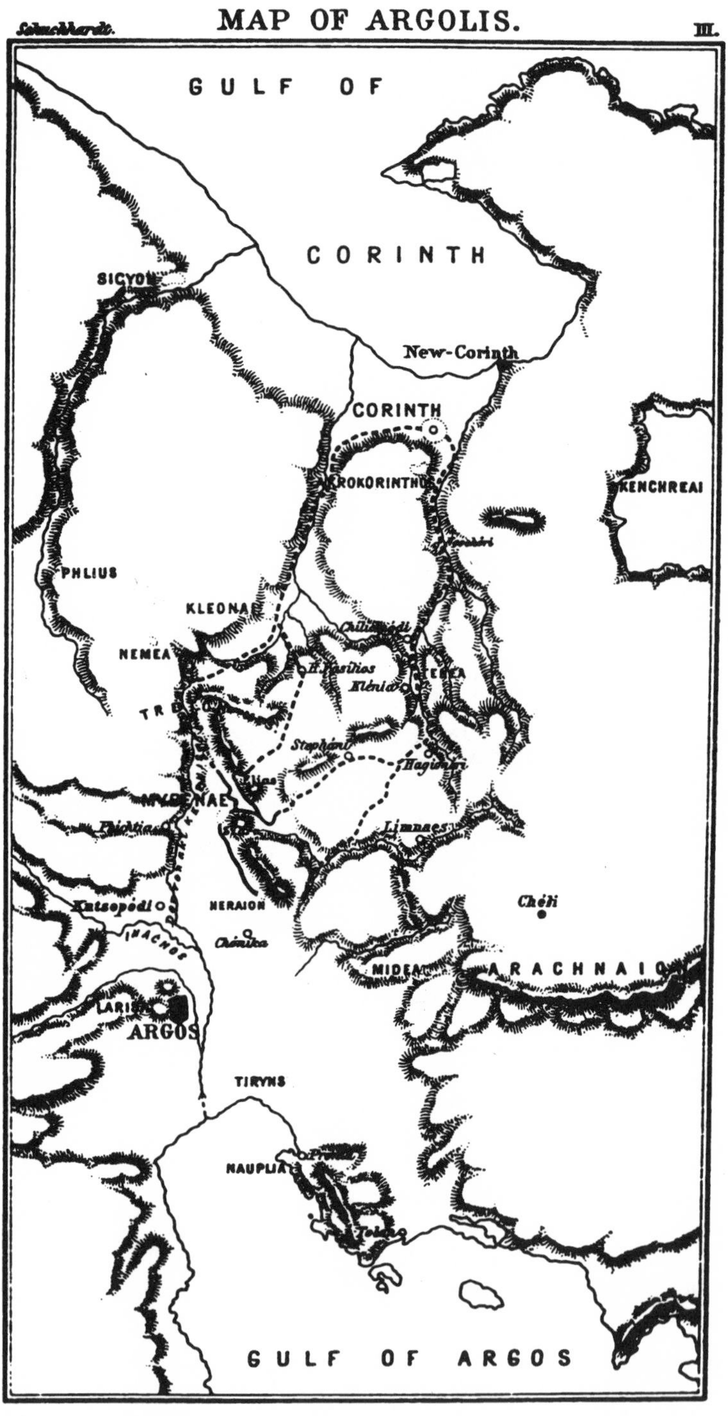

Schuchhardt

GULF OF

CORINTH

SICYON

New-Corinth

CORINTH

AKROKORINTHOS

KENCHREAI

PHLIUS

KLEONAE

Calimaki

NEMEA

H. Basilios

TEGEA

Klenia

TR

Stephani

Hagios

MYCENAE

Nea

Phichtia

Limnaes

Katsopodi

HERAION

Chéli

INACHOS

Chonica

ARACHNAION

MIDEA

LARISA

ARGOS

TIRYNS

NAUPLIA

GULF OF ARGOS

Map 3. Map of the Argolid, showing roads from Mycenae.
After H. Steffen, Karten von Mykenae *(Berlin, 1884).*

Natural defensibility was enhanced by human technology. In the Late Bronze Age, walls some 900 meters in length ringed the entire crest of the hill, enclosing an area of more than 38,000 square meters. Because the wall consisted largely of enormous rough-hewn blocks and unhewn boulders reaching a width of eight meters in places, Greeks of a later age referred to such walls as Cyclopean and told the tale of how Perseus, the legendary founder of Mycenae, employed giant Cyclopes from Lycia to construct the walls (Strabo, 8.6.11; Pausanias, 2.7, 7.3).

The main entrance into the citadel is in the northwest corner of the circuit—the famous Lion Gate, a massive post and lintel construction with a monumental relief of lions rampant against a pillar. On the south side of the gate, the wall projects outward some fifteen meters running parallel with the main circuit to provide a vantage point from which archers and spearmen could attack the unshielded

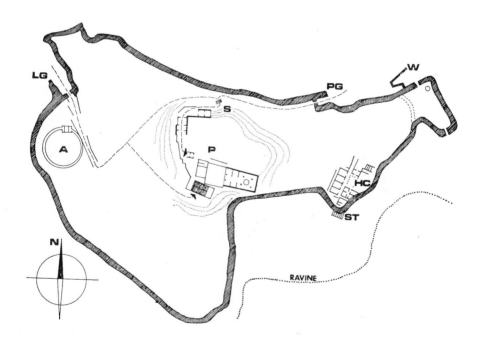

2. Sketch of the Third Citadel of Mycenae. A: grave circle A; LG: lion gate; PG: postern gate; W: underground cistern; S: north staircase; P: palace area; HC: House of Columns; ST: southeastern tower (drawing Garvey). *G. Mylonas (1966, 31). Reprinted by permission of Princeton University Press.*

right flank of any force attempting to storm the gate. Defensive concerns also led to a similar projection at the Postern Gate in the north wall, and an extension in the northeastern section of the wall gave access from within the walls to an underground reservoir supplied by runoff from the surrounding hills funneled into it through a system of terra-cotta pipes. Since the only year-round source of water, the Perseia Spring, lies several hundred meters beyond the walls, the construction of this extension solved a major weakness in Mycenae's defensive system.

Less sound from a strategic point of view is the great curving sweep of the circuit to the south and west, which throws a generous, protective arm around the cluster of graves known as Grave Circle A, creating an increase in the amount of wall space that must be defended. It is probable that, like the Lion Gate, this extension served as an announcement, or advertisement, of power.

Within the walls, the extant building foundations cluster in four distinct areas. Directly to the north and northeast of the Lion Gate is an area composed of a number of buildings occupied only for a relatively short period in the second half of the thirteenth century and destroyed in the difficulties ca. 1200. Their purpose is unclear, though one, a four-room structure, may have served as a guardhouse, and others may have been storerooms. Despite the nondescript nature of the architectural remains, a number of important finds have been uncovered from this sector, including statuettes and a large female figurine, a bronze hound, some ivory-work, a Linear B tablet, and a faience plaque bearing a cartouche of the fourteenth-century Pharaoh Amenhotep III.

Inside the circuit of the Northeast Extension lie the foundations of a small complex of buildings constructed at the same time as the enlargement of the wall in the second half of the thirteenth century. The strategic nature of the extension suggests a similar purpose for the buildings, inasmuch as the angle of the walls here contains the stairway to the subterranean cistern and two narrow openings which may have been used as sally ports or escapes. All the buildings in this area show signs of destruction by fire at the end of the period (ca. 1200).

Perhaps the largest and most complex area of occupation within the citadel is that which occupies the southwest slope of the acropolis between the Great Ramp leading from the Lion Gate and the southwest courses of the Cyclopean Wall. Though occupied during the early centuries of the second millennium, this area, except for the Grave Circle, appears to have been deserted during much of the Late Bronze Age until the thirteenth century. The wall in this area dates from the second half of the fourteenth century, while the buildings seem to date to the first half of the next century. These buildings were apparently devoted to cult practice and included a shrine in which parts of a fresco have been discovered, depicting what may be a female figure holding aloft ears of grain in each hand. Within the shrine were benches or platforms built out from the walls on which stood figurines usually thought to be either goddesses or worshippers. Building "Gamma," containing an altar and an unworked boulder set in the floor, was characterized by its excavator, Mylonas, as a site of cult activity, and particularly of animal sacrifice, since ash and animal bones were found around the altar. Southeast of this building was a large complex of rooms separated by long corridors which also reveal strong cult associations—an interpretation supported by the fresco fragments found there, depicting female figures. One room of the complex features a rectangular altar-hearth raised a quarter of a meter above the floor level and stone benches on the surrounding walls.

This complex shows signs of destruction twice during the thirteenth century. Several structures indicate earthquake damage, after which a number of them appear to have been filled or sealed and soon built over, with the new structures retaining the same purposes as the old. Other buildings were simply abandoned. A second destruction occurred at the end of the century and was accompanied by widespread burning in other parts of the citadel. While substantial rebuilding took place in the following period, the new structures were less sturdy and often did not follow the earlier ground plans. It cannot be determined whether the southwest section persisted as a cult center or whether the buildings were given over to residential use.

The fourth sector is the palace complex with its associated structures. Situated on the very summit and upper slopes of the acropolis, it is the most prone to damage by weathering, erosion, and slipping into lower levels, making it difficult to understand in terms of its archaeology. Other problems in understanding the palace area have been caused by the leveling of part of the area during the late Dark Age for the construction of a small temple, and by the intensity (and varying quality) of excavation done in the area since 1876.

In spite of these problems, the remains do yield a picture of the area. The palace seems to have been in a state of continuous growth from the mid-fourteenth through the late thirteenth centuries. The older extant portions of the complex, located just west and south of the summit, include a massive terrace supported by a long wall, which provided the entry way into the palace complex. Several substantial rooms seem to have opened onto a corridor running in the same direction. A number of basement rooms are believed to have been used for storage. They also opened onto a corridor which bordered a substantial two-story building (called the "Xenon," or Guest House by Mylonas) and led to the Main Court, then a large open area, and finally the Great Hall or Megaron.

Restored in the present century, the Megaron now forms a long rectangle some 23 by 11.5 meters; originally it may have been a two-story building. Crossing the Main Court, one would pass through a deep, covered portico at whose end a massive double door led to a large vestibule. The architectural focus of attention in the nearly square chamber (ca. 13 by 11.5 meters) was a great circular hearth, approximately 3.7 meters in diameter, around which four stout columns supported the high roof. At least one of the walls of the Megaron held a fresco of warriors with chariots and horses and a group of women standing on rocky ground in front of a walled citadel or town.

East and north of the Palace are two large building complexes. The "House of Columns," named for its many column bases, is a long, uneven rectangle, divided into three sections. The two outer sections are labyrinthine combinations of rooms and corridors of various dimensions. Roughly in the center of the building stood a large colonnaded court approximately 190 meters square. The second building was nearly square, some 750 square meters, divided roughly into two sections of squarish rooms separated by an interior corridor. Among the rooms' debris were ivory chips and shavings, fragments of gold leaf, small nodules of copper ore, and fragments of semi-precious stones—all materials used in the manufacture of luxury items and responsible for its name, the Artists' Workshop and Quarters.

The close proximity of these two buildings, their communication with one another, and the possibility that they had a common entrance suggest that the two structures were built roughly at the same time during the second half of the thirteenth century. Given the labor involved to erect a complex of these proportions, it is difficult not to agree with Mylonas' argument that these buildings represent the extreme east wing of the Palace. Thus the House of Columns may well have served as the residence of the king (or *wanax*), and it was directly linked to the other buildings of the Palace complex spreading over a series of artificial terraces on the summit. Both buildings, like so many other structures within the citadel, appear to have been destroyed by fire at the end of the thirteenth century, although just possibly the palace proper on the summit escaped destruction until about 1125 B.C.E.

Society at the Beginning of the Dark Age

Thus would Mycenae have appeared on the eve of the disruptions of the late thirteenth century. But what precisely was the nature of this site: a fortress, a palace, both at once, a city? These are not idle questions, for as we shall see, the nature of thirteenth-century Mycenae is something quite different from the Mycenae of the twelfth, and both are different yet again from the other sites of the ensuing Dark Age which we shall be examining in subsequent chapters. These questions, then, address the issue of continuity, or the lack thereof, between Bronze Age social structure and economy and that of the Dark Age.

Among the four distinct sectors within the Cyclopean Walls, only one, that of the Southwest Slope, could possibly have contained a large residential area. Yet even here, nearly a third of this area was taken up by the Granary and Grave Circle A, and several buildings are thought to have been devoted to either cult practice or personnel. Nor is it clear that the other buildings were in fact of a residential character. If Mycenae was a city, it would seem that it was a city without many permanent residents, and therefore unusual among cities ancient and modern.

Many of Mycenae's structures—the walls, the two gates, and the Northeast Extension—had a defensive military function; others—such as the Palace, the Artists' Workshop, and the House of Columns—convey a political and administrative function; the structures on the Southwest Slope fulfilled a cultic function. Those in residence on the citadel must have been linked to these functions: they were people either directly or indirectly in the service of the person who dwelt in the Palace.

It is a widely-held opinion that the citadel of Mycenae, as well as other palace complexes both on the mainland and on Crete, began as centers for the storage and redistribution of agricultural surpluses. Earlier in the Bronze Age, villages of peasant farmers, perhaps spurred by increases in population brought about by favorable climatic conditions or agricultural innovations, began coming together in a process known as village nucleation.[4] The entrenched, precautionary habit of setting aside their small surpluses as a hedge against occasional famine years continued, especially since the peasants now had the manpower to construct centrally located storage facilities to be used in common.

Such storage facilities, containing the hoarded wealth of the community, became the nucleus of the future palace center and the focus of a new economic and social system which temporarily submerged the old *demos*, essentially a settlement consisting of a few families, each led by a family head. It is likely that one of these heads, by any of a variety of means, established a patronage over his fellows, and thus was in a position to initiate or further the process of nucleation, thereby gaining control over the pooled surpluses. Through the accretion of such unheard-of power, he would have quickly emerged as something greater than a mere village leader, while a particular village with its new concentration of power and wealth, might eventually become something greater as well. Such a polity would have acted as a redistributive center, gathering in the surpluses of the farmers in the district, some of which would be stored, some retained for the personal use of the village head (termed by anthropologists and archaeologists, a "big man"), and some to be rendered by leverage into an even greater accumulation of wealth.

By the fourteenth and thirteenth centuries, the palace centers clearly had become something more than redistribution centers, although this function remained vital to the farmers dwelling in villages and hamlets, and even on isolated farmsteads in the surrounding plain. The abiding importance of storage is attested as late as the mid-thirteenth century. All across the northern side of the site are foundations identified as storage magazines. Within the palace itself a number of rooms opening on the north corridor are thought to have been used for storage, and certain free-standing buildings, such as the Granary just south of the Lion Gate, have this same function. Furthermore, Mycenae appears to have been the hub of a small network of well-constructed roads connecting the citadel with outlying agricultural regions, particularly to the northeast. Anton Jansen (1997, 1–16) argues sensibly and persuasively for the role of agriculture in both the construction and location of these roads. Though previously they were thought to have been used primarily for military purposes, Jansen believes that three of the four roads identified so far were built to facilitate communication between the citadel and the hilly region to the north and east, where conditions for crop production and grazing of flocks were good. The roads would also have served as arteries to important clay beds and stone quarries.

Later not only agricultural produce but also raw materials and finished products were stored in and distributed from the central source. The power of the chief "manager" was enhanced by his ability to command the activities of local craftsmen, and in turn, his control over crafts, especially luxury goods, enabled the "manager" to enter into all sorts of favorable exchange relationships. Through the process of gift giving, he could attract and maintain an elite following, whose members could fill top military and administrative posts. Possessing a productive life far exceeding that of stored grain, craft products could be used as key elements of long-range planning in such matters as marriage, military, and trade alliances. Evidence is plentiful that the Mycenaean export trade depended largely on such items as richly dyed textiles and quality ceramics. And of course, some of the stored items were used to maintain the manager, his family, and his retainers.

At the center of such diverse activity, citadels like Mycenae, with their resident elites, gained great political and symbolic importance. Centers and elites alike stood at the peak of a socioeconomic pyramid. At its base, the great majority of the population labored in their small fields to produce a surplus, which was gathered for collective storage within the protected citadel. Between the base and apex was a smaller though still sizable group of craftsmen and merchants, much of whose labor would have been monopolized by the palace in return for rations produced by the peasants. At the top of the pyramid were the administrative and military elites and the central manager, named in the palace records as the *wanax*. This group would have been the chief consumers, as well as the controllers, of craft goods and luxury items. In return for these benefits, the *wanax* and his peers provided security against famine and protection against enemies for those situated lower on the pyramid.

Such a system would be flexible and durable enough to withstand the occasional poor harvest or even two lean years in a row if they had been preceded by a run of good harvests. But a third lean year would necessitate either the killing off of flocks and herds for food or the importation of grain at the expense of at least a portion of the citadel's hoarded wealth. The citadel might survive a fourth lean year if there were luxury items remaining to be traded for grain, but a fifth bad year is likely to have spelled disaster, given the pressure of increasing population on the marginal land of much of Greece.

It was this kind of society that flourished during the thirteenth century and that withstood three separate destructions at Mycenae. The first destruction seems to have taken place during the mid-thirteenth century, affecting only the areas to the north, west, and southwest of the Cyclopean Walls, where there is evidence of settlement going back as far as the third millennium. By the Late Bronze Age it is probable that the total population of this outlying area or lower town was greater than that of the citadel. Most of these settlements were little more than small crofts and farming hamlets consisting of only a few houses. There were, however, larger complexes; one, the House of the Oil Merchant complex, comprised five distinct sections and a multitude of rooms.

When this complex, along with other settlements in the vicinity, was destroyed, the area was apparently not reoccupied. While a few of the settlers would have been killed in the destruction and others may have abandoned Mycenae altogether, many more may have moved within the walls of the citadel. The impetus behind the sudden expansion on the previously unoccupied Southwest Slope of the citadel, may have been the destruction outside the citadel. Only two or three of the buildings have conclusively been identified as "cult buildings." Certainly some of the other buildings in this area may have housed refugees newly uprooted from outlying farms.

In any event the citadel itself suffered no apparent harm in this episode, and indeed far from ushering in an unalterable decline, the final decades of the century saw Mycenae continue with an ambitious building program which included the Artists' Workshop, the House of Columns, and the Northeast Extension with its secret passage down to the underground cistern. The wave of growth and prosperity that had begun a century or more earlier billowed even higher for those resident at Mycenae. Its position among other citadel communities in Greece seems to have grown more impressive, and it played a prominent part within the lively political, economic, and cultural interaction in the eastern Mediterranean sphere. So wealthy and powerful did Mycenae seem that some scholars have described it as the center of a Mycenaean Empire.[5]

While we believe that there are serious difficulties with this description, the evidence suggests that those in power at Mycenae were more successful in consolidating their control than their contemporaries in other parts of Greece. As early as the sixteenth century, Mycenae seems to gain an advantage over other sites in the Argolid: the shaft graves of the two grave circles testify to the wealth and importance of the few people interred within them. With an earlier start in establishing themselves, the powerful few at Mycenae soon gained a monopoly on another form of burial—the *tholos*, or beehive, tombs. From the early thirteenth century, *tholoi* are found only at Mycenae and not in neighboring sites in the Argolid, and they become increasingly impressive both in form and as expressions of command. In other mainland regions, such as Messenia, *tholoi* are not concentrated at a single center. A distinctive masonry style, utilizing conglomerate stone cut and set in regular courses with close-fitting joints, is found in the latest *tholoi* as well as in the major rebuilding of the fortifications and can be interpreted as "part of a well-conceived building program by the reigning group at Mycenae to advertise itself as the sole and legitimate heir of power" (Wright, 1987). The advertisement carried beyond Mycenae, if Wright's reconstruction is correct. It is also found at Argos and Tiryns, where it may reveal the extension of control from Mycenae.

That Mycenae was viewed as unique in the eyes of other con-

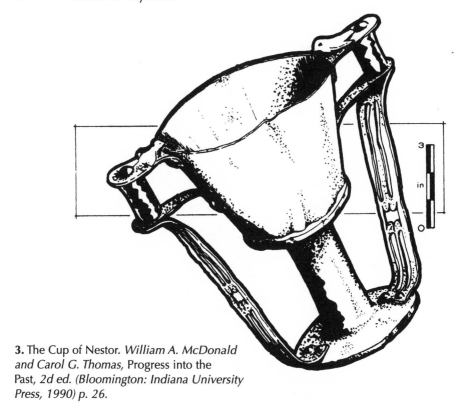

3. The Cup of Nestor. *William A. McDonald and Carol G. Thomas,* Progress into the Past, *2d ed. (Bloomington: Indiana University Press, 1990) p. 26.*

temporary powers is shown by Egyptian objects found in Greece in a fifteenth-century context. Eric Cline has argued persuasively that faience plaques inscribed with the names of Amenhotep III and Queen Tiy and found at several Aegean sites, but at Mycenae in particular, correlate "with the emergence of Mycenae as a dominant power in the Aegean world" (Cline 1987).

Vast construction projects like the *tholos* tombs of Mycenae speak of control over large sectors of the economy and large numbers of laborers. James Wright calculates construction of the Aegisthus *tholos* alone required approximately 57,600 man-hours, excluding the masonry work (Wright 1987, 174 n. 131). The Lion Gate, the massive *tholoi*, and the expanding fortifications are "badges" of power functioning to glorify the ruler of Mycenae. Drawing the shaft graves of Circle A within the walls, which involved an awkward extension of the fortification, may be seen as a deliberate effort to strengthen kingly power by association with heroic ancestors.

Such powerful kings may well have begun to subdue those near peers who were acknowledged leaders in neighboring regions. We have noted the system of roads extending from Mycenae. While it is true that these roads are confined to "a region within easy walking distance of the citadel of Mycenae" (Jansen 1997, 8), it is possible that these regional roads were linked to others leading to more distant places. Legend gives to Elektryon, son of Perseus and king of Midea, kingship of Mycenae as well. Legend also speaks of Heracles of Tiryns' rivalry with and humiliation by Eurystheus, King of Mycenae. Is there an historical reflection of Argos' dependence on Mycenae in the subordinate relationship of Diomedes, leader of Argos, to Agamemnon in the *Iliad*? Agamemnon's position in the *Iliad* may reflect both the remembrance of political development in the Age of Heroes and the uncertainty of others regarding such claims to superior status.

Problems ca. 1200 B.C.E.

If Mycenae's rulers did extend their control over other sites, their strength was short-lived, occurring only in the last century or two of the Bronze Age. And the very greatness of Mycenae contained the seeds of decline, perhaps even hastening it: the great southwestern extension of the walls may signify new power or the fear of that of another. In the case of the former, the nearly simultaneous refortification of Mycenae, Tiryns, and Midea take on the qualities of a costly exercise in status emulation. But would there have been any need either for an extension of the wall south of the Lion Gate to provide the opportunity to attack the flanks of enemy forces or for construction of the extension providing safe access to a water supply if the walls were merely emblems of status? And beyond the Argolid, what of the fortifications partially straddling the Isthmus of Corinth which date from the same period? Are they perhaps the remains of a defensive wall, originally intended to guard the overland approaches to the Peloponnese against intruders?

Even if we ignore the defensive aspects of the walls themselves, there are plenty of other signs, some obvious, some less so, that all was not well. Mycenaean Thebes was destroyed, probably during the early thirteenth century. Buildings outside the citadel of Mycenae were destroyed perhaps only ten or twenty years after the completion of the building program on the Southwest Slope.

Among the less obvious, but in a way more sinister, signs of decline is the evidence of a breakdown in communications and trade in the later thirteenth century, clearly seen in the beginning of the fragmentation of Mycenaean cultural uniformity. The near universality of pottery in terms of fabric, shape, and decoration, achieved both on the mainland and among the Cyclades during the fourteenth and early thirteenth centuries, weakened.[6] Now new shapes appear, especially the deep bowl; some older shapes disappear, including the "stirrup jar" and painted *kylikes* or cup-shaped vessels; decorative motifs are still based on earlier types, but their number declines from forty to twenty-seven and their execution is inferior. Patterns begin to take on a geometric quality, with more of the surface empty of design, a style that persists into the twelfth century. For our present concern, most striking is the occasional absence beyond the Argolid of Argive late thirteenth-century shapes and motifs; the farther away from the mainland one ventures, the more pronounced is their absence. In the Cyclades, the Dodecanese, and the Ionian Islands not only are there few imports of these forms, but the local ware derives all of its inspiration from preceding periods. Only a severe breakdown in communications could account for these developments. In addition to this apparent weakening of contact there are also signs of a decline in population in the Argolid. Evidence from burials suggests a decline in the number of people using cemeteries at Mycenae, Argos, Prosymna, and Tiryns.

All of these portents must be considered within their temporal and spatial contexts—namely the severe and widespread conflagration that occurred at Mycenae around 1200 B.C.E. Destruction was nearly universal within the citadel at Mycenae: only the Granary seems certainly to have been spared. The Northeast Extension is also a likely survivor, and the Palace on the summit may also have escaped destruction at this time. But aside from these areas, there is hardly a section of the citadel which has not yielded a layer of ash deposited around 1200 B.C.E.

The damage was not confined to Mycenae. In the Argolid both

Tiryns and Midea suffered substantial damage, with the latter apparently being abandoned at this time. Other sites which were either destroyed or abandoned included Prosymna, Zygouries, and Berbati. Far beyond the Argolid, most of the palace centers and many smaller settlements show signs of destruction: in Boeotia, Gla suffered damage by fire and appears to have been abandoned shortly afterwards, and Orchomenus also shows signs of fire damage, although it is not known whether the destruction can be attributed to this period. The Palace of Nestor at Epano Englianos (Pylos) in Messenia was destroyed around 1200, and there is hardly any sign of resettlement following the destruction.[7] Though not destroyed, Athens experienced difficulties at approximately the same time.

Nor were Greece and the Aegean alone in this time of trouble. At about the same time that Mycenae was extending her walls to provide a safe access to water, the Hittite Empire was beginning to experience an inability to cope with simultaneous disturbances on virtually all of its frontiers, and the Pharaoh Merneptah was gathering forces to meet the first wave of "Sea Peoples." A few decades later when the entire Peloponnese was subjected to destruction or abandonment, the Hittite empire collapsed and the prosperous city of Ugarit on the east coast of the Mediterranean was destroyed so suddenly that modern-day excavators found pots that were being fired when disaster befell the city. Those powers that remained intact, such as Assyria and Egypt, shrank into their heartlands.

Some Mycenaean sites experienced the same result: shrinking but not disappearing. Mycenae itself shows substantial signs of reoccupation following the destruction of ca. 1200 B.C.E., and each year brings more such evidence to light. Almost every sector which suffered destruction, particularly the Southwest Slope and the House of Columns, had some reoccupation during the twelfth century. Later activity on the site of the Palace presents special problems in interpreting its situation after the conflagration, as we have seen.

Who were the people trying to rebuild on the citadel? If we examine their pottery, it seems obvious that they were Mycenaeans. Shapes and decoration draw heavily on earlier periods for inspiration to produce the "Close Style" and "Granary Style," both of which characterize the middle phase of the twelfth century at Mycenae. The first, which has been condemned by many as "busy" or "fastidious," refers simply to the introduction of natural and geometric motifs into every available surface space. When well executed, the product can be quite elegant and not at all inferior to much of thirteenth-century material. The "Granary Style" represents something of an antithesis to the "Close Style": found on shapes small and large, it favors the application of two or three linear bands of paint on the external rim, shoulders, and belly of the vase. Decorations include the tassel, the loop, and especially the wavy line. If there is anything new in this material it is a certain lack of expertise in the application of paint.

A number of more general conclusions may be drawn from these developments. One is that there has been a general lack of innovation during this period. Neither the "Close" nor the "Granary" style is substantially different from previous styles: they use earlier shapes and motifs, and only their application is somewhat different. While some decline in technique is noticeable in some shapes and motifs, this is not pervasive.

One class of pottery, though found in association with early twelfth-century material, is claimed by some to be totally unrelated

4. LHIIIC close style vase. *V. R. d'A. Desborough (1964, plate 4d). Courtesy of Oxford University Press. Used by permission.*

to it or any other Mycenaean ware. This is the so-called "Handmade Burnished Ware," or sometimes "Barbarian Ware," which seems to be confined to the earlier decades of the century.[8] A number of scholars have claimed that this ware is consistent with the rough fabric and unlovely design one would expect to be produced by survivors of a disaster who were suddenly forced through circumstances to produce their own pottery. Others point not only to the unique fabric and decoration of this ware, but to its resemblance to material found further north in the Balkans, particularly Bulgaria, and to the "Coarse Ware" of Troy VIIb (dated to the twelfth century), arguing that it signifies the arrival of a new people.

In any case, it is possible to conclude that Mycenaean culture and probably some Mycenaeans continued to live on in the citadel. The citadel itself, however, assumed quite a different appearance. In its heyday, it was a fortress, a residence for rulers, and a center for the collection and redistribution of agricultural and other goods. After 1200, more of the erstwhile rural population was drawn within the walls, altering its character to that of a makeshift, crowded refugee town, although some of the Citadel's former glory may have been retained in the rebuilt portion of the House of Columns.

What happened to the pyramidal sociopolitical structure after this destruction? Did a *wanax* oversee changed conditions? If so, did he have assistance from members of the former, now largely unemployed, administrators? Was he perhaps an ambitious peasant who saw an opportunity and took it? Whoever now lived in the restored House of Columns, it is clear that the administrative structure underwent at least a partial collapse. Linear B records came to an end and, although there are a few scholars who believe otherwise, it is generally assumed that literacy, never very well established in Mycenaean Greece, went the way of the ruling structure. As for the power of Mycenae abroad, the Citadel was no longer in a position to exert control much beyond its own walls. Power became fragmented and local.

Though survivors remained, others departed for far distant lands. There is increasing evidence for two waves of new Mycenaean settlers on Cyprus in the late thirteenth century, and it is likely that the Argolid contributed refugees to this emigration. Other "refugee" centers included the northern and central Peloponnese (Achaea and Arcadia), the Ionian Islands, parts of Attica, and Euboea. Unlike earlier contacts, however, these movements did not result in regular trade activity. Regionalism quickly replaced the internationalism of the thirteenth century.

Causes of Destruction

Theories to account for so complete a collapse fall into three fundamental schools. There are those who believe that the Mycenaean civilization was the victim of external factors such as invasions, migrations, and raiding. Others argue that internal conditions arising from within Mycenaean society were primarily responsible for the collapse. A third school stresses the larger context of collapse and demands that the situation in Greece be viewed in relation to its Mediterranean orbit.[9]

The once standard explanation was that of an invasion instigated by Dorian tribes and lead by the Heraclidae—the Sons of Heracles. According to legend, poor relations between Heracles and the royal house of Mycenae resulted, after the death of the hero, in the banishment of the Heraclidae from the Argolid. One version of the tale has them wandering until they arrived in Doris, where they obtained land on which to settle from the Dorian king, thus establishing the friendship between the Heraclidae and Dorians. Resolved to return to their homeland, the Heraclidae and their Dorian allies made two attempts, the first unsuccessful but the second securing access to the Peloponnese. Thucydides says that this invasion occurred eighty years after the capture of Troy, an event which the Hellenistic scholar Eratosthenes pegged at 1184 B.C.E. Thus the Dorian Invasion would have occurred late in the twelfth century.

But whether one chooses the low chronology of 1184 or Herodotus' high chronology of 1250 for the destruction of Troy, Thucydides' placement of the Dorian Invasion eighty years later is not supported by modern archaeological evidence of the various destructions at Mycenae and elsewhere in the Peloponnese. The date 1184 suffers on two counts. If both the first and second destructions at Mycenae date from the late thirteenth century, with the second occurring, at the very latest, in 1190, then Mycenae could not possibly have been in any kind of condition for conducting a lengthy siege at

Troy or at any other overseas site. But even if 1184 were an accurate date for the fall of Troy (assuming all the while that such an event even took place), the date of 1104 yielded by Thucydides' assertion that the Dorian Invasion occurred eighty years after 1184, places the invasion too late by fifteen or twenty years for even the last of the Mycenaean destructions—that of the Granary Fire now commonly dated to around 1125. While Herodotus' date of 1250 for the fall of Troy fares better insofar as Mycenae's military capabilities are concerned, the subtraction of eighty years from this date presents us with the same problem raised by the later date: judging from the latest archaeological findings, a date of 1170 for the Dorian Invasion is at least twenty years too late for the second, major destruction at Mycenae, and forty-five to fifty years too early for the third destruction.

Certainly such inconsistencies are not fatal to the notion of a Dorian Invasion. All of the ancient chronologies could be wrong. But even if we abandon the traditional chronology, a simple migration theory does not account for the extent of the collapse. This is not to dismiss all movement in and out of Greece, which was an on-going phenomenon.[10] However, supposed hallmarks of newcomers have been shown to have come into use gradually during the transitional years of the later Bronze Age. The "Handmade Burnished Ware," may be an intrusive element; but even so, as evidence for northern intruders the case is still not proved. And, as we have seen, it joined rather than replaced, pottery that continued the earlier Mycenaean tradition.

There are other claimants for agents of destruction from beyond the Mycenaean world, particularly the fluctuating groupings known as the "Land and Sea Peoples." The names of some of the allies who made up the motley hordes are preserved in Egyptian documents; possible identifications such as Lycians, Sardinians, Tyrrhenians and Sicilians have supporters. The effectiveness of these groups in other parts of the eastern Mediterranean is clearly documented in cries for help against them by the king of Ugarit. Some scholars have found reason to propose Viking-style pirates coursing through Aegean waters: Robert Drews, for example, suggests that revolutionary military changes in the Late Bronze Age brought new weapons and tactics to groups of people hitherto on the fringes of high civilization (Drews

1993). With their great numbers and new skills as foot soldiers they accomplished the destruction of previously superior powers. Traveling light and fast, these marauders would leave little if any trace of their presence in the archaeological record, thus explaining the lack of evidence for intruders during this period. What is not explained is the destruction done to such heavily fortified sites as Mycenae, a feat hardly consistent with the image of lightly armed raiders practicing hit-and-run tactics.

Despairing of ever finding positive evidence of foreign invaders, scholars have increasingly sought factors from within Mycenaean society or inherent in the physical setting of Bronze Age Greece, such as geological or climatic phenomena, to explain the collapse of Mycenaean power. The theories of this "Internalist" school look to civil war within kingdoms or warfare between kingdoms, as well as such physical catastrophes as massive earthquake, drought, and consequent famine resulting from major climatic change, deforestation, and erosion of scarce agricultural land.

In a society as burdensome for the peasantry as Mycenaean Greece is likely to have become by the thirteenth century, the idea that civil wars and revolutions may have been responsible is understandable and perhaps even attractive from a moral perspective. It has even been suggested that the Dorians, rather than northern intruders, were in fact the oppressed underclass who rebelled successfully, toppling the Mycenaean regimes and eventually imposing their own social structure and dialect on most of the Peloponnese (Chadwick 1976b).

However, the concept of civil war or armed uprising does not explain the extent of the destructions, the failure to rebuild destroyed sites, the abandonment of many sites, or the subsequent depopulation of many areas. It is difficult to imagine how an unarmed, untrained, and unorganized peasantry could hope to prevail against a heavily armed, highly trained, and well-organized military elite.

Scenes of warfare occurring commonly in Mycenaean artistic representations have combined with Homeric and later Greek traditions concerning the Heroic Age to earn for the Mycenaeans a reputation for unbridled pugnacity. Whether or not this reputation is entirely deserved, one must admit that the Mycenaeans themselves are likely culprits, responsible for a number of earlier destructions such as those at Thebes and Knossos, and in association with the Mycenaean penetration of the Cyclades. Clearly warfare between Mycenaean states was a factor in the political and social evolution of Bronze Age Greece from at least the end of the fifteenth century. But unless we are prepared to entertain the notion of a political situation in which the palace centers, like so many gingham dogs and calico cats, ate each other up, then we must admit that even endemic warfare between Mycenaean states would not be sufficient by itself to cause a collapse.

Of the three possible natural disasters which could have befallen Mycenaean society, two can be quickly dismissed. Greece, the Aegean, and West Anatolia form one of the most seismically active areas on the planet. Earthquakes—sometimes quite powerful ones—are common in the area, and a number of major Bronze Age sites, among them Knossos, Phaistos, and Troy, at some time in their history sustained considerable earthquake damage. And yet always, following even the most destructive earthquakes, cities were rebuilt and reoccupied, and life went on until the next earthquake. Even if the palace centers were leveled by a truly massive earthquake, or series of quakes, why are there signs of intense and widespread burning at so many sites? Only since the last century, because of the laying of gas mains and urban electrification, has burning on a wide scale become the common companion of earthquakes. If the quake struck at night, isolated fires might have flared up from spilled oil meeting the occasional overturned lamp, but truly widespread burning such as is encountered at Mycenae and Pylos seems more consistent with intentional rather than accidental destruction.

As for ecological degradation through deforestation resulting in massive erosion, studies indicate that this is a recent phenomenon, occurring only within the last couple of centuries (Bintliff 1977; Wright, et al. 1990). More compelling is the argument that climate change resulted in prolonged periods of drought. First proposed in 1966 by Rhys Carpenter, the cause of such a climate change is argued to have been the displacement northward of the jet stream during the autumn and winter months (Carpenter 1966). Thus rain-laden clouds, which would normally visit Greece and the Aegean beginning in the month of November, would have passed over Central and Eastern Europe instead. Such a shift, the result of a contraction of the polar ice caps, would cause widespread and catastrophic drought throughout much of Greece. Where this hypothesis encounters difficulties is not in demonstrating that such a climate shift could have happened—the so-called Little Ice Age of the thirteenth and fourteenth centuries C.E. is evidence enough to show that such changes are real. The trouble with Carpenter's scenario is in the time of the climate shift: there is at present no evidence that such a climate change did in fact take place during the twelfth century B.C.E.

As we have seen, one of the attractions of the climate-shift hypothesis is its ability to account for the evident decline of the entire eastern Mediterranean region at the end of the Bronze Age. Yet another hypothesis, not dependent on anything so unpredictable as the weather, but with the same ability to explain the Mycenaean destructions within their eastern Mediterranean context, is that of "systems collapse." The growing complexity and specialization of Late Bronze Age political, economic, and social organization placed hitherto unknown stresses on the entire structure upon which Mycenaean kingdoms were based. Any sudden difficulty, such as crop failure or disruption of trade, would affect every aspect of the system. The old redistributive system, originally designed to support a relatively small number of peasant farmers with perhaps a few "big men" and their households, was ill-suited to bear up under the weight of several layers of administration and the increasingly lavish court of the *wanax*. Once the state had reached the point beyond which it could not expand territorially, as the Mycenaean states appear to have done some time in the thirteenth century, the maintenance of an extensive mechanism of management, a large royal palace, and possibly a standing army would have rendered the political structure top-heavy and the lines of communication sclerotic. Even in the best of times such a state would appear systemically distorted. Response to a crisis such as crop failure is likely to have been slow, and if its result was to apply even more pressure to the already burdened peasantry, the distortion would increase until its effects were felt throughout the system.

Thus while interruption of trade and crop failure do not explain the actual destruction of the palaces, the collapse of an effective system does suggest an answer. The ambitious program of construction toward the end of the thirteenth century can be seen as a case of weakness as well as a sign of strength. The extravagance of the thirteenth-century Mycenaean palace elites overextended the entire system on which centralization rested. The citadel was in direct competition with the farmers for manpower. The extension of the walls alone must have consumed an enormous amount of labor, and for every man used in the construction of Mycenae's walls there would be that much less of a crop sown or harvested. Even if slave labor were used for construction, the results would have been the same: the slaves represented an increase in population which, so long as they were working on Mycenae's walls, were dependent on the Mycenaean farmers. Increased burdens borne by the peasantry may have brought about an intolerable imbalance between the rulers and the ruled which resulted in the disintegration of the state as the peasantry abandoned the land, rose up in rebellion, or aided and abetted external enemies.

One scholar, Joseph Tainter, has suggested that complexity itself carried with it the seeds of social collapse (Tainter 1988). Social complexity, he argues, should be viewed as a survival strategy—one of a number of such strategies employed by human groups. Like any strategy, complexity as a survival technique succeeds only to the extent that its benefits outweigh the costs incurred in making the strategy work. Such a strategy is typically employed to solve problems of food supply or to meet threats posed by enemies. In the case of Mycenae, the development of a redistributive economy represented a substantial increase in complexity while establishing an adequate and secure food supply.

This complexity, however, was represented not only by the construction of storage facilities for grain and other produce, but by innumerable unintended consequences set in motion by so fundamental a change in the economy. The stockpiles would require protection against thieves and raiders, first perhaps by armed guards, then by walls. New layers of administration would be needed to administer the facilities and to commandeer more foodstuffs as supplies were depleted. Most important, however, would be the consequence of higher population levels resulting from any improvement in eased access to food. Larger numbers would require more intensive exploitation of existing farm lands and the bringing of new land under the plow. Eventually, however, as the intensity of exploitation of farm land reached the point beyond which it could no longer provide an adequate return for the labor invested, this strategy would become less and less rewarding.

Two possible solutions to this dilemma lay in the expansion of the polity through military conquest or by colonization, and there is evidence that both solutions were attempted. But conquest carries with it obvious risks, while it does not appear on present evidence that colonization was pursued on a scale large enough to alleviate Mycenae's population problem. Meanwhile the absence of monumental *tholos* tombs everywhere in the Argive plain save in the neighborhood of Mycenae seems to indicate the consolidation of authority in the citadel all through the thirteenth century. In other words, Mycenae had not renounced the strategy of pursuing complexity despite the probable social and economic stresses resulting from this process. Nor is this persistence surprising, for complex polities rarely if ever initiate programs leading to reduced complexity, and the phenomenon of controlled collapse is very likely unknown in human history. Instead societies are usually overtaken by events and are forced into a state of collapse, often with catastrophic results.

Having catalogued some of the most prominent among the numerous theories concerning the chaotic ending of Mycenaean power, it is important to remember that all such explanations are hypotheses only, lacking the evidence necessary to call them historical fact. Perhaps the answer is to recognize that there is merit in many of these hypotheses, that a great number of problems arose in a narrow space of time. Actual agents of destruction would have varied from one region of Greece to another.

Mycenae without a Kingdom

In the end, we must admit that we do not know what happened at Mycenae at the end of the thirteenth century, but we can feel the weight of the difficulties, for they press us down to the brink of the Dark Age. Thus poised, what might life have been like for the twelfth-century survivors at Mycenae?

Unlike Pylos, whose destruction appears to have been total and irreparable, Mycenae shows substantial signs of reoccupation following the destruction of ca. 1200. However, despite this brave effort at rebuilding and the probable continuity of population, the situation at Mycenae in the twelfth century was vastly different from that of previous centuries. While the partial rebuilding of the House of Columns may indicate a restoration of governmental authority, and perhaps even a continuance in power by a member of the old ruling dynasty, we cannot avoid the conclusion that authority and power had become sharply curtailed. Practical, if negative, evidence of this inability to re-establish a secure hold over the surrounding territories is found in the paucity of twelfth- and eleventh-century settlement material from beyond the Cyclopean walls. Desborough concluded from this evidence of continued Mycenaean weakness that the invaders whom he thought to be responsible for the thirteenth-century destructions, while not staying to settle in the newly conquered territories, nevertheless must have remained in the neighborhood, where their disruptive presence would be sufficient to limit recovery. Here again, however, we are faced with the unwholesome prospect of hunting for evidence which resolutely refuses to be found. Following the initial destructions of ca. 1230, evidence becomes rare. Where the odd scattering of sherds and bits of wall indicate that the surrounding plain was not completely deserted, most of the twelfth- and eleventh-century evidence comes from burials and so cannot be used to indicate settlement beyond the walls. Whatever the reason, it is apparent that the Argive Plain had ceased to be safe for settlement, and whatever authority survived at Mycenae either could not or would not make it otherwise.

If the plain was no longer safe for settlement, how safe could it have been for the peaceful pursuit of agriculture? However complex and wide-ranging the Mycenaean economy and trade patterns had been in previous centuries, it must be remembered that the Citadel's survival had never ceased to depend on its agricultural base. Persistent and repeated interruption of the agricultural cycle could only have dire consequences for the community at large. Thus, life within the walls would have been radically altered. The fact that a good deal of rebuilding occurred shows that some semblance of order was restored early in the twelfth century, and the introduction of the Close and Granary styles attests to a revival of pottery production. There even seems to have been a partial resumption of inter-regional trade toward the middle of the twelfth century, evidenced by the spread of the style of pottery known as mature Late Helladic IIIC. None of these indications of a return to more settled conditions, however, adds up to more than a temporary resurgence. Of all the areas of Mycenae visited with destruction, none was completely restored, and what rebuilding did occur was of a relatively flimsy nature. In addition, the increasing regionalism in Mycenaean pottery indicates a chronic instability in the realm of trade and communications.

Internally, social interaction must have become greatly simplified. One indication of this change is the almost certain loss of literacy, perhaps within a generation of the destructions at the end of the thirteenth century. From the evidence at hand, the Linear B script was used almost exclusively for administrative and accounting purposes, and its use was confined to a small group of administrators and clerks. Even so, since Linear B served an important purpose in the redistributive economy of the thirteenth century, its loss represents a sure token of a collapse of that economy and system, and a return to a simpler mode of governance and exchange.

As life became simpler, if more precarious, society grew more fragmented. Though remnants of the old central officialdom may have survived for a time, they would almost surely have been cut off immediately from their colleagues further afield. What became of these latter we can only guess, but the survival of the old Mycenaean title *qa-si-re-u* (employed for local officials round about the kingdom) in the form *basileus* may indicate that some were able to set up on their own as local lords and petty chieftains. As we shall see in later chapters, Dark Age sites at Nichoria in Messenia and Lefkandi on Euboea may have been seats of authority for such men. Communities like Asine in the Argolid or Perati in Attica, whether or not they were governed by a *qa-si-re-u*, may have maintained an independent existence from the early twelfth century, providing more proof of the increasing political fragmentation of the age.

At Mycenae itself, the presence of the Granary (if that is indeed what it is), the rebuilding efforts on the site of the House of Columns, and the construction of a viaduct spanning the Chavos ravine outside the Citadel, all attest to a restoration of order and a renewed vitality. Lacking evidence to the contrary, we could speculate that parts of the old Mycenaean redistributive economy, and with it elements of the Mycenaean political structure, also achieved a partial renaissance during the first half of the twelfth century. Thus we would not be speaking so much of a total collapse of the old system as of a severe reduction of that system to match the comparative poverty of the new circumstances.

If this was in fact the case, we can imagine the remnant of the peasantry, now housed within Mycenae's walls, still cultivating the fields beyond and yielding up a surplus for storage in the Granary. This surplus, far more modest than in earlier days, could have been used as a security against future poor harvests, perhaps as a medium of exchange for scarce craft products or raw materials, and to support, on a greatly reduced level, the household of whoever it was who now dwelt in the House of Columns.

To the extent that it continued to exist at all, the Mycenaean organization would have become greatly simplified and much smaller. If the occupant of the rebuilt portion of the House of Columns was indeed the ruler of Mycenae, he may have been called *wanax*,

5. Linear B tablet. *Drawing ©Anne Lou Robkin. Used by permission.*

and members of his own family may have been selected to fill positions of the near moribund officialdom. The act of governing would have become a far more direct and personal matter as a result of the reduction of offices and the loss of literacy. Hence the gap separating the rulers from the ruled, a veritable chasm during the Mycenaean heyday, would have narrowed substantially. This radical simplification of the governing apparatus, when coupled with the fact that most of the population would now have resided within the citadel walls, would result in a polity which resembled somewhat less the Mycenaean redistributive center and perhaps rather more the small egalitarian community of the Dark Age headed by a "big man," or *basileus*.

The blow caused major changes in all aspects of life, but it failed to dispatch its victim immediately. Though weak, Mycenae lingered, and even rallied, for a brief period before succumbing to a final destruction. This last destruction at Mycenae, known as the Granary Fire, occurred sometime between 1130 and 1120. Compared with the earlier destructions, this one does not seem to be as widespread. Indeed it has been suggested that the Granary Fire was accidental and not the work of enemies. Whatever the causes of the ultimate destruction, Mycenae ceased to be a site of importance. The Southwest Slope, seemingly a religious area in the early thirteenth century and possibly a haven for refugees in the twelfth, now became a cemetery, inhabited only by the dead. Although the citadel appears not to have been completely abandoned, the evidence from the Southwest Slope would seem to indicate a further depopulation. The Granary Fire effectively removed any further opportunities for restoration. In fact, by the early or mid-eleventh century, Mycenae appears to have become something of a cultural colony of Attica: at this time pottery decorated in the new Attic Protogeometric style begins to appear in the Argolid alongside the debased forms of Granary Ware, or Submycenaean ware, then current among native potters. Other borrowings may include the change from multiple burials in chamber tombs to single or double burials in cists and pit graves, although it should be remembered that such features of funerary practice were not unknown during previous periods in the Argolid, and in any case may simply represent a common response to unsettled conditions.

Again it must be stressed that in the period following the Granary Fire there is little or no incontestable evidence to suggest the presence of intruders. The Citadel again sustained damage without being destroyed and lost population without being abandoned. It seems to have lost every battle, with one shadowy, insubstantial foe after another, and yet always remained in possession of the field. When we speak of such things as systems collapse, it is easy to get the impression that the Mycenaean Age ended violently and suddenly. While this impression might be accurate if applied to the destruction of Pylos around 1200, it would be highly inaccurate if applied to the Argolid. As we have seen, the events of the late thirteenth century

6. Artist's reconstruction of Mycenae burning.
Drawing ©Anne Lou Robkin. Used by permission.

did not suddenly plunge Mycenae into darkness, but rather into a twilight age in which it was still possible to dream of and strive toward a restoration of greatness. The destruction of 1200 may have made the final demise of Mycenaean culture a foregone conclusion, but it is doubtful that the Mycenaeans of the time believed so. In the end it took yet another violent episode, the Granary Fire, to plunge Mycenae irredeemably into the Dark Age.

2

Nichoria

The Darkest Period of the Dark Age

Mycenae's fate in the twelfth century defines the beginning of the Dark Age. While many settlements, large and small, were destroyed, others endured the times of trouble, emerging as much simpler cultures. On the mainland, continuing occupation is attested at the once major centers of Tiryns, Athens, Iolkos, Thebes, Argos, and the Menelaion as well as at Mycenae. Some smaller sites, such as Teikhos Dymaion in Achaea, became substantial settlements for a century or so, their populations perhaps increased by refugees fleeing difficulties in other areas. The resilience of many sites in each category fades toward the end of the twelfth and the start of the eleventh centuries.

Taking their place were tiny hamlets, nearly inconspicuous through their size and by choice of their inhabitants. In some cases where the archaeological record is fairly clear, it is likely that former inhabitants of these sites became at least partly nomadic for a generation or more, returning to their ancestral villages only occasionally, to bury their dead, for example. All these conditions mean that surviving evidence is scanty both in numbers of sites and amount of data. Fortunately one such location has been carefully studied: known as Nichoria in modern times, the hilltop site provided a home for communities of people since the early centuries of the second millennium. In the Late Bronze Age it was drawn into the expanding kingdom in the southwestern Peloponnese that was increasingly controlled from Pylos. During the height of the Mycenaean Age, its counterpart in the Argolid would have been one of the larger villages drawn into the orbit of Mycenae. In this role, Nichoria may have been fairly typical of mainland towns in the Late Bronze Age. However, in enduring after the collapse of the Pylian kingdom, it was unusually fortunate: it was one of very few Mycenaean towns of the region to become a Dark Age settlement.

Vincent Desborough's description of the southern Peloponnese as virtually "empty of life" is a useful definition for much of the Greek mainland during the second century of the Dark Age—not many people, but there were a few. Although survivors of the catastrophe possessed little of the wealth or sophisticated organization of their predecessors, and few of the foreign contacts, they forged their simpler societies from what remained, often on the same sites that had served as Mycenaean centers.

The Site

Excavated from 1969 to 1975, the finds in their quantity, variety, and larger contextual setting furnish what was described in 1983 as "incomparably the most dependable record that has so far been recovered" (McDonald, Coulson, and Rosser 1983, 318). The site itself is a flat-topped ridge, 500 meters long and 95 meters in elevation.[1] Its north and south edges are precipitous, making the position defensible. A single main approach is from the northwest; a steeper path climbs from the northeast, passable but not easily so. The site is obscured by the leading edge of low hills in the lower valleys of the five-rivers region where it stands and so is neither prominent nor conspicuous—valuable qualities during the insecurity of the early Dark Age. The location is strategically sound in a number of other ways. Nichoria is a pivotal point in a land transportation system, and at two kilometers from the Messenian Gulf, it can take advantage of sea transport as well. The rivers of the region do not permit ship traffic, but their water supply provides irrigation for agricultural land that is without springs.

These features made the ridge town valuable in the expanding Pylian kingdom during the flourishing centuries of the Mycenaean Age. It may have been the regional center of one of the two provinces of the realm—known as the Further Province—in an extension of centralization similar to the process we have examined for Mycenae. However, the relationship between Bronze Age Nichoria and the palace center at Pylos is likely to have been different from that between the dependencies which lay scattered about the Argive plain and Mycenae. For Mycenae, the centralizing tendencies of the fourteenth and thirteenth centuries seem to have bound small peripheral communities ever more tightly to the palace center, thus limiting, perhaps even suppressing, local inclinations toward autonomy. Although forces of consolidation are in evidence at Pylos also, the occupants of the palace center seem not to have been so successful in reducing local independent action.[2]

We have seen in the case of Mycenae during the fourteenth and thirteenth centuries that the center apparently was able to monopolize the construction of those badges of power, the *tholos* tombs, while Messenia shows a wide distribution of such tombs, none of which is so grand as the Argive examples. The relative quantity and grandeur of the tomb remains can be explained by the degree of central control: the lords of Mycenae could command the manpower of the entire Argolid and restrict the use of tholoi to the palace vicinity, but local lords throughout Messenia drew on forces in their immediate neighborhoods to broadcast their status.

Thus it seems fair to speculate that Nichoria, though small by standards of the centers, was nevertheless the home of some wealth and power. Evidence from the local Linear B tablets suggests that the town was the seat of a local official, or *qa-si-re-u*, and those rather numerous *te-re-ta*—whom John Chadwick sees as "a class of local land-holders" (1976a, 76)—must have been spread throughout the kingdom. The tablets also show that the power of the palace was not unlimited: there was a range of production and exchange in which the palace did not participate; bureaucratic accounting was limited; and the very adjective *wa-na-ka-te-ro*, something like royal, seems principally associated with personal privileges of the *wa-na-ka* rather

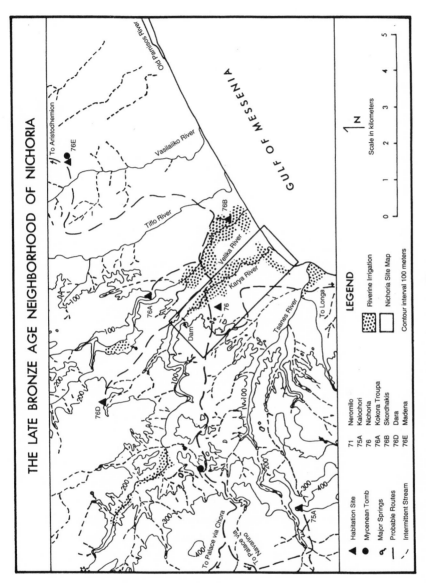

Map 4. Late Bronze Age neighborhood of Nichoria. *William G. Loy (1970, figure 40). Reproduction permitted by the U.S. government.*

than with official responsibilities. In Messenia, then, regions may have acted as semi-autonomous feudatories rather than units of a fully centralized kingdom. We may imagine such Messenian towns as Nichoria behaving at the local level somewhat in the manner of Pylos at the larger regional level, with the singular difference that Pylos, even in theory, answered to no greater power. And so Nichoria may have served as a redistribution center in miniature with agricultural and other surpluses being collected in a central storage facility, some to support the local population and increase the wealth of the local leader, some to be sent on to Pylos.

Physical remains, including an impressive *tholos* tomb and a wide street, affirm this postulated role, a surmise that is born out by evidence of a rise in population to between 600 and 800 people. Another testament to its position within the kingdom is Nichoria's fate in the time of troubles since, like other sites, it suffered in the widespread collapse. Thus, it was significant enough to be involved in the problems affecting so much of Greece. Its excavators believe that it was deserted for about a century from ca. 1200. However, a thin, random scattering of twelfth-century sherds may attest to uninterrupted occupation. The remains of the town itself, however, did not disappear, and seasonal herdsmen may have visited the ridge top without taking up fixed habitation.

The history of Nichoria in the Dark Age has been divided into four periods:

Dark Age I (1075–975)
Dark Age II (975–850)
Transition (850–800)
Dark Age III (800–750).

Beginning in about 1075 a small group of people did settle down permanently on the ridge. Some thirteen or fourteen families, numbering about sixty people, used portions of the remaining stone foundations to erect their individual one-room houses. This settlement lasted about a century, its members surviving more by hunting deer and pasturing animals—especially cattle—than through intensive agriculture. Homes were scattered on the ridge top, but the largest concentration emerged in the north sector, the most secluded portion of the hill. Judging from the remaining stone foundations, buildings were oriented haphazardly in something like a retracted

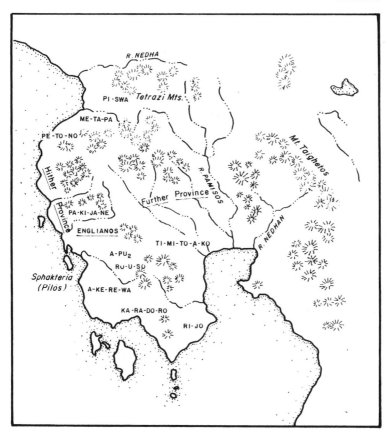

Map 5. The region of the Bronze Age kingdom of
Pylos. *Drawing © Alice Alden. Used by permission.*

form of the Mycenaean pattern of the settlement (Rapp and Aschenbrenner 1978, 95). Their form is known only from the remaining
stone foundations. Upon the groundwork of ruined houses from the
Mycenaean Age, the new inhabitants threw up "flimsy superstruc-
tures of organic materials" (McDonald, Coulson, and Rosser 1983,
57). Over time, timber frames with mud brick walls replaced the
wattle and daub used in the first settlement. Wooden rafters covered
with branches or reeds and, later, thatch provided roofs, while hard-
packed mud constituted floors of the buildings.

Population tripled in the settlement known as Dark Age II, which
succeeded the first without break and lasted from ca. 975 to 850.

7. Artist's reconstruction of Nichoria. *Drawing*
© Anne Lou Robkin. Used by permission.

Forty families, about two hundred people, dwelt on the ridge, many clustering their small apsidal homes around a larger structure. This building, originally 10.5 meters in length, was remodeled in the ninth century with the addition of an apse and a courtyard that increased the length to 15.9 meters. The new rear room was used for storage and some cooking after the large cooking pit in the center of the first structure went out of use, while a large main room accommodated all the other main household activities including, probably, family cult rites. Placed at the west end of the room, a stone-paved circle (about 1.60 meters in diameter) may have served as the place of sacrificing burnt offerings; sheep and goat bones together with a layer of carbonized material point to this conclusion, and the walling off of the circle in the remodeling of the building emphasizes its special significance.

In a period of transition in the settlement lasting from about 850 to 800, people drew themselves together ever more closely. The families congregated tightly around the central structure, a pattern that continued during the third and final settlement, Dark Age III

(800–750 B.C.E.). The community's size shrank to about twenty families, or one hundred people, but the central structure became even more massive, achieving a length of 20.2 meters, including the courtyard. Half of the complex was open to the air, and the amount of coarse pottery ware found in this area indicates that it was the collection and distribution center for the community. Two covered rooms may have served as a residence. This third settlement was the last, ending in fire near the middle of the eighth century. The excavators mention the possibility that the traditional enemies of Messenia, the Laconians, may have been responsible for the destruction of Nichoria. There is no definite evidence in favor of this speculation aside from the strong likelihood of Laconian trade with Nichoria during the preceding period, DAII. Even that link seems to have waned in DAIII. (McDonald, Coulson, and Rosser 1983, 216).

By and large, homogeneity marks the other evidence from Nichoria. Pottery provides the largest category of evidence: in the excavation publication, 198 pages are devoted to pottery, compared with 51 given to architecture and 42 to small finds. In DAI, pottery was "fired to a dirty white color with a rather soft and crumbly texture"; its two decorative motifs were the wavy line and an undecorated zone (McDonald, Coulson, and Rosser 1983, 110). Pottery remains increased in number in the second settlement; the range of shapes was the same as that of DAI, but decorative motifs were more varied. Most popular were concentric semicircles or cross hatched triangles painted with black color on clay which had been fired to a reddish yellow color (McDonald, Coulson, and Rosser 1983, 72). In the transitional period, potters took a greater interest in form and shape, although they used fewer decorative motifs. During the life of the final settlement, small shapes and coarse ware generally increased while the range of decorative motifs declined even more.

Accompanying pottery were small metal objects, chipped stone pieces, and spindle whorls. The metal objects are small and unimpressive: of 79 bronze pieces, 16 are no more than formless pieces of scrap or small droplets of waste metal. Those objects with recognizable shapes include 25 small personal objects such as rings, beads, and pins; 21 small tools and rivets; and a few statuettes. In addition, excavation produced 8 lead objects; 32 iron pieces of which 9 are scrap pieces and 6 are nails; and a single twist of gold wire (McDon-

8. Upper profile of a deep bowl, Dark Age II. *McDonald, Coulson, and Rosser (1983, plate 3–50). Courtesy of William A. McDonald and the University of Minnesota Press. Used by permission.*

ald and Wilkie 1992, 274ff.). Most of the metal goods were associated with the largest dwelling. The majority of stone and bone objects found at Nichoria come from Bronze Age deposits, although some were evidently reused in the Dark Age.[3] By contrast, whorls for spinning are abundant during the Dark Age: 44 are certainly Dark Age in date, another 34 probably are, and yet another 26 may belong to these centuries (McDonald, Coulson, and Rosser 1983, 287f.). Six rough spools, also dating to the Dark Age, may have been loom weights used in weaving.

In all categories, materials and design are essentially local, with some possible "foreign" goods deriving from other regions of Greece. Daily activities such as farming on the plain below the hilltop, tending of tree crops on the ridge itself, pasturing of animals, and production of secondary goods from plants and animals seem to have consumed the attention of all alike.

Living members of the community buried the dead in cist graves in a cemetery northwest of the ridge in a location overlapping a cemetery dating to the Mycenaean Age. Meager finds from two burials (bronze rings and pins, vessels and fragments of vessels, clay whorls) match the finds from the settlement of those dwelling in the first

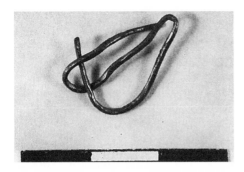

9. Dark Age gold wire. *William A. McDonald, "Excavations at Nichoria in Messenia,"* Hesperia 41 (1972) plate 51f. Courtesy of William A. McDonald and the American School of Classical Studies at Athens. Used by permission.

Dark Age settlement. Some burials in *pithoi*, or large vases, have also been found in the general area of the cists. Nearby, a small Mycenaean *tholos* was reused in DAI: close to the body were two vases, two bronze rings, bits of an iron pin, and a clay whorl. Another small *tholos* (2 meters in diameter) appears to date originally to the Dark Age.

Causes of Change

The eleventh century, at least at Nichoria, was thus a time of noticeable cultural continuity, despite its much lower level of sophistication. Dark Age Nichoria was situated on the very foundations of Mycenaean buildings, the deceased were interred near the Mycenaean cemetery and sometimes even in reused Mycenaean tombs. The repertoire of pottery shapes and designs descended from the wider range of Mycenaean ware. But were those who lived at Nichoria and made pottery reminiscent of earlier types the true descendants of Mycenaean Greeks? Or were they newcomers who borrowed from those whom they had displaced?

As we have already seen in considering the problems at Mycenae, the question of intruders is vexed. The traditional explanation of a "Dorian Invasion" does not fit neatly into the framework dictated by modern archaeological discoveries. Similar difficulties cloud a reconstruction of developments in Messenia. Here, too, a traditional reconstruction survives in Pausanias' curious story in the section of his guidebook dealing with Messenia (4.3.3–8); it *could* explain the fall of Pylos and the repopulation of the southwestern Peloponnese.

Two generations after the fall of Troy, the tale begins, the Peloponnese was successfully invaded by the Dorians, led by the Heraclidae. Upon arriving in Messenia, they expelled the descendants of Nestor, who had ruled Messenia from their palace center at Pylos. It happened, however, that the Heraclidae were in disagreement over which of them should rule in Messenia. Kresphontes was particularly anxious to gain the country for his share, but the others, with the exception of the eldest, Temenos, were equally keen to deny him the kingship. So Kresphontes persuaded Temenos to aid him in achieving his desire by means of a trick: Temenos commanded that lots should be drawn to decide the ruler of Messenia, and he placed a clay lot for each of the Heraclidae into a water-filled *hydria*, a vessel specially used for liquids. While the lots of the other contenders were of sun-dried clay, Kresphontes' was fire-baked, with the result that his lot was the only one not to dissolve in the water. Thus Kresphontes gained the sovereignty of Messenia. Pausanias goes on to say that the rule initiated by Kresphontes was just and not overly burdensome on the subject population. In fact, the Dorians divided the land equally with the Messenians. Moreover, the newcomers had ousted the Neleids, who had themselves been distrusted as outsiders, coming as they did from Thessalian Iolkos.

Though popular with the common people, the account continues, Kresphontes incensed the Messenian nobles, causing them to murder not only Kresphontes but also all of his sons save the youngest, Aipytos, who was safely out of the country at the time of the uprising. On reaching manhood, Aipytos returned to Messenia at the head of a large army raised from other parts of the Peloponnese. After taking vengeance upon the leaders of the massacre of his family, Aipytos became king, gaining such respect "that his descendants were called the descendants of Aipytos rather than of Heracles" (4.3.8; trans. Levi 1971).

This combination of folktale, charter myth, and saga assumes the reality of two events for which there is little or no archaeological evidence—perhaps an early instance of historians attempting to fill a void of evidence by manipulating and interweaving "in delicate gossamer the purported evidence of myth and legend" (Starr 1992, 2). While Pausanias speaks of the Dorian entrance into Messenia as part of an organized invasion that resulted in the conquest of the entire

Peloponnese, there is no archaeological evidence, aside from ruined citadels and handmade pottery, for any large intrusion followed by settlement. Moreover, the variable pattern and chronology evidenced at different sites undercuts the validity of a single cause for the difficulties. The tale also assumes the survival in Messenia of a substantial number of Mycenaeans, while the archaeological evidence attests to massive depopulation. Not only is there no sign of Dorians in Messenia in the twelfth and eleventh centuries, there are few signs of Mycenaeans either.

The Nature of Dark Age Nichoria

In spite of continuous elements, the world of Dark Age Nichoria was very different from that of the Bronze Age settlement. A major change occurred when links to the larger state directed from Pylos collapsed. In fact, by the eleventh century Pylos was no longer occupied. Although a few people continued to live among the ruins of Pylos in the early twelfth century, the site was soon deserted and remained forgotten until the twentieth century C.E. All the elements that constituted the increasing centralization of the Late Bronze Age disappeared: administrative regulation carried out with the aid of written records, production for an interactive system of exchange and redistribution, exposure to products and ideas alive in the larger Mycenaean and eastern Mediterranean orbits, increasing wealth manifested both in improved standards of daily life and in material luxuries.

Life in the eleventh century changed in other ways in response to the great difficulties. Mobility replaced permanency in much of Greece. Anthony Snodgrass has concluded that the apparent desertion of hundreds of Mycenaean sites, together with later reoccupation and memory of their names, could be explained as the result of intermittent visits by pastoralists (1987, 190–209).[4] The thesis does not assert that Greeks of the early Dark Age reverted to complete nomadism or even seasonal transhumance but that they placed greater reliance on pastoral resources than had been practiced in the Bronze Age or would typify the Classical Greek economy.

As we have seen, a rise in the proportion of cattle bones in early Iron Age Nichoria points to greater reliance on animal husbandry.

Nor is Nichoria the only example of such signs: several sites, including Eretria and Lefkandi on the island of Euboea, have remains of small, simple structures beneath the more permanent buildings of the later Dark Age. The small structures could be explained as seasonal abodes of short-term visitors, and the crude handmade pottery, sometimes attributed to newcomers, could be the product of migratory people who did not regularly use a potter's wheel.

Animal husbandry offers several advantages in an unstable environment. Animals are sources of food, labor, and secondary products that can be stored until they are needed. In addition, animals are movable wealth and, as such, can serve as objects of exchange. Thucydides remembered an earlier time when

> The people were migratory and readily left their homes whenever they were overpowered by numbers. There was no commerce. . . . The several peoples cultivated their own soil just enough to obtain a subsistence from it. But they had no accumulations of wealth and did not plant the ground. (1.2; trans. Jowett 1900)

It is impossible, of course, to date the period described by Thucydides; however, archaeological evidence indicates a good fit with the early Dark Age. As Snodgrass proposes, the high proportion of sheep and oxen figurines dedicated at Olympia in the earlier part of the Dark Age but declining in the later centuries may help in assigning general dates to the period of increased pastoralism. This tendency is not evident throughout the entire mainland; as we will see, Attica is a good example of different developments.

The evidence from Nichoria shows clearly that animals played a great role in sustaining the lives of the inhabitants on the ridge. Analysis of cattle bones (McDonald, Coulson, and Rosser 1983, 323) suggests that the proportion of beef in the diet at Nichoria fell from about 20% in the flourishing Mycenaean Age to about 11% at the end of the Bronze Age, and then rose steadily to 45% in Dark Age III. By comparison, the proportions of sheep, goats, and pigs seem to have declined after the Bronze Age. On the other hand, more dogs lived in the small community. Bones of the red deer, and later the roe deer, are proportionately greater in Dark Age Nichoria than they were during the Mycenaean Age. These finds combine to suggest that settlers on the ridge spent a good bit of time pasturing domesticated animals in the bottomlands near the ridge and hunting wild

10. Helicopter photo of Nichoria from the northwest. *Rapp and Aschenbrenner (1978, plate 9.5). Courtesy of William A. McDonald and the University of Minnesota Press. Used by permission.*

animals in lands that, with less intensive cultivation, were reverting to woodlands. Dogs would be invaluable aides to humans in both occupations, especially since human numbers were so few. In fact, pasturage and hunting require less labor than farming.

Nevertheless, evidence shows that some crops were grown: grains (wheat and probably barley as well), grapes, olives, legumes of the pea family, figs, wild cherries, and acorns are part of the archaeological record. As in the case of deer bones, there is a strong suggestion that some foodstuffs were gathered, not produced. Others, particularly the long-lived olive trees, may have been an inheritance from Mycenaean times. Cereal grains, vegetables, and some fruits were planted, harvested, and stored on the site itself. Certain animals, too, would have been kept in the settlement—for example, the more vulnerable young and pregnant females; there was plenty of space unoccupied by humans available on the ridge top. That Nichorians did not venture more widely for possible resources is shown by the few remains of shellfish in the record, even though the Gulf was only two kilometers distant.

In addition to farming and herding, another ongoing task was carrying water to the settlement from the river bed or springs at the base of the mound, for there was no source of water on its top. Not quite so regular were several fundamental household crafts: pottery making, spinning wool and weaving it into textiles, leather working, and care of the buildings of the small village. Some cooperation is shown by the large buildings, and specialized production is probable for metal goods, the better pottery, and perhaps objects fashioned from chipped stone and worked bone. These more specialized skills show no change in tradition but rather continuity from the Bronze Age, although both quantity and quality had declined. The spindle whorls, for example, are clumsy, asymmetrical, handmade, and plain fired, it seems, in the family oven or hearth. They are thus both "symptoms of hard and troubled times" (McDonald, Coulson, and Rosser 1983, 291) and indications of adaptation of remembered technology to suit the new conditions.

Social Organization

Our picture of the physical community and the nature of subsistence for its members does not produce an image of complexity in any aspect of life. While we can only speculate about the organization and organizers of Nichoria, the picture is one of a close community. However, the larger building at Nichoria demonstrates some distinction among members of the community, implying the residence of a slightly more significant family. Its interior hearth (the stone-paved circle described above) may have been the scene of gatherings of the adults to discuss affairs that concerned them all, or it may have been the communal hearth for cult activities. In fact, it probably served both of these purposes and others as well. Since most of the metal scraps were associated with this building, we may regard its inhabitants as wealthier and, perhaps, of higher status in the community. Even so, the building was a dwelling set amidst other similar, though smaller, dwellings; not variety but homogeneity characterizes the community. If a single leader directed the affairs of the group, he did so living in the midst of others and possessing wealth of much the same order. And he communicated directly with others since, as we have seen in examining twelfth-century Mycenae, the administrative tool of written records vanished with the last palaces. Reliance on direct speech and oral tradition filled the needs of communal memory. The spoken word was crucial to Dark Age life: the age provides a rare example of a culture operating in conditions wholly dependent upon speech.[5]

With the collapse of the Mycenaean centers, the limited literacy provided by the Linear B script disappeared with the administrative systems that had called it forth. Literacy, ever symptomatic of complexity in society, ceased to have a function when that complexity ended. It is at present impossible to pin down exactly when the knowledge of Linear B was lost. Our evidence indicates that the script ceased to be used quite suddenly around 1200, at the time of the destructions of the citadels; although Mycenaean civilization lingered at a number of sites, there is no indication of further use of any sort of writing. It may be that people did not simply "forget" the script or that the palace administrators engaged in its use were all casualties of the destructions but rather that the new, simpler circumstances no longer required the sort of documents for which it had been employed.

However, even the simplest of societies needs a form of communication between its members and a means of passing knowledge to its young. Instruction, norms of social and religious behavior, acceptable land use, and definitions of status are no less necessary for simple societies than for complex societies. In the absence of literacy, the rules of society must be passed on by word of mouth.

Because the spoken word is impermanent, it must be made memorable. Among the Greeks, speech was patterned in form and in subject. Ideas were shaped into groups of words that fit into an elaborate poetic meter dependent upon variation of long and short syllables. Once an idea was suitably shaped to the poetic form, it could be inserted into longer accounts. Since long accounts are even more difficult to recall than shorter stories, their usual form draws heavily on devices to ensure memorability, both for the narrator and for the audience. In addition to poetic form, successful oral traditions are

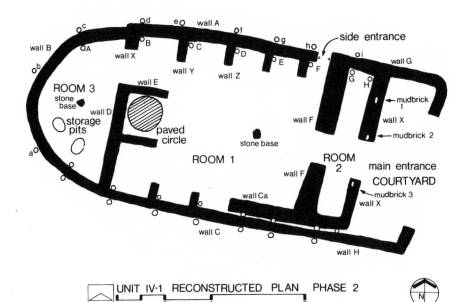

UNIT IV·1   RECONSTRUCTED   PLAN   PHASE 2

marked by larger-than-life events and figures that have immediate significance for the audience. Although individual narrators are important to the creation and retention of an oral tradition, they are controlled by the interests of their community; their efforts would go for naught without communal acceptance. It is telling that individual shapers of the tradition are, for the most part, anonymous.

We are fortunate in having the end product of the oral tradition of Dark Age Greece fixed in writing when literacy returned to Greece at the very end of the centuries of darkness. Dubbed the "Encyclopedia of the Dark Age" by Eric Havelock (1963, esp. 61–84), who first defined its crucial role in society, the epic poetry of Homer allows us to glimpse the mentality of those who created it and passed it on to their children.

Nonliteracy and the epic encyclopedia open a number of windows looking in upon Dark Age life. Beyond showing life to be without the level of complexity that generally accompanies the development of literacy, complete reliance on the spoken word fosters

11a; 11b. Unit IV (Nichoria): Reconstructed plan and recreation of exterior. *McDonald, Coulson, and Rosser (1983, figures 2.18 and 2.19). Courtesy of William A. McDonald and the University of Minnesota Press. Used by permission.*

certain features of communal organization and perceptions about the world. Praise poetry, for example, honoring the deeds of local ancestors, would have encouraged the present generation to strive to emulate them. Just such an effect seems to have been produced by the Homeric corpus. Nonliteracy, then, was one of the basic forces that defined the ways people interacted with one another, both formally and informally. Its influence is visible in the form of community and relationships with other communities, as well as in the very conceptions about the proper ordering of life.

In all of the communities we are considering, smallness of territory and of population has been a notable characteristic. Direct communication between members of such tiny communities was both possible and natural. Recognition of the importance of communal discourse is nicely captured in Hannah Arendt's definition of the later Greek community as "the organization of the people as it arises out of acting and speaking together" (1958, 198). More equal participation in the affairs of the community is often a feature of oral societies. Yet since effective speech is so vital to communal well-being, a mark of higher status may well be verbal eloquence. It is not amiss to suggest that the "Big Man" in Nichoria was skilled in words as well as in action, in the fashion of Homeric leaders. Reliance on discourse molded fundamental conceptions of the world and the role of humans in it.

Maintenance of proper order was the priority of the entire community, both as agents of defining that order and as its enforcers. Justice was communal business from the time of our first evidence in the *Iliad* and *Odyssey* and remained so throughout the Classical period. It is not surprising that gods participated equally in the process of securing order for the community, for in societies reliant upon the spoken word, divinity is neither remote nor separate from the human world.

The conception of gaining a livelihood was partly shaped by the value placed on direct communication: from the Dark Age through the Classical period, economic activity was essentially local, personal, limited in specialization, and characterized by little sophistication of management. In sum, dependence upon direct communication conditioned every aspect of Greek life as it moved through the centuries of transformation.

If, as we suspect, the art of writing disappeared, there is little concrete evidence of the operation of oral discourse in the Dark Age communities, apart from the end product, the Homeric epics which were captured by the newly rediscovered web of writing at the end of the eighth century. We may glimpse this world in the Homeric epics, although the issue of the poems' historicity has been hotly debated for centuries.[6] While some have seen the epics as ahistorical, completely fictitious, others are convinced that they reflect true conditions of life in early Greece. Further complications arise from the disagreement about the period thought to be reflected: a case has been made for the Mycenaean Age itself; others have identified "Homer's world" with the difficult times of the tenth and ninth centuries; many argue for the ninth and eighth centuries; and, finally, a case has been put for the Archaic period.

One solution is to recognize the several "chronological" levels that coexist in the poems as they were captured in written form toward the end of the eighth century: layers discernible in the tales show that they had evolved for centuries through oral transmission. Archaeological evidence, for instance, has shown that certain "antiquities" were retained, and the list of Greek forces mustered at Troy has hallmarks of a Mycenaean catalogue. In spite of these retentions, however, a feature of oral tradition is gradual modernization: to succeed with his audience, a singer must weave new and old threads together to create an immediately intelligible account.[7] If a specific passage is puzzling, the flow of the account collapses—a disaster when the only tool of transmission is the spoken word. Many believe that pieces of information intended to be preserved must be linked to the existing corpus of information within one or two generations or they will be lost. Thus, we are persuaded that much of the backdrop of the *Iliad* and *Odyssey* was understandable to audiences of eighth century Greece. Consequently, the modern historian can use the poems to provide glimpses of that world.

On this premise, let us return to the way of life of preclassical communities. Homeric kings are known as *basileis* (each one a *basileus*), and there are a great many of them collected together at Troy in the *Iliad* or attempting to reestablish a normal life at home in the *Odyssey*. These leaders of society are marked by two primary qualities: they are redoubtable fighters, always standing in the forefront of battle, and because of their own wisdom, they are able to provide useful counsel to others. Specific adjectives identify a *basileus* as one who gives the sign, sets to order, regulates, and shows his strength in his very physical appearance. Mental powers are demonstrated by fluency of speech, useful advice, presiding over assemblies, and sharing opinions with others who are also recognized as wise. The outstanding heroes of the epics gain renown in their local communities through these traits and show their status by means of greater possessions, especially land and its products, as well as herds of animals.

Though a *basileus* has a role that transcends immediate family concerns, his basis of strength is his own household, or *oikos*. At least in the epic world, these households were the largest kinship groups. When Odysseus seeks to reassert his power in Ithaca, for instance, he has the aid of his son and two household slaves. By preserving and enriching his own *oikos*, a man draws other families—through their own leaders—to his following. He keeps the allegiance of other heads of families as long as he is successful in battle and counsel, demonstrating his skills by means of material acquisitions. When he fails, leadership passes to the person giving the best advice or best proving himself in combat.

The physical picture of Nichoria accords well with such a situation. The community is virtually an extended family, and the village leader, the head of the most important family. The community of Dark Age Nichoria, numbering some two hundred individuals during the tenth and ninth centuries, appears to be founded on a more stable foundation than its immediate predecessor. Too large to have supported itself by hunting and herding alone, the DAII settlement shows the first signs of renewed social differentiation and complexity. The large building occupied during this period and named by the excavators Unit IV-1 seems not to have been used solely as a center for cult activities or communal stores; its primary purpose may have been the residence of an exceptional person, known to modern anthropologists as the "Big Man" of the community, along with his immediate family.

We have mentioned this anthropological conception in connection with the emergence of certain centers and their leaders in the earlier Bronze Age.[8] The term first came into common use in the 1960s in the scholarly literature dealing with the anthropology of the Melanesian islanders of the southwest Pacific. Referring to no formal office, the term indicates rather a type, much like such terms as "captain of industry" or its negative "robber baron." Not offices to which people may be appointed or elected, instead the terms reflect a state of being which people attain through their own deeds or misdeeds. The term Big Man carries some of the same informal, *ad hoc* quality in its meaning. Any man, if he is energetic enough and has valuable connections and luck, can be a Big Man.

The motive that drives aspirants to this condition is the attainment of status, the desire to be influential. Since societies of the Big Man type commonly occur in situations in which there is a low population and a relative abundance of land or other vital resources, the control of land and resources is not sufficient to make a Big Man. Instead it is people that the aspiring Big Man must collect; by attracting a following, a network of clients among ordinary men, one achieves status. In addition, such a person becomes a man of status in the eyes of his peers by striking alliances with them and engaging with them in competitive generosity—activity which seems to be central to the creation and maintenance of the Big Man status. The Big Man initially attracts and maintains his following through such displays as feast-giving or by providing a bride-price for the marriageable sons of his followers. He forges alliances with the Big Men of neighboring regions through ritual gift-giving and establishes superiority over them by besting them in a potlatch or competitive display of generosity. Such displays are governed only in part, if at all, by a desire to be an aid and comfort to others; the real wellspring of the Big Man's generosity is the search for status and influence. A by-product of these displays is redistribution of goods.

To call a Big Man a chief is incorrect; a Big Man society is distinct from a chiefdom in a number of important respects. Foremost is the personal, rather than institutional, character of the Big Man's power. He is in every respect a self-made man; an ordinary man becomes a Big Man solely by means of his own personal actions and attributes. He is not born to the role as a prince is born to be king. So personal is the Big Man's power and so bound up is it with his status that the Big Man's status and influence are virtually identical to the role of Big Man itself. Thus, should the Big Man ever lose status, he would in effect cease to be a Big Man. When he dies he cannot pass this status on to his sons.

By contrast, the status of a chief is not completely dependent upon his own deeds—one can be born into this role. Thus a chief can lose status and even behave shamefully without necessarily ceasing to be chief. When the chief dies, there will always be another to take his place, whether through election or the succession of his son. A chiefdom has an institutional quality that is totally lacking in a Big Man society. The latter lacks complexity in that anyone can become Big Man, while a chiefdom displays the ranking of a more complex society. The greater structure provides a continuity and stability to the community.

While the consensus among scholars of early Greece seems to be that the evidence does not favor a classic Big Man society in all its details, the model is suggestive enough to fuel arguments for either a modified Big Man leadership or a low-level chiefdom.[9] In other words, there is a variety of positions between the classic Big Man and the institutionalized chief as originally described into which Greek polities of the Dark Age could fall; given the pronounced regional character of life in the Dark Age, variety is to be expected. Yet all descriptions emphasize the noninstitutional, personalized nature of leadership and a dependence on personal loyalty and alliance, guest-friendship, ritual gift-giving, and redistribution disguised as generosity. The instability of Dark Age leadership and its unimpressive record of achievement are regularly stressed as well.

James Whitley (1991a), for example, draws upon durability of settlement as a means of defining political and organizational distinctions. In his view, Dark Age sites should be viewed either as "stable" or "unstable." Stable sites are those such as Athens and Knossos, which show continuous occupation through the Dark Age and into succeeding periods. For Whitley, the longevity of such sites is an indication of a stable leadership that allowed the community to withstand not only the vicissitudes of the Dark Age but the cultural revolution at the end of that era. Unstable sites are those sites which were occupied only for a short duration and which, in most instances, did not survive the Dark Age. Their instability arose in part from their political and social structure as Big Man societies. The great weakness of Big Man societies is the ephemeral character of the personal loyalties and charisma upon which the Big Man's power is based. In a true Big Man society, the location of the community—the land upon which it is based—is of much less importance than the ties of the community to the Big Man himself. Upon the death of the Big Man, the community tends to drift apart or is attracted to the neighborhood of another Big Man.

Among the sites matching this description Whitley includes Nichoria and, in another slightly different category, Lefkandi (to which we will return in chapter Four). We argue that Nichoria is both stable and an instance of a Big Man society. In Whitley's view, short duration alone places it among the unstable sites, a means of categorization that is not compelling: excepting the possible seventy-five- to one-hundred-year hiatus following the destruction of Pylos around 1200, Nichoria enjoyed more or less permanent occupation from the late third millennium to ca. 750 B.C.E., or nearly 1500 years. Nor, as Whitley admits, does Nichoria belong among those sites which display spatial instability. The most noticeable "shifts" occurred in the expansion or contraction of the community's core, and during the three centuries of the Dark Age settlement the site seems on present evidence to have been stable. Furthermore, during all of DAII (975–850) there existed only one building of sizable proportions, which though remodeled and expanded was never abandoned for the sake of another structure. Its DAIII successor was erected virtually next door to the older building, its east wall actually abutting the apse of the earlier unit.

Even in DAI (ca. 1075–975), when the site boasted a population of no more that fifty or sixty souls, there is likely to have been some man, or set of men, who assumed leadership functions. In fact, if there ever was a Big Man at Nichoria, he is likely to have gained his status during this early period. In these years conditions were beginning to calm following the disasters of the late thirteenth and twelfth centuries, allowing a resumption of settlement at Nichoria after the hiatus.

The scanty evidence allows no definitive explanation, but the following scenario may be plausible. Nichoria was abandoned, not destroyed, and it seems improbable that the entire population was put to the sword or led into slavery or died of natural causes. In fact, the inhabitants may have been forewarned of whatever danger was approaching and made a successful escape. Archaeological evidence points to a stronger Mycenaean element in Arcadia following the destructions, and former Nichorians may have been part of that influx.

Having arrived safely in Arcadia, the Nichorian émigrés will have been forced by circumstances to adopt a transhumant life of herding and hunting, typical of Arcadian populations down to late Classical and Hellenistic times and even beyond. Under such transient conditions, the survivors would likely have split into bands in which a premium would be placed on mobility. The small size of such bands would favor egalitarianism over social ranking, and such leaders as they had will have attained their positions owing to their skill as hunters and warriors.

That the wanderers maintained some contact with their ancestral home is entirely possible. The very presence of LHIIIC sherds is proof that someone was making occasional visits to Nichoria. The mixed nature of DAI pottery, the reuse of a Bronze Age *tholos*, and

particularly the construction in DAII of a small new *tholos* are perhaps indicative not merely of a continuity of tradition, but of a return
of the descendants of the Bronze Age population.

With the passing of the immediate threat, perhaps within a generation or two, people may have begun moving back into the area
on a seasonal basis. By the turn of the eleventh century, it is possible
that several small groups were maintaining seasonal camps within
the neighborhood. The resettlement of Nichoria sometime around
1075 may have been no more than a small-scale village nucleation,
or an early example of "synoecism," that is unification of smaller
settlements into a single community—a process which has occurred
time and again under various appellations in Greek history and prehistory as Athens and Corinth show even more plainly.

It is at this point, at the beginning of DAI or shortly thereafter,
that the rise of a Big Man becomes possible. For a Big Man to thrive,
conditions can not be so unsettled that all are left to their own devices, yet neither can they be so settled and prosperous that leadership becomes institutionalized. Most important, however, a Big Man
society requires the production of a surplus. A would-be Nichorian
Big Man could attain power only by producing a surplus of his own
which he could then redistribute by holding banquets and through
other displays of generosity, thereby gaining status while putting the
rest of the community under an obligation.

Strangely, the particular circumstances of eleventh-century Nichoria may have fostered a transformation from a Big Man order,
characteristically unstable, to a stable chiefdom quite early. Big Men
seem to thrive on conditions in which there is an abundance of resources, including land, and a scarcity of people. In the case of Nichoria, there may have been such an abundance of empty land and
such a scarcity of people that the role of the Big Man became institutionalized for lack of either internal or external competition. Big
Man societies are said to be dependent upon large and complex kinship groups to act as the Big Man's core of support, but the archaeological evidence for Dark Age Nichoria points to smaller units, the
nuclear family. Nor does the evidence suggest the presence of external rivals: Nichoria was isolated, especially in the early Dark Age.
Thus, without rivals, the same family may have retained the highest
status in the community for more than a single generation.

By the mid-tenth century, consequently, when the first phase of Unit IV-1 seems to have been built, we can no longer argue for the presence of a Big Man at Nichoria. The construction of large, rather complex, permanent structures such as Units IV-1 and IV-5 presents strong evidence of a continuity of position quite uncharacteristic of a Big Man society. To the extent that such buildings represented the power of a leader, their permanence throughout DAII and III is persuasive that the Nichorian villagers had learned to regard leadership as an entity separate from the men who filled it. Just as there was now a continuity of function, there must also have been a growing continuity of men exercising that function, brought about either through the election of a new Big Man upon the death of the old or by the succession to Big Man status by the son of the former holder.

The population of Nichoria had grown to around two hundred inhabitants, a number perhaps too large to be controlled or easily influenced through ritual gift-giving alone, but not so large that loyalty, obedience, command, and power would cease to be personal. A chief will have retained personal qualities in his exercise of power while being freed somewhat from the pressures imposed by continual displays of competitive generosity. This is not to say that the leader was no longer expected to be generous and open-handed: but using the Homeric epics as reflective of Dark Age conditions, the portrayal of Agamemnon's greed and duplicity suggests that the chief, however flagrant his behavior, would not cease to be chief.

The archaeological evidence from Nichoria is good validation of the Homeric picture. One larger dwelling where communal functions took place was nestled among a group of homes, and their inhabitants, that progressively drew more tightly together. Minimal distinctions separated the families. Cooperation was necessary to ensure that the herds grazing in the bottomlands were safe, that leather was properly divided among every household, that the gods received their due portion of the olives. Signs of cooperation in battle are not readily apparent at Nichoria, but desire for safety is shown in the very location of the settlement.

In some early Dark Age communities, distinction was greater. We will consider the case of Lefkandi in some detail, but to anticipate, a tenth-century burial there offers evidence of very high status attached to two unusually rich inhabitants, a man and a woman. Such variations are to be expected since regionalism is an increasing mark of Dark Age Greece. Localism was always characteristic of the ancient Greek world, tempered by growing consolidation only in the Late Bronze Age, and even then Mycenae seems to have outstripped other regions in tightening control over the surrounding villages. During the Late Bronze Age, however, a cultural uniformity spread, at least among palace sites, so that art, architecture, craft products, and even the Linear B script show little variation from region to region. From the eleventh century onward, by contrast, regionalism was woven into the very fabric of life, encouraged by several factors. The huge decline in population on the mainland of Greece resulted in tiny, scattered groups of people. Vincent Desborough described the southern Peloponnese during these hard times as nearly uninhabited (1972, 83f.). That is not quite the case, but it is nearly correct. Fear promoted seclusion, and the low level of culture acted as a barrier to traders from more advanced societies beyond the Aegean.

The eleventh century, then, is a time of collapse back to the usual form of community in ancient Greece, the village. Life was hard, without pretension, regular in its demands from one day to the next. Families of four or five lived in simple homes where they were self-sufficient for many of their needs. Some labor was invested in common concerns, as shown by the stored surplus food in the latest large building of Nichoria. Heads of families gathered around the hearth of the most powerful villager to discuss and plan these common concerns.

The glorious Mycenaean past was very much a part of their world, but more as a memory passed to children through song than as a true imitation. We can imagine a parent encouraging a child to envision the grand street that once crossed the ridge top from end to end, linking the site to a glorious palace in the distant realm of the "hither kingdom." It must have been difficult for the child or even the parent to form a clear image of that palace. Yet, a level of continuity is clear: one of the communities drawn into the Pylian kingdom survived even when the palace center was destroyed. The material culture of the villagers was Submycenaean in both senses of the term: that is, it derives from Mycenaean products but in less-accomplished forms. Continuity also seems to mark the inhabitants of Dark Age Nichoria; a strong case can be made that survivors of the catastrophe led a less settled life for two or three generations until they eventually returned to their ancestral settlement.

3

Athens

Tenth Century
Breath of Spring

Mycenae and Nichoria represent two points on the spectrum of Dark Age sites. Mycenae, perhaps the most powerful citadel center among its mainland contemporaries during the thirteenth century, endured three disasters to continue a lesser existence through most of the twelfth century. Then, around the last quarter of that century, the citadel was largely abandoned, although some habitation is indicated during the Submycenaean and Protogeometric periods. An indication of its final altered status is found in the Greek muster list for the battle against invading Persians in the fifth century: the former home of Agamemnon, leader of the host at Troy, could contribute only eighty hoplites.

Though Nichoria was an important town in its own right in the Late Bronze Age, it was caught up in the process of centralization reaching out from Pylos. Thus its status, size, and population were far less than Mycenae's. In the twelfth century, too, Nichoria's history was just the reverse of Mycenae: virtually abandoned for two or three generations after the time of troubles, it became home to a few people dwelling amidst ruins of its past life in the eleventh century. Through the Dark Age, the settlement grew in size and, presumably, stability, but it was abandoned in the late Dark Age and, thus, did not become an independent *polis* in the Classical period.

Both of these sites illustrate the most prominent single characteristic of the first two centuries of the Dark Age: destruction of places, people, and institutions. That the destruction was not complete is nicely shown by another site: Athens had a significant role in the Bronze Age, and it would become the "school of Hellas" in the Classical period. Its Dark Age history distinguishes it in that age as well.

While there was a sense of insecurity in Athens during the general destructions of the late thirteenth and early twelfth centuries, the site did not suffer the fate of either Mycenae or Nichoria: settlement continued uninterrupted from the Mycenaean into the Submycenaean era. In fact, it may have been a refuge for Mycenaean Age survivors from other parts of Greece. By comparison with other settlements of the Submycenaean era, Athens was vigorous, attracting the attention of craftsmen and traders, even from places as distant as the Levant. Its vigor did not persist through the whole of the Dark Age, however: by the early eighth century the prominence of Athens, even within Attica, had been lost. Thus, unification of territory that became the *polis* of the Athenians began anew in the Archaic period (see Table 2).

Table 2: Athenian Dark Age Periodization

Late Mycenaean	ca. 1200–1125 B.C.E.
Submycenaean	ca. 1125–1050 B.C.E.
Protogeometric	ca. 1050–900 B.C.E.
Geometric	ca. 900–700 B.C.E.

Late Bronze Age Conditions

Attica experienced the process of unification attested for several regions in the Late Bronze Age. Akin to circumstances in Messenia and the Argolid, numerous small sites were gradually drawn within the sphere of a single citadel site as centralized rule subsumed the authority of local leaders. The existence of written records confirms the accuracy of this reconstruction for Mycenae, Pylos, and Thebes. Although no Linear B tablets from Athens survive, evidence of pottery shows a growing uniformity, and architectural remains from the Athenian acropolis, though meager, have features similar to those of other centers. A major difference between Athens and other centers lies in the time when unification reached its height: only toward the very end of the Mycenaean Age did Athens rise in prominence. *Tholos* tombs at several sites (such as Menidi, Thorikos, and Marathon) suggest the strength, as well as the wealth, of individuals of considerable stature well into the thirteenth century. Individual sites retained ceramic distinctions through most of the age; and one view of the architectural innovations on the Acropolis dates them to the twelfth century. Regionalism remained a potent force in Attica far longer than it did at Mycenae.

Yet Athens did extend its authority in the twelfth century.[1] One indication is the new influence of Athens in the pottery of other sites, especially that of Salamis. It is noteworthy that several important sites, such as Perati and A. Kosmas, ceased to exist in the Submycenaean period (ca. 1125–1050 in Athens), while Salamis came within the cultural sphere of Athens. In fact, Athens and Salamis are the only well-established sites during this period. Although the cultural superiority of Athens was not extraordinary and Attica, measured by absolute standards, was not a markedly prosperous region, in terms relative to the rest of twelfth-century Greece, conditions here were unusual. Athens grew strong, withstanding the difficulties of the Late Bronze Age while few other sites—either inside or outside the territory of Attica—were so fortunate.

The territory of Attica is more conducive to unification than are many other parts of the mainland. A peninsula jutting into the Aegean, it is bounded by sea on two sides and mountains on the third, features that lend a natural cohesion. Though encompassing some 2500 square kilometers, the area is not sharply divided into smaller compartments; even the interior mountains of Aigaleos, Pentelikon, Hymettos, and Laureion are not massive divides. They serve rather to define the three major plains of the peninsula—the western Thriasian, the central Mesogeia, and the western plain around Athens—where basic crop production permits a degree of self-sufficiency. The presence of silver and lead, abundant clay, and building materials (particularly fine marble) also encourages the self-containment of the region.

Still, these same features can push in just the opposite direction—that is, toward regionalism. Differences in the nature of the land throughout the peninsula create various economies: while the plains are good agricultural land, the shallow soil of the hills and mountains is suited to olive trees and grazing. The areas in which unusual resources are located have yet another economic character. The peninsula's very size along with its several interior mountains, can promote localism, especially in times of low population or serious pressures, whether of human or natural agency. Attica's history in the period we are considering moved between these two poles of unity and regionalism.[2]

When conditions favor unity of the area, Athens is a likely candidate for the agent of unification. The plain of Athens is the largest of the three Attic plains, and it is enclosed on the north, west, and east by hills. To the south it opens to the sea. Athens itself is favored with two seasonal rivers, the Kephisos and the Ilisos, and with natural springs on its acropolis. That outcrop, too, is a special gift of nature: reaching 120 meters above the plain, it is suitably high and steep-sided to be a defensible stronghold but not so lofty or craggy as to prevent use by humans. Two natural paths—a gentle slope on the west and a deep cleft on the north—lead to a level plateau on the northwest sector, which offers a fair amount of habitable space.

In fact, the Acropolis was inhabited as early as the late Neolithic, and evidence of habitation continues from the Early Bronze Age through the Late Bronze Age without interruption into the Submycenaean era. The most substantial building and settlement occurred during the thirteenth and early twelfth centuries.[3] Spiros Iakovidis has identified three separate building periods during the Late Bronze Age.[4] The earliest is marked by the remains of a single room on the plateau. During LHIIIB, or the thirteenth century, a second burst of activity resulted in five artificial platforms of unequal size carved into the stone. These platforms were surrounded by retaining walls of considerable height, constructed of sizable stones bedded in shallow trenches. During this phase stairs were carved in the cleft forming the northeast ascent, which may have become the

12. Artist's reconstruction of Athens. *Drawing ©Anne Lou Robkin. Used by permission.*

main access to the summit. Also dating to this phase was the creation of an artificial descent from the summit to the lower plateau in front of several caves on the northwest slope. A palace may have rested on this platform.

During the late thirteenth century, a massive project resulted in a cyclopean wall with a perimeter of 700 meters. Constructed of large irregular blocks with surfaces roughly dressed, it may have been 9 to 10 meters high and 3 to 6 meters wide. Remains of a massive tower in the southwest segment define the location of the principal gate and main access to the citadel heights. The new fortifications blocked the northeast access. Within the 25,000 square meters enclosed by the wall stood the palace, of which very little survives. Even so, the few traces, together with the plan of the site and the nature of its fortification, are sufficient to convince such experts as Iakovidis that the architects of Mycenaean Athens modeled their construction on citadels of the Argolid, and perhaps also the stronghold at Gla. A shaft cut into the rock of the north slope, leading down eight flights of stairs to a spring chamber, echoes similar shafts at Mycenae and Tiryns.

The population of late Mycenaean Athens dwelt in houses on the Acropolis slopes, in the Kerameikos area to the northwest of the Acropolis, and also south of the Acropolis. What would become the agora of Athens in the Classical period was the main cemetery for Mycenaean Athens, though graves have been found in all areas. It is difficult to estimate the size of the settlement or of its population. Hope Simpson suggests that Mycenaean Athens was comparable in size to Mycenaean Tiryns, which he describes as "widespread and quite densely inhabited in the LHIIIB and LHIIIC periods at least" (1981, 43).

In seeking an explanation for this almost unique position of relative strength during the time of troubles for much of Greece, it is important to notice an intensification of contact with the Argolid reflected in Athenian pottery and in that of the new site established at Perati in eastern Attica. Later Greeks described this contact in more human terms:

> The sons of Pallas, who before were quiet upon expectation of recovering the kingdom after Aegeus's death, who was without issue, as soon as Theseus appeared and was acknowledged the successor, highly resenting that Aegeus first, an adopted son only of Pandion, and not at all related to the family of Erechtheus, should be holding the kingdom, and that after him, Theseus, a visitor and stranger, should be destined to succeed to it, broke out in open war. (Plutarch, *Theseus* 13; trans. Dryden 1932)

Another tradition traces the flight of Neleids from Pylos to Athens; descendants of the first Pylian refugees—Melanthos and Kodros—became kings of Athens (Strabo 9.1.7 and Pausanias 2.18.7). Such legends, coupled with the physical evidence of outside influence on Late Bronze Age Athens, suggest that this site served, for some reason, as a strong point, withstanding the difficulties of the late thirteenth and early twelfth centuries while few other mainland sites were so fortunate. Thus, the relative strength of Athens during the early Submycenaean period may have occurred by default: other settlements did not survive to impede an extension of power and cultural influence, or if they did survive, they were too weak to pose an obstacle to Athenian expansion.

It is impossible to identify the conditions that created such special status for Athens inasmuch as an answer is wrapped in the larger questions surrounding the cause(s) of difficulties throughout the eastern Mediterranean. If we knew that Dorians or other invaders were the culprits for the destruction of sites in the Argolid, for example, it would be arguable that Athens somehow foiled the would-be captors. Following this line of reasoning, Sarah Immerwahr has argued that Athens was "chosen as part of a central Mycenaean plan to defend the whole southeastern part of Greece north of the isthmus from threatened attack, . . . a kind of pan-Mycenaean strategy" (1971, 153). If, however, we ascribe the collapse of Mycenaean citadels to internal warfare, we might target Athens as a relatively insignificant center that was not yet worthy of attack by more powerful Mycenaean kingdoms. Thus, it has been suggested that the earlier destruction of Thebes allowed increased Athenian commercial activity in Boeotia, enhancing both the prosperity and the power of Athens. The site grew belatedly to a position of strength and its inhabitants were able to utilize that strength in the face of collapse elsewhere.

Although the explanation is uncertain, the result is not: Athens increasingly controlled the population of Attica through the Submycenaean into the Protogeometric period as late as the ninth century. As Desborough concluded, "the orderly nature of the community suggested by the standardization of culture and customs presumably meant a well-organised and strong city which gave it a prestige and primacy in the Greek world" (1972, 159).

Dark Age Conditions

The Dark Age settlement does not merit the title of city—hardly that of town; instead, groups of graves and the location of wells indicate several small concentrations of homes. In the Submycenaean period five groupings are apparent, while the Protogeometric period may have seen a slightly greater concentration in the area of the Agora, a trend that would continue. No substantial buildings remain to provide clues to the kinds of structures that housed Dark Age Athenians. Grave goods, on the other hand, reveal the continued extension of influence by these people into Attica: as the number of communities increased in the late eleventh, tenth, and ninth centuries, the remains recovered from them, especially pottery, show strong, persisting Athenian connections.

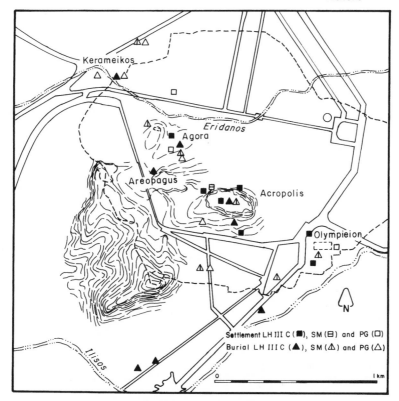

Map 6. Principal remains of LHIIIC—Protogeometric Athens. *Drawing © Alice Alden, after J. Vanschoon-winkel (1991, figure 3). Used by permission.*

Indeed, pottery documents Athenian prestige and primacy even beyond Attica. Continuity of the potter's craft is certain: at Athens itself, all phases of Late Helladic pottery are represented, with the last yielding to Submycenaean, which, in turn, is superseded by changes that mark Protogeometric ware in the mid-eleventh century. This Athenian material "constitutes the greatest amount of recorded and illustrated settlement pottery of this period. Nowhere in Greece or the Aegean," in Desborough's estimation, "is there anything to approach it" (1964, 13). It is not, however, the sole evidence from Attica: cemeteries on Salamis and in the Kerameikos provide additional material of the Submycenaean phase, while the large cemetery of Perati on the east coast, dating to the late thirteenth and twelfth centuries, has produced more than 800 vases of LHIIIC character (Desborough 1964, 115). The transition from LHIIIB to C is represented by a few vases, and at the later end, some examples can be termed Submycenaean.

In addition to revealing ongoing habitation or, in the case of cemeteries, use of the same location for burial, the pottery points to contact beyond Attica. The material from Perati reveals Aegean contacts, particularly with Naxos and the Dodecanese but also with the Argolid. In Desborough's words, "it displays a remarkable fusion of Argive, Naxian and Dodecanesian elements" (1964, 13). At Athens, connections with Cyprus seem to have been especially pronounced. Certain shapes that are characteristic of the Cypriot style (bottles, duck vases, ring vases, and pilgrim flasks) are found in Athens, as well as Lefkandi, at the time of transition to Protogeometric. A link between Athens and Crete is evident in the development of the Cretan Protogeometric style "with its direct Attic inspiration" (Snodgrass 1971, 80).

These connections to the outside world, along with unbroken ties to the earlier tradition, were key factors, in the eyes of Desborough, in locating the momentous change from shapes and designs of the Mycenaean tradition to techniques and conceptions that would produce the Geometric style. On the basis of clear evidence of continuity of settlement, he first concluded that Protogeometric style originated in Athens in ca. 1025 (1952, 294). Later, revising his position to accord to Thessaly an independent role in the rise of the new style (1964, 258ff.), he nevertheless continued to assert the significance of Athens in the development: even the largely independent process occurring in Thessaly owed an "initial debt to the Athenian Protogeometric style" (1964, 263). These developments, begun at Athens, marked a significant turning away from the "dead end of Mycenaean" (Desborough 1972, 145). As we have seen in examining the twelfth-century developments at Mycenae, Desborough stressed the importance of newly arrived intruders on the Greek mainland (1964, 259ff.). We believe that the new elements were due more to the measure of outside contact preserved in a few places, particularly Athens.

The ceramic development was, in part, a result of technical advances: the use of a faster wheel to throw the pottery produced more disciplined shapes, while the employment of the compass and the multiple brush created more careful decorative elements. Equally, however, potters seem to have approached their craft with a changed attitude about shaping and making the vessel. As Günther Kopcke has remarked, "The potter seems to have found a new aim in his craft" (1977, 36). Application of zoned decoration now clearly marked the divisions of the pot: simple geometric shapes occupied roughly a third of the surface, generally on the shoulder and/or neck of closed vases and the upper body of the open shapes. "The notion that each part of the pot had its own proper, separate function to perform, but that in doing so it should nevertheless preserve a harmonious proportion to the pot as a whole; and that the main decoration had its own proper place on the pot, to which it should be confined—these are among the qualities that distinguish the new style" (Snodgrass 1971, 46f.).

These innovations may appear insignificant in any effort to uncover the essential history of the Dark Age, but to the specialist's eye they reveal that potters and painters of the simple shapes had imposed order on their products (Hurwit 1985, 58). And they had begun to experiment with shapes and with decoration: living creatures join the wavy lines and concentric circles of Protogeometric vases. In a word, conditions in Athens now made it possible to spend time on

13. Protogeometric Amphora (ht. 52 cm.). © *Deutsches Archäologishes Institut Athen; negative number KER 3421. Used by permission.*

nonessential activities—a vase without a painted figure serves its purpose just as well as one with a figure.

The introduction of iron technology into the Aegean also underlines the importance of Athens.[5] In this development, as in the rise of Protogeometric pottery, continuity from the Bronze Age and contacts with the wider Mediterranean world played major roles. As our understanding of the spread of iron technology increases, the certainty grows that Cyprus served as an intermediary between the eastern Mediterranean and the Greek mainland and that one of the main points of contact was Athens (Desborough 1964, 25f.; 1972, 230f.).

A useful scheme for following the development of ironworking technology in the Mediterranean sphere is to discern three stages. At first, as an expensive commodity, its use was mainly ornamental; in the second stage iron was employed for practical tools and weapons, but bronze still predominated over iron; finally, those ratios between the two metals were reversed. Initial, largely independent, steps in this process are now located in the Levant, particularly in Palestine and Cyprus. "It seems that the Cypriot success . . . provided the vital breakthrough for the Iron Age in the Mediterranean area and indeed for the Old World generally" (Snodgrass 1980, 344f.). Intensive experimentation is evident in the twelfth century, interestingly at a time marked by a growing presence of Mycenaean objects—and probably Mycenaean people—on Cyprus; the full Iron Age on that island is dated to the mid-eleventh century. Diffusion of the Cypriot discoveries moved both eastward and westward in the twelfth and eleventh centuries.

A likely scenario is that the Aegean followed the Cypriot pattern of transition from bronze to iron, propelled at least at the start by imports of ready-made products from Cyprus, especially iron knives: some of the earliest Aegean examples of the new metal were iron knives modeled on Cypriot types. Influence from Cyprus continued, represented by two iron swords from Athenian graves dated to ca. 1050. Now, however, the link apparently weakened as different patterns emerged in the two regions. Local Aegean developments are apparent even in the twelfth century objects—in iron daggers and finger rings, for example—but from the mid-eleventh century Aegean ironworking followed a course of its own.

Athens stands out prominently in quantity of finds and in the rise of new uses of iron. A table of bronze and iron examples from Athens gives these ratios (see Table 3). Snodgrass calls attention to the use of iron for pins and fibulae, something "not often encountered anywhere else" (1980, 348).

Table 3: Comparative Use of Bronze and Iron in Athens during the Protogeometric Period

Type	No. of bronze examples	No. of iron examples
Swords	0	8
Spearheads	4	4
Daggers*	0	2
Knives*	0	4
Dress-pins	13	47
Fibulae	9	12
Axes, tools, arrowheads	0	3

(Snodgrass 1980b, 348, Table 10.2.)
*The dagger in Kerameikos I, 192, plate 76, tomb 17, is classified by Snodgrass as a knife.

Certainly Athens was not the only Aegean site active in the early stages of ironworking: Tiryns, Lefkandi, Naxos, Crete, and Macedonia were also important in the transition from bronze to iron. The current picture suggests that developments in Macedonia were largely independent, due in part to links with the Balkans or Asia Minor (Desborough 1972, 254f.), and in turn, these northern developments influenced Epirus (Desborough 1972, 261). Crete seems to have been in direct contact with Cyprus (Desborough 1972, 251; Snodgrass 1980, 349). By contrast, developments in southern Greece link Athens, Lefkandi, and Tiryns—perhaps also Naxos—showing that they interacted with one another as well as with Cyprus.

It is true that iron ore is present in all these regions; but it is also present in parts of Greece where ironworking developed only much later. In the western regions of central Greece and the Peloponnese, for instance, there is little ironwork dated before about 900 (Snodgrass 1980, 351f.). Beyond the raw material, the new technology required the acquisition of skills from pioneers in the art of ironworking. And it needed a community in which some specialization could be supported. The relative stability of Athens in the eleventh and tenth centuries provided both conditions.

The Ionian Migration

Another category of evidence underscores the importance of Athens as a conduit to the larger Mediterranean and Aegean sphere: traditional accounts of migration from the Greek mainland to the coast of Asia Minor name Athens as the point of departure.[6] On the authority of Pherekydes, whose fifth-century account has not been preserved, Strabo reports that "Androklos, legitimate son of Kodros the king of Athens, was the leader of the Ionian colonization . . . and he became the founder of Ephesus" (Strabo 14.1.3; trans. Jones 1927). Pausanias supplies more detail, telling how the eldest sons of Kodros—Neileus and Medon—quarreled over the kingship of Athens; the Delphic oracle was required to decide the issue. When the oracle awarded the kingship to Medon, "Neileus and Kodros's other sons were sent away to found a colony, with any Athenians who wanted to go with them" (7.2.1; trans. Levi 1971). Though most modern scholars would agree with the verdict of Carl Roebuck that "there is much, of course, to object to in this tradition" (1955, 62f.), evidence of several sorts allows the conclusion that "the movement of the Ionians eastwards from Attica and elsewhere, is real enough" (Snodgrass 1971, 302).

The traditional evidence quite uniformly makes Attica a point of refuge for various peoples: when the Ionians of Achaea were dispelled from their lands, they moved to Athens (Herodotus 1.145, Pausanias 7.1.4), where they were received as fellow citizens by King Melanthos. Melanthos himself was, on the conventional view, a newcomer to Athens. A descendant of one of Nestor's brothers, Melanthos joined other Pylians in fleeing from Pylos when it was burned. He himself became a king—in Athens. Herodotus may provide evidence for a great variety of refugees in Athens since he lists as participants in the Ionian migration Abantians from Euboea, Minyans from Orchomenus, Cadmeans, Dryopes, Phocians, Molossians, Arcadian Pelasgi, Dorians from Epidaurus, "and many others" (1.146). Moreover, as we have argued above, the archaeological evidence from Submycenaean Athens suggests strong contacts between that center and the Argolid.

Physical remains confirm the tradition that the migration occurred in the aftermath of the Late Bronze Age disturbances. A new community in the vicinity of the destroyed Bronze Age foundation

Map 7. Attica, Euboea, and Ionia. *Drawing ©Alice Alden. Used by permission.*

at Miletus dates to the first half of the eleventh century, and other Ionian sites have produced similar evidence dating their origins to the century between about 1050 and 950.

To these categories can be added several common elements found on both sides of the Aegean: a shared dialect of Greek, the same names for tribes, observance of the festival of the Apaturia, the similar nature of the cult of Poseidon Helikonios, and certain shared names of months of the calendar.

Developments at Athens itself provide the final piece of evidence. As Snodgrass concludes, "the fact that Athens seems to have been as active and populous a centre as any in Greece in the dark days before 1000 B.C.E. makes it credible that she should have provided the focus for much of the migration" (1971, 374). Athens weathered the time of troubles; thus, if others of the mainland sought a safe haven, as tradition recounts that they did, Athens was an obvious choice. Nor was it so intimidating as far-off Cyprus, which received large influxes of people identified as Aegean, or more specifically Mycenaean, judging from their products and their language. We have seen that Athens seems to have extended its control at the very end of the Bronze Age and maintained a strong position well into the Dark Age; in doing so, it may have continued to draw together a considerable population and to attract even more newcomers.

If this is in fact the case, we can answer the questions posed by Desborough: "Why did they go so far afield? Was there not plenty of space in Attica?" Recent studies suggest that space may well have become more limited in Attica in the eleventh century, as it would elsewhere three centuries later, when the recourse taken by most communities was to export a portion of the surplus population. The picture of Dark Age settlement in Attica drawn by James Whitley strengthens this supposition.[7] From two communities in the Submycenaean period (Athens and Salamis) "it would appear that we are witnessing the beginning of an expansion of settlement from Athens into the Attic countryside," movement that would produce more than twenty-eight settlements dotting the Attic peninsula by the late eighth century (1991b, 55). Whitley believes that the actual population of Athens was still low; thus factors other than scarcity of land would have been in operation.

We seem to be confronted by a paradox: a small Athenian population which nevertheless is engaged in a process of colonization of the Attic hinterland. One explanation of the puzzle may lie in the simple fact that in the eleventh century Athens retained characteristics of the old Mycenaean palace/citadel. As we saw in the case of Mycenae, such places were significant storehouses of communal and royal wealth as well as military strongholds. They were essentially storage facilities within walled palace precincts and not meant for the habitation of large populations. If Athens had retained these characteristics into the eleventh and tenth centuries, one would expect to find a densely settled area surrounding the fortress-crowned Acropolis, as was the case at Mycenae and Tiryns through the late thirteenth century and into the twelfth. But as we have seen, at Athens, both on the Acropolis and in the immediate environs, there is evidence of low population at the very time that Attica began to fill up. Again we return to our paradox.

14. Impression of Dark Age Athenian settlement. *After late eighteenth-century c.e. drawing by Stuart and Revett from west end of Acropolis.*

Perhaps we should look further afield, in time and in space, to seek solutions. We have referred to the depopulations characteristic of the early Dark Age on several occasions. While some of the estimates made not too long ago regarding rates of settlement abandonment and a population loss reaching nearly ninety percent (Snod-grass 1980, 20) now appear to have been overdrawn, still it seems that most areas in mainland Greece suffered measurable and pro-longed depopulation. To match events so severe and long-lasting, we can look to Western Europe during the century and a half following the first outbreak of the Great Plague in the mid-fourteenth century C.E. Among the peasantry in the southern French province of Lan-guedoc, the mortality rate due to plague reached and exceeded fifty percent during the initial onslaught of the disease.[8] Within monastic communities, the closely confined living arrangements caused mor-tality rates to soar in some instances beyond ninety percent. Nor were the populations of Western Europe able to rebound from these setbacks. The plague became endemic within the population and outbreaks of the disease occurred with clockwork regularity dur-ing much of the period between 1350 and 1480.

Among the practical results of these grim statistics were the abun-dance and extraordinary cheapness of land left vacant by the death of its owners, an expansion both of wild forest and grazing land at the expense of arable acreage, and the concentration of large tracts of land into a few hands as the number of possible inheritors within each kinship group dropped dramatically. All but the last of these consequences would benefit the survivors among the classes of ten-ant farmers and landless farm laborers in the acquisition of land. In-deed, by the turn of the fifteenth century, the encroachment of the wild upon settled areas became such a threat that it prompted for-esters, whose duties previously had included the prevention of the poaching of game animals and fish by the local peasantry, to urge them to "Go into the forest, cut the trees . . . break the soil to the plow . . . graze your sheep and cattle, hunt stags . . . and other wild animals; fish . . . to your heart's content" (Ladurie 1974, 18).

Even the concentration of large holdings due to the scarcity of inheritors acted indirectly to aid in the resettlement of vacant land. Large holdings required large inputs of labor, and as labor was scarce, land owners either had to commandeer the aid of the entire extended family down to the third generation or commit large out-lays of cash and in-kind wages to pay for hired help. Post-plague wages paid to landless farm laborers were higher in real terms than those paid prior to 1350 or after the turn of the sixteenth century.

The combination of depressed land prices and high wages allowed a sizable group of men to buy land and farm equipment, build houses, and start families.

The picture of southern France in the fifteenth century C.E. shows us an open landscape recently denuded of people and yet simultaneously the scene of property aggrandizement by surviving landowners along with scattered but widespread pioneer settlement by erstwhile tenant farmers and landless laborers. Here we have another paradox, but one which is explicable because of our knowledge of the cause of the depopulation, supplemented by the meticulous record keeping of the late Medieval French tax assessors.

For Attica of the eleventh and tenth centuries B.C.E. there is no such fund of knowledge. We know that depopulation occurred but are unsure of the cause. Although plague has been put forward as a possible cause of the general collapse of Mycenaean civilization in the twelfth century, other evidence argues strongly against plague as the primary factor. Plague that becomes endemic to a population will of course act to decrease the numbers of that population, the evidence of which will be seen in the abandonment of settlement sites. But plague will not cause the physical destruction of cities, and at the end of the thirteenth century we have nearly as many site destructions as abandonments.

While we do not yet know the reason for the depopulation in mainland Greece generally and in and around Athens particularly, we can hazard a few intelligent guesses based on our comparison with events in late medieval France. Let us assume that, for whatever reason, during the twelfth century time of troubles Attica, including Athens, suffered a sharp decline in population. As a result, not only were large tracts of the Attic hinterland abandoned, but the densely settled areas surrounding the Athenian Acropolis were also thinned of population, in spite of the arrival of refugees from other parts of Attica and from the wider Greek mainland. While the abandoned areas in Attica were reverting to scrub or forest suitable only for grazing, the kinship groups settled on the lands surrounding the Acropolis had suffered their own demographic crisis and were producing fewer surviving inheritors. Thus there developed a situation characterized by the concentration of properties in a few hands while in more distant areas of Attica land was being abandoned altogether.

So far this scenario resembles that of southern France in the fifteenth century C.E. But there is one crucial difference. While the twelfth century B.C.E. witnessed a general decline in Attic population, the region in the next century seemingly faced population pressure. This phenomenon can be ascribed to the role Attica had played as a magnet for refugee populations from the Peloponnese, particularly from the Argolid and Messenia. Admittedly refugee groups are inherently transient in character and many would have stayed in Attica only a short time before moving on, perhaps to the islands of the Sporades and ultimately to the new foundations in Ionia. As we will see in the next chapter, many of the wanderers are likely to have settled at Lefkandi on Euboea.

However, some would have stayed in Attica. According to our model of general depopulation throughout Attica, coupled with the concentration of large holdings in the vicinity of Athens, it is unlikely that much of the refugee community would have settled within sight of the Acropolis. The Athenian leaders, whoever they may have been, would have made the refugees welcome to the abandoned territories in the region but would have firmly denied them settlement rights on lands near Athens for the very reason that these lands, open as they might appear, were in fact held in ownership by survivors of families whose occupancy reached back to the Mycenaean Age.

Other factors would have encouraged the resettlement of the countryside. Bronze Age Athens, like Pylos and other contemporary centers, may have had a sizable landless population. Whether these were primarily slaves attached to the land or freemen who earned their livelihood as craftsmen or by performing farm work for in-kind wages, we do not know. Judging from the Pylos Linear B tablets, types of land were granted in conditional use but not given over in ownership. While no specific evidence describes the fate of this population during the century of turmoil from 1200 to 1100, it seems reasonable that some will have survived to take advantage of the altered situation, assuming control over lands abandoned after the demise or flight of their former masters.

In sum, our argument is that the depopulation of the Attic countryside caused by the troubles of the twelfth century began to be reversed during the eleventh by the resettlement of these lands by various refugee populations as well as by groups long resident in the region. Some were "refugees" from parts of Attica, drawn to Athens for the safety it offered; others were surviving members of the elaborate Mycenaean socioeconomic hierarchy. This resettlement occurred not because conditions in Greece had suddenly improved but because Athens and Attica generally had withstood the troubles of the previous century. By the mid-eleventh century, therefore, a situation had arisen in which Attica found itself reaching a crisis of overpopulation which could only be alleviated by means of overseas colonization.

Our picture of a stable community in Athens suggests that there was a supervisory mechanism to organize a communal enterprise that sent settlers into Attica and even across the Aegean to Asia Minor. Thus, we may reevaluate Snodgrass's view that settlement of Ionia was not an official enterprise "dispatched or even sponsored by a state" (1971, 373). To be sure, the size of the early settlements indicates that the numbers of settlers were few. Before the development of the "penteconter," or fifty-oared ship, boats were both smaller and more rudimentary. And persistent traditions that the settlers took native wives support this picture of small-scale ventures. However, even limited enterprises need some organization.

Though tiny and even precariously held, these settlements would play a momentous role in subsequent developments in the Aegean. Most immediately apparent is that these new settlements, along with Doric and Aeolic settlements in southern and northern Asia Minor, began the conversion of the Aegean into a Greek lake. Assuredly the Mycenaean Greeks made their presence felt in Asia Minor; perhaps they were the "Ahhiyawans" recorded in the Hittite tablets. Even if this identification is incorrect, Mycenaean presence is well attested at Miletus, where excavation has revealed a megaron of more than 200 square meters, as well as other living quarters and agricultural buildings dating to the fourteenth century. Settlements of Mycenaean character are also affirmed for Samos, Iasos and a site near later Erythrai; fifty clustered Mycenaean chamber tombs, discovered in 1962 west of Bodrum, contain pottery ranging between about 1500 and 1200. Pottery and tomb finds dating to the Late Bronze Age have also been made at several other locations, including Ephesus (where unstratified Mycenaean material has been found and dated to the thirteenth century) and sites further inland. Though important, this was a *limited presence*, not permanent, widespread habitation. By contrast, the Dark Age migrations eastward from the mainland would join both sides of the Aegean and eventually spread to that sea's northern coastline, completing the circuit of Greek settlement. At the time of early settlement it is notable that, in the words of Snodgrass, "the more advanced regions (of Greece) are united in that they share a natural and easy access to the Aegean Sea" (1971, 375). The importance of that access in subsequent Greek history—lasting even to the twentieth century C.E.—is a continuous thread.

Results of Migration

Beyond defining the sphere of Hellenic life, the settlement became a constant conduit to non-Greek cultures of Anatolia and even beyond. Interaction was initially limited by the weakness both of the Greek communities and of the Phrygians, who inhabited west-central Anatolia. In the eighth century, contact with Phrygia intensified, and when that kingdom collapsed, its role in Greek affairs was assumed by Lydia. Through Lydian culture, the Greeks would learn of coinage, hoplite armies, and tyrants; and through Lydian mistakes, the Asia Minor Greeks would confront the even greater force of Persia. When the settlements were first carved into the rugged coast, such influences and consequences were in the distant future, but the stage for them was set by the Dark Age migrations.

The very precariousness of the early settlements had huge significance in yet another respect. Forced by their situation among native peoples to guard themselves, the settlers formed tight, closely knit communities in which the cooperation of all was essential to survival. In their physical form and their sense of corporate responsibility, these little settlements have been seen as the ancestors of the Classical *polis*.[9] In nominating Ionia as the source of this type of political community, Victor Ehrenberg stressed the settling of Greeks among an alien population and the usual location of settlements on peninsulas and isthmuses, both factors promoting compactness. A mudbrick circuit wall—like that of Old Smyrna, dated to Middle Geometric times— "defended an entire city, albeit a small one" unlike the Mycenaean walls that "were *par excellence* citadel defences enclosing a palace and its surrounds" (Nicholls 1958–59, 117).

Though "a city is not yet a state," Ehrenberg wrote, "exercising its sway over barbarians, it must have become a state" (Ehrenberg 1964, 11; J. M. Cook 1958–59). There is no need to assign absolute priority to the eastern or western Aegean inasmuch as straitened conditions existed in mainland communities as well. Yet these very similarities make it a reasonable prediction that the forms taken by these communities would not be greatly different in most regions of the Aegean "lake."

A fourth consequence of the eleventh- and tenth-century migrations is that Ionian institutions derived from a Submycenaean cultural base.[10] That evolution, consequently, begins with the form of community existing in Athens in the eleventh and tenth centuries. Since we have argued both for a late consolidation of the Bronze Age kingdom around Athens and for its continuity into post-Mycenaean times, it is reasonable to envision a central administrative organization connected with the palace on the Acropolis. And if Athens resembled the other Mycenaean kingdoms, a single *"wanax"* would have occupied a central position in that organization. In a fashion not unlike that of Mycenae, the power of a single figure seems to have diminished during the twelfth and eleventh centuries; at least no such powerful individual is noticeable in the physical record.

Reasons for this diminution, however, are likely to have varied between Mycenae and Athens. If we have correctly reconstructed the situation in Attica during the time of troubles, it may well have been the arrival of other powerful individuals—from Attica and beyond—that reduced the authority of a single local *wanax*. Signs of a stratified society appear in the archaeological evidence in the late twelfth century: as early as 1100, funerary evidence indicates competition for recognition among inhabitants of Athens, and by 1050, formal cemeteries were being reserved for those of high status (I. Morris 1987, 172f.). By the second half of the eleventh century, society appears to have been ordered according to age and sex, with early features of an increasingly significant aristocratic element. Using the account of the Athenian constitution ascribed to Aristotle (the *Athenaion Politeia*) as a guide to general developments, it may have been during the early Dark Age that a life kingship was limited in duration, divided among several holders, and curbed by a select council of powerful figures.

Tradition reinforces the physical evidence of emerging aristocracy in describing the role of individuals in the migrations across the Aegean, the leaders who became *basileis* in the twelve new settlements. Legends indicate that there were many willing—and presumably qualified by status—to undertake this position. Androklos, legitimate son of Kodros the king of Athens, founded Ephesus. Miletus owed its establishment to Neleus, of Pylian descent. Myus was founded by a bastard son of Kodros, Kydrelos; Lebedos by Andro-

15. Bronze statuette from the Ath (ht. 20.5 cm). © *Deutsches Archä Institut Athen; negative number I Used by permission.*

pompos, a name found in the Pylian genealogy; Colophon by Andraimon, another Pylian; Priene by Aipytos, a son of Neleus; Teos, initially by Athamas; Erythrai by Knopos, another bastard son of Kodros; Phocaea by Philogenes; Clazomenai by Paralos; Chios by Egertios; Samos by Tembrion. Later accounts emphasize the power of these leaders and their descendants—for example, the leader of Ephesus who was especially active in waging war on Samos, assisting Priene, and capturing Larissa from the natives.

The local histories relate, however, that community affairs were soon directed by prominent familial groups: the *basilidai* of Ephesus and Erythrai and Chios; the Neleids at Miletus; the forty families of Teos. When "historical" evidence exposes the nature of Ionian life in the Archaic period, it reveals social, economic, and political domination by aristocratic families. In the words of C. J. Emlyn-Jones, Ionian development shows "the early elimination of the kingship in favour of aristocratic rule which comprised or included members of the regal family" (1980, 25).

By associating the source of migration with Athens, we may also gain a better understanding of the origins of an unusual body in Ionia: a league of twelve individual states. Since the evidence for its early activities is dependent upon scattered traditions, a certain date for its emergence cannot be assigned. Carl Roebuck (1955) argues convincingly for an early association of towns for purposes of mutual assistance against enemies, an original nucleus that enlarged as more settlements were made in the later eleventh and tenth centuries. During the tenth and ninth centuries, the league can be described, in Roebuck's words, as a "loose quasi-feudal organization . . . with considerable friction among its kings" (1955, 64). As the tiny towns became larger *poleis*, the organization grew into the Ionian League of twelve city-states that is better known from evidence of the Archaic period.

Roebuck sensibly asks, "Is it not possible that in this early Ionian league we may have the transference of a post-Mycenaean kingship to Ionia?" (63). We can be even bolder. If new settlements in Attica and Asia Minor were being made concurrently, or nearly so, links between the newly founded Ionian communities may mirror the bond between Athens and the recently settled Attic villages. A difference between the situations on either side of the Aegean was that no single Ionian community had the established status of Athens. Even so, tradition suggests that Ephesus won preeminence as the center of the early league: its founder and first king, Androklos, might very well have emulated his father, King Kodros of Athens.

Both internal developments and outside pressures would cause paths to diverge as the Dark Age progressed through the ninth and eighth centuries. Regional distinctions apply as much to Attica and to the Ionian communities as they do to other parts of the Greek world.[11] In fact, Athens appears to have become more, rather than less, isolated as events quickened in many parts of the mainland, and by the eighth century its preeminence had disappeared. Even within Attica, Attic graves surpassed Athenian examples in their richness (Whitley 1991, 57). A declaration of independence from Athens is detectable in the development of hero cults in several communities that "chose now to emphasize their local origins, their local autochthony, rather than their links with Athens" (Whitley 1991, 60). Traditional accounts echo the material evidence by telling of the aristocratic factionalism so prominent in the Archaic period of Athenian history (Sealey 1960). From roughly 730 Athens was no longer an outward-looking city with major maritime and commercial interests; Attica now circumscribed its concerns. At the same time, Athenian artistic initiative was lost.

Consequently, conditions in Attica came to resemble those prevailing throughout most of the Greek mainland, even though the similarity appeared only late in the Dark Age. During the early Dark Age, an unusual twilight persisted in Athens, not the brilliance of thirteenth-century Mycenae but an unusual—perhaps unique—situation by comparison with much of the Aegean world. It was reflected in cultural, perhaps political, control over other parts of Attica and adjacent regions of mainland Greece. The perceived security offered by Athens drew others to the area, as tradition recalls. And from the late eleventh century, the community was a conduit for the movement of ideas, products, and people into and out of Athens. Although these traits disappeared, the earlier achievement was remembered through oral tradition and marked by physical evidence, not to be entirely forgotten. In fact, Athens' strength during the early Dark Age would be a significant factor in its huge, better-known role in the Classical period.

4

Lefkandi

*New Heroes
of the Ninth Century*

We have seen how three communities coped, or failed to cope, with
the profound reversal of fortune dealt to them in the closing decades
of the Bronze Age, examining the strategies used by each community
to make a new life in the face of changed circumstances. Many sites,
some of the most powerful among them, suffered destruction, often
on a massive scale, and when the inhabitants cleared away the rubble
and reconstituted their communities, they did so, as at Mycenae, at
a reduced level, maintaining a shadowy existence among the ruins.
Scores of other communities were abandoned, their inhabitants fleeing to the hills or overseas; when these sites were again occupied the
settlers may have had no memory of the old community, and the old
blood lines were most likely intermingled with new ones. In the case
of Dark Age Nichoria, there are indications both of continuity with
the old population and of the addition of new elements. A handful of
sites managed to weather the storm, suffering only slight social and

economic dislocation, and even, as in the case of Athens, seeming to profit from the straitened circumstances.

The site of Lefkandi on the island of Euboea bears certain similarities to each of the communities we have considered. Like Mycenae, this community suffered multiple destructions during the twelfth century and, like Nichoria, was eventually abandoned. However, its similarity with Athens may be most significant: like its neighbor, Lefkandi was able to withstand, or was bypassed by, the upheavals occurring at the end of the thirteenth century. Moreover, its proximity to Athens seems to have drawn Lefkandi into the sphere of Athenian cultural dynamism. An ongoing dialectic between cultural isolationism and expansionism is paralleled by a waning and waxing of Athenian influence.

Not simply outside influence but internal developments as well pushed this tiny community to reach well beyond its own territory, away from the island of Euboea and even well outside the Aegean. Lefkandi's precociousness is an early glimpse of the energies of the Archaic *poleis*.

The Site

At over 150 kilometers, the island of Euboea is prodigiously long, lying close to the mainland, opposite east Locris and south coastal Thessaly in the north and Attica in the south. Despite its proximity to the mainland, however, the island from prehistoric times has maintained periodic connections with the Sporades islands to the northeast (particularly Skyros), the west coast of Anatolia in the east, the Cyclades and Crete in the south, and Cyprus and the Levant in the southeast.

The modern village of Lefkandi is situated on the western shore, about equidistant from the northern and southern extremities of the island. The ancient settlement, which may have been named Lelanton, was situated atop a long, broad ridge or hill 500 meters long by 120 meters wide a few hundred meters east of the modern town. The hill comprises the only eminence of a shallow promontory thrust into the sea midway between the towns of Chalcis to the west and Eretria to the east. Although greatly eroded, its ancient contours can be esti-

Map 8. Euboean sites. *Popham and Sackett (1968, plate 3).*
Reproduced with permission of the British School at Athens.

mated with some confidence: the summit would have risen somewhat less than the present 17 meters and will have been less spa-
cious than today. The south face was steep enough to provide defense without fortifications, while the inlets to east and west of the
valley behind the hill were larger than is presently the case and would
have provided some protection for the gentler north slope.

Strategically the most serious drawback to the site is its lack
of water—its later name, Xeropolis, means "dry-town." Water had
to be fetched from the Lelas River, which empties into the sea a
few hundred meters west of Xeropolis. Judging from the numerous

Table 4: Chronological Periods

Late Helladic IIIC	twelfth century B.C.E.
Submycenaean	1125–1050 B.C.E.
Protogeometric	1050–900 B.C.E.
Early	1050–1000 B.C.E.
Middle	1000–950 B.C.E.
Late	950–900 B.C.E.
Subprotogeometric	900–750 B.C.E.
Subprotogeometic I	900–875 B.C.E.
Subprotogeometric II	875–850 B.C.E.
Subprotogeometric III	850–750 B.C.E.
Late Geometric	750–700 B.C.E.

sherds of large *pithoi* found at the site, the solution was to store large quantities of water within the settlement. Despite the difficulty of access to water, the location held other perhaps more important attractions, especially its proximity to the sea and its position at the southeast edge of the fertile Lelantine Plain, which gave access to the entire central portion of the island.

For a variety of reasons the archaeology of the site is difficult to interpret. Rising land values attendant upon a booming tourist industry have made it increasingly difficult to obtain excavation permits or to purchase land for long-term research. Increasing competition between landowners and archaeologists has led, in at least one instance, to the malicious destruction of a site. As a result, only a small fraction of the hill has been excavated.[1]

Another problem arises in trying to correlate the cemeteries with settlement areas: the five cemeteries and burial groups unearthed since 1968 do not match the settlement areas chronologically. To date, no cemetery has been found corresponding to the Bronze Age settlement for which there is substantial evidence, although a number of intramural burials dating from the twelfth century have been found and studied. The earliest cemetery evidence dates from the Submycenaean through Middle Protogeometric periods (roughly 1125–950)—a period for which there exists no settlement evidence. The cemetery evidence ceases around 825, even though the site continued to be occupied down to about 700.

The Settlement

The site was occupied from Mycenaean times into the late Dark Age.[2] Finds from trenches include a good deal of LHIIIC material and significant Geometric evidence with Protogeometric layers below it. The main excavation in the northeast sector revealed the walls of an apsidal building dating to the latest phase of the site (ca. 825–700) built over an earlier building dating to the twelfth century. Mixed with Late Geometric sherds recovered from a refuse pit just west of the building was one bearing alphabetic graffiti. A wall paralleled the east wall of the building and abutting the wall on either side are three circular stone structures, perhaps used for processing grain, as a stone pounder was found in one of the structures. Two large rubbish pits east of the wall contain materials extending from Mycenaean times to the first half of the ninth century. A smaller, later pit containing tenth century material is referred to as the "Molds Deposit" since it held fragments of discarded clay molds used in bronze casting, apparently for the casting of decorated legs for bronze tripod stands.

South of the rubbish pits, several sets of disjointed walls were discovered which may be the remains of a building or perhaps a long terracing wall. Other walls in the area are thought to have served as animal pens. This collection is of Late Geometric date, although some lengths incorporate remains of earlier walls.

Some distance north of the hill, a concentration of burnt sherds grouped in five separate find spots has been interpreted by the excavation team as marking the location of a building, or buildings, where pottery was stored until the area was abandoned, or perhaps destroyed, sometime in the late ninth or early eighth century. The possibility that Lefkandi had storage facilities for pottery is important since such a facility would be of little use for a site the size of ninth-century Lefkandi, unless the pottery were being used in trade.

The Cemeteries

The slopes leading to the Lelantine Plain immediately to the north of Lefkandi and about 600 meters northwest of Xeropolis seem to have been given over to cemeteries during the Dark Age. There are

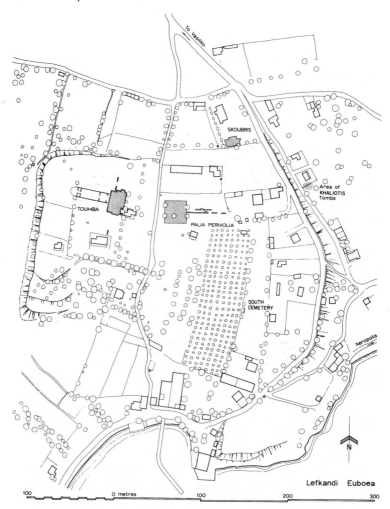

Map 9. Regional map of Lefkandi with ancient sites. *Popham, Sackett, and Themelis (1980, plate 1). Reproduced with permission of the British School at Athens.*

three large cemeteries and two smaller burial groups. Closest to Xero-polis is a small group of tombs. Since they were thoroughly robbed and have not been formally investigated, they cannot be precisely dated, but there is a possibility that the area was in use for funeral purposes as early as the twelfth century. Of the larger cemeteries, that situated in the field of A. Skoubris contains the earliest known evidence, a high proportion of which is Submycenaean and early Protogeometric material. The excavated area of roughly 175 square meters represents possibly no more than a quarter of the cemetery area. Between 1968 and 1980 a total of sixty tombs and nineteen pyres was examined.

About 100 meters south of the Skoubris cemetery is the cemetery of Palia Perivolia. Since this cemetery has been much more thoroughly explored, the excavators are confident that the forty tombs and forty-seven pyres unearthed represent all or most of the cemetery. It contains pyres and shaft graves dating mostly to the Protogeometric and Subprotogeometric periods. A series of trenches extending beyond the Palia Perivolia site have uncovered a separate group of four tombs and three pyres, with three of the seven certain cases of inhumation (in contrast to cremation) found in all of the cemeteries. One tomb, notable for its double burial, is identified as a warrior grave by weaponry found in it dated to around 880–870.

The final burial location lies on the hill of Toumba, about 50 meters west of Palia Perivolia. Although Toumba is roughly contemporary with Palia Perivolia, there is no comparison in terms of wealth between the two sites. Even without the monumental "tumulus" burial on the summit, Toumba is by far the wealthiest of the three major cemeteries. It is followed by Skoubris, while Palia Perivolia ranks a penurious third.

Historical Survey

The settlement area on Xeropolis has yielded evidence of continuous occupation from the second half of the third millennium down to the end of the twelfth century. After a hiatus, occupation resumed by the early or middle tenth century, continuing until the end of the eighth century. The earlier periods of the settlement indicate stability, longevity, and a modicum of prosperity. The pottery associated with the site derives not from the contemporary pottery found on the mainland, but seemingly from Early Bronze Age pottery from West Anatolia. The first known inhabitants, then, may have been recent emigrants from Anatolia.

Although the end of the Early Helladic period (2100/2000 B.C.E.) is associated on the mainland with the widespread destruction of settlements, no such destruction appears to have been visited on Lefkandi. Nor does there appear to have been radical change in material culture in the rest of its Bronze Age life. Even in the twelfth century, when mainland centers were going up in flames and their populations put to flight, Lefkandi presents the image of a bustling, populous town rather akin to contemporary Athens.

The excavators at Lefkandi have identified three distinct architectural and ceramic phases associated with the site's twelfth-century levels. Phase One bears all the hallmarks of a refugee town, thrown up quickly and haphazardly. The pottery of this phase, while competently executed, is limited in shape and decoration. The general conflagration that ended this phase brought forth the Phase Two community, a relatively large and prosperous town laid out on regular lines. While most of the pottery of this phase represents a continuation of Phase One, a few craftsmen were willing to extend the range of shapes and decoration, returning to figured decoration featuring both human and animal shapes. There is even a reemergence of the old griffin motif, familiar from Mycenaean contexts.

The Phase Two community was also brought to an end by destruction, after which the town was quickly rebuilt. Soon, however, the site underwent a general, unreversed decline. The Phase Three settlement shows signs of population loss and a careless arrangement of buildings interspersed with refuse heaps and pottery of limited shapes, decoration, and technical competence. Despite the settlement's final abandonment around 1100, we are confronted with evidence of a substantial cemetery some 600 meters northwest of Xeropolis, but no settlement on Xeropolis itself—a situation just the opposite of that of the twelfth century. It may be that the settlement that produced this cemetery has yet to be discovered. Another possibility is that the area was abandoned for several generations and that this cemetery was used beginning shortly after 1100 by a semi-nomadic, transient population, a situation akin to that at Nichoria.

Matching the apparent discontinuity of settlement is a true discontinuity of ceramic styles. The latest Mycenaean ware tends to be of a rather coarse fabric, light in color, and the most common drinking vessel is a small conical bowl. The Submycenaean material tends to have a dark ground, with the globular cup most common. Although the new material still represents what Desborough calls "the dying stage of the Mycenaean tradition," it is ultimately an alien, rather than Euboean, school of that tradition (Popham, Sackett, and Themelis 1980, 283–93).

The material remains bear all the signs of what has in the last few decades come to typify the early Iron Age Greek "cultural kit": a debased pottery derived from Mycenaean forms, burial of the dead in single cist graves, long pins and arched fibulae to fasten clothing, and iron tools and weapons. Some gold found its way into this early Dark Age community: six datable tombs and two pyres (out of a total of sixty-four tombs and twenty-one pyres) contained that precious metal.

During the eleventh century, developments in pottery indicate a gradual improvement in quality of life and the establishment of more distant connections. In the later eleventh and early tenth centuries, technique improved, ceramic shapes witnessed a general standard-ization, and something approaching an artistic canon of decoration emerged. At the same time, imports appear: a juglet of Syro-Pales-tinian derivation, a flask, and a "*pyxis,*" or unguent jar, which may have derived either from Cyprus or from Crete, and an iron dirk found in the same tomb as the Syro-Palestinian juglet which may have come from the same area. A small number of locally crafted items are obvious imitations of foreign originals.

Although their "foreign" origin cannot be doubted, the circum-stances of their importation is unknown. It is not unreasonable to suggest that the Lefkandians themselves may have initiated these for-eign contacts, given earlier though sporadic contacts with the south Cyclades, Crete, and even Cyprus and the later evidence of Eubo-ean and specifically Lefkandian contacts with Crete, Cyprus, and the Near East. Long distance trade to the south and east also appears less surprising if it is seen in the context of trade routes with nearer regions. Finds attest increasing Euboean interest in Thessaly, Skyros in the Sporades, and Naxos in the south, and Desborough has sug-gested that Euboean trading contacts with these areas had become so consolidated in the late eleventh century that they formed a new cultural *koine* (Popham, Sackett, and Themelis 1980, 283–93). It is equally possible that the seafarers came from the eastern Mediterra-nean. Although the cities of the Syro-Phoenician littoral had suf-fered devastation roughly contemporary with the Aegean disasters, by the mid-eleventh century, they had recovered sufficiently to again become centers of commerce and trade.[3] Yet another possibility is that Cypriots and Cretans acted as middlemen for Phoenician and even Egyptian goods.

After this brief flurry of activity around 1050, however, there is as yet no evidence of further long distance contacts for several decades. Judging from the cemetery material, there seems to have been a decline in prosperity at Lefkandi during these years: gold and other high-status goods found in tombs cease almost entirely. A necklace of thirty-six faience beads is the sole luxury item from the tombs of this period. But more remarkable than this find is the puzzling evidence that during this less prosperous period all three of the area's major cemeteries were being used. Why this community should require three cemeteries, when one sufficed for the most prosperous early eleventh-century community is not known. Toumba, the latest of the three cemeteries, signals the third and last remarkable development of this period. Excavations on a low hill on the southern edge of the Lelantine Plain a few hundred meters north of modern Lefkandi, revealed a cemetery with initial finds of thirty-six tombs and eight pyres. New excavations showed that walls discovered in 1980 belonged to a building of monumental proportions: a long, narrow, multiple-room structure about 45 meters long by 10 meters wide with an apsidal west end, a peaked roof, and surrounded, probably on all but the east side, by a veranda. The east entrance was masked by a wall running north to south; between the wall and the doorway there was a shallow porch only 1.5 meters deep. The doorway itself, at 4.8 meters in width, was probably too wide to be closed by actual doors; possibly skins or cloth draperies were stretched across it in foul weather.

A smaller doorway in the center of the west wall of the East Room led into the Central Room, architecturally the heart of the building, with a length of 22 meters. Two stub walls in the room's northeast corner may be the remains of a staircase, which would have led to an upper storey or loft. This room produced the most startling discovery in the building, indeed within the entire Toumba site. In its center were two large burial shafts, side by side. The shaft nearest the south wall contained a double burial, a combination of inhumation and cremation. A large, richly tooled bronze amphora (perhaps

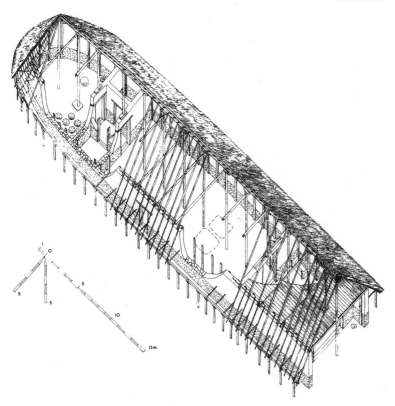

16. *Heroön:* Axonometric drawing of building as reconstructed. *Popham, Calligas, and Sackett (1993, plate 28). Reproduced with permission of the British School at Athens.*

an antique even at the time of burial) held the cremated remains together with a long, tube-like robe or shroud of rich cloth. Next to the amphora was a warrior's kit consisting of a sword along with the badly decomposed remains of a wooden scabbard, a spearhead, razor, and whetstone—all but the whetstone and scabbard of iron. Accompanying the cremation burial was the inhumation of a richly clad woman, laid out on her back, her head to the west. The amphora containing the bones of the warrior sat next to her right leg. The lady was bedecked in gold: she wore gold earrings; a necklace of gold, faience, and crystal; a gold pendant; and sheet-gold disks were placed over her breasts. The position of her hands, placed close together over her abdomen, and of her feet, also close together, has raised the

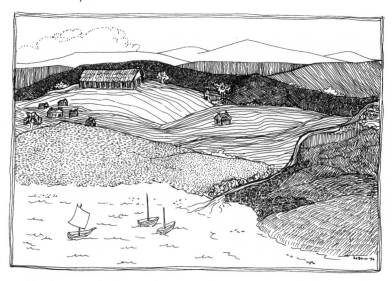

17. Artist's reconstruction of Lefkandi. *Drawing ©Anne Lou Robkin. Used by permission.*

suspicion that she may have been bound, perhaps a victim of suttee. A study of her dentition has indicated that she was probably in her late twenties at the time of her death. The man was probably older—between the ages of thirty and forty-five.

The other shaft contained the skeletons of four horses, the iron bits still in their mouths. These animals were apparently thrown headlong into the shaft as a funerary sacrifice to accompany their late master into the next world. This is not the only instance of horse sacrifice at Toumba.[4]

Signs of ancient damage appear on the interior walls of the two small rooms adjoining the central room; moreover, these rooms and the apse appear to have been left unfinished when the building was abandoned. Within a short space of time, to judge by finds associated with the building, the upper walls, roofing, and support posts were dismantled, the interior filled in, and a tumulus raised over the whole site. Some of the excavators have concluded that the building was never used as a residence, for there are few signs of heavy use, no trace of a hearth, and no indication of food preparation or consumption. Thus, the edifice may have been intended for destruction from the beginning—as a *heroön*, or hero shrine. Furthermore, the burials of the Toumba cemetery, which began soon after the mound was raised over the site, huddled close to the tumulus as if to bask in the reflected glory of its occupants. However, P.G. Calligas, a member of the excavation team, has published a minority report which maintains that the building was indeed the residence, for however short a time, of a patriarchal clan chieftain or head of an *oikos* (Popham, Calligas, and Sackett 1993; and Calligas 1988).

Not long after the warrior's burial—probably by 950—there are signs of unparalleled wealth at the Toumba cemetery and of reoccupation of the settlement on Xeropolis Hill. The Late Protogeometric period (ca. 975–900) opens with another brief phase of cultural and commercial expansion, more brilliant and profound in its consequences than that of the earlier epoch. From the start, the new settlement at Lefkandi was inundated by alien influences, and local craftsmen absorbed these new influences and experimented with new shapes and designs. Such conditions mark the opening of a long period of commercial expansion overseas with prosperity and seeming stability at home which Calligas has termed the *Lefkandi Period*. Not only Lefkandi but the entire island of Euboea played a leading role in the commercial and cultural affairs of Greece and the Aegean, centering, at least initially, around the settlement on Xeropolis.

The evidence at Lefkandi consists mainly of potsherds, but their wide scatter indicates an enlarged settled area and population. Evidence of greater socioeconomic complexity accompanies the increase in population. The molds deposit described above indicates the existence of a bronze foundry that manufactured large tripods or tripod-caldrons, precursors of the ceremonial caldrons of the eighth and seventh centuries. If the caldrons were intended for home consumption, we can surmise the existence of a ruling family or a small aristocratic group with the means to acquire such items. If they were to be used primarily in trade, we have some indication of the nature of that trade. Both conclusions may be essentially correct.

The evidence from the cemeteries is more spectacular and similarly indicative of renewed long-distance contacts. The wealth and vitality of the period is reflected mainly in the amount of pottery found in the tombs, its quality, and numerous indications of foreign influence and contact. One tomb at Palia Perivolia (Tomb 22) yielded a veritable potter's inventory of ceramic objects: no fewer than twen-

18. Bronze cauldron (ht. 1.5 m.)
© *Deutsches Archäologishes Institut Ather*
negative number 74.115. Used by permiss

ty-nine vases of various shapes and a thirtieth object in the form of a bell-shaped "dolly" with movable legs. Tomb 26 at Toumba, one of several "warrior graves," produced eleven vases in addition to an iron sword and a "quiverful" of arrows.

New shapes flourish alongside older shapes. The favored *skyphos*, an open, two-handled bowl, for example, retains its earlier Attic-inspired form even while new versions appear. Evidence of outside influence comes notably from Thessaly and Cyprus, two areas with previous histories of contact with Lefkandi. There is solid evidence of contact with Vergina, in southern Macedonia, where late Protogeometric Euboean pottery has been found; and a gold pendant from Palia Perivolia Tomb 22 has an analogue discovered on the island of Skyros. Lefkandian pottery has been identified on the north Cycladic islands of Tenos and Andros. The site's pottery now shows substantial Athenian influence in motifs, and the number of direct Athenian imports is higher than at any previous time.

Attic influence spilled over into the more conservative area of burial customs. The remains stored in the two funeral amphorae of a rare double-urn cremation were almost certainly of a man and a woman, for one of the amphorae was of the belly-handled variety used in women's cremations, while the other was neck-handled, signifying a man's cremation.[5] That identification was made easier since it was found in association with a spearhead and a "killed" sword—that is, a sword intentionally made useless by firing the blade and bending it double. Such "warrior graves" are more common at Athens.

All of these developments occurred during a brief period, perhaps no longer than a decade. Just as suddenly they ceased. The later tenth and ninth centuries show a marked return to conservatism.[6] Native pottery shapes and decorative systems re-emerge, and only the hardiest of imports are retained. In funerary terms, the return to conservatism meant a return to the shaft grave and the pyre. The one or two urn burials later than those already described date from the end of the tenth century. However, foreign contacts were maintained, and there is no indication of a decline in prosperity.

Nothing could better illustrate this continuity than the remarkable centaur statuette found in the Toumba cemetery in 1969.[7] Dating from the closing years of the tenth century or the early years of the ninth, the statuette is something of a hybrid: its animal body is a wheel-made terra-cotta cylinder common in the late Mycenaean period, while the human torso and front legs resemble a series of Cypriot centaurs and bull-men manufactured from the late twelfth century down to the late eighth century.

Following M. L. West's suggestion, we might even name the centaur. Though its left arm is missing, the irregular surface of the statuette's left shoulder makes it likely that the left hand was grasping an elongated object which rested there, perhaps a branch or club, the centaurs' weapons of choice. Of even greater significance is the deep incision just below the centaur's left knee, made prior to the firing of the statuette. Tradition has it that the leader of the centaurs, Cheiron, accidentally received just such a wound at the hands of Heracles. The intent of the artist may well have been to produce a likeness of Cheiron, which, at 36 centimeters in height and 26 centimeters in length, is the largest and most impressive work of sculpture to survive from the Dark Age and fairly represents the continuing commercial and artistic vitality of the community even during a period of supposed cultural conservatism.

The explosion of wealth implied by objects recovered from the cemeteries, particularly from Toumba, is puzzling. Even the old Skoubris cemetery experienced something like a renaissance, with

19. Lefkandi centaur (ca. 900). *Popham, Sackett, and Themelis (1980, plate 22). Reproduced with permission of the British School at Athens.*

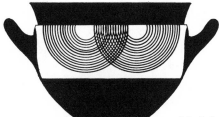

20. Subprotogeometric *skyphos* with semicircle decoration. *Popham and Sackett (1968, plate 60).* Reproduced with permission of the British School at Athens.

five gold finds in tombs dated to between 875 and 825. In addition to indicating wealth, many of the rich finds are imports and imply a level of trade unprecedented at Lefkandi or elsewhere in Greece. The faience necklaces are all Near Eastern or Egyptian in derivation. A bronze jug and bowl, described as a wine-service set, also have an Egyptian or Phoenician derivation.

The possibility that a Euboean carrying trade was involved is supported by the numerous local products that have turned up in foreign quarters. Euboean enterprise in the latter half of the ninth century is well represented by exports found on Cyprus, at Al Mina in Syria, and for the first time, in Italy and Sicily to the west. Perhaps the most popular Euboean export of the time was the ubiquitous pendant semicircle *skyphos*, a shape whose decorative scheme was already over a century old at the time of the establishment in the later ninth century of the Al Mina trading station. In a list of contacts, one region is missing during this period: Attic imports are almost totally absent. The new Geometric forms and motifs of the ninth century current in Attica were either unknown or ignored on Euboea.

This strange mix of parochialism and prosperity lasted to about 825, when signs of trouble appear: use of all of the known cemeteries ends; surface sherds that seem to date from the later ninth century show definite signs of burning; and on Xeropolis there are signs that the settlement may have been losing population and that the area of the site was contracting. The reduced settlement on Xeropolis survived another century or more, managing to continue foreign contacts and even renewing contact with Attica: Attic imports and products of local manufacture with Attic characteristics are much in evidence. Some sort of equilibrium seems to have lasted down to about 750, when another profound change occurred. Lefkandi finally entered the Geometric Age: inspired primarily by Athenian examples, it began developing a late Geometric style of its own. This apparently sudden change of heart after a century and a half of stubborn resistance illuminates Lefkandi's continuing interest, despite its reduced circumstances, in overseas trade. To preserve its markets, Lefkandi may have adopted the tool of its Athenian and, more recently, Corinthian competitors: Geometric pottery.

By the late eighth century Lefkandi was no longer the sole, or even principal, population center on the island. For some decades it seems to have been losing primacy, and perhaps population, to the new settlements of Chalcis and Eretria at either end of the Lelantine Plain, settlements that grew increasingly prominent after the disturbances at Lefkandi in about 825. With this development, Lefkandi would have found itself in the unenviable position of having a potential enemy on either flank. The site appears to have been destroyed and finally abandoned at the close of the eighth century because of this very situation: it may have been caught literally in the middle of a struggle for control of the plain between Eretria and Chalcis, a victim of the first Greek war of which we have record, an event that closes the door to the Dark Ages. The final destruction of Lefkandi around 700 B.C.E. coincides so closely with the most recent dating of the half-legendary Lelantine War that we hardly need look further for the circumstances of the demise of the settlement on Xeropolis Hill.

Social Organization

James Whitley included both Nichoria and Lefkandi in his list of "unstable" settlements, so named because they did not survive the Dark Age and indeed seemed to flourish only within a Dark Age political and social setting. Lefkandi was also singled out as spatially unstable, as demonstrated by a supposed shift in population locus from Xeropolis to Toumba at about the time of the construction of the monumental building. According to Whitley, the reason for this shift was that Lefkandi was a Big Man society and the Toumba building was his dwelling (1991a). Since this kind of society is founded on the prestige of one Big Man, it is inherently unstable: should this person lose prestige or die, his power would be dispersed.

There are chronological problems with this hypothesis, for Whitley suggests an unbroken sequence of events from the twelfth-century settlement of Xeropolis to a tenth-century establishment at Toumba, and then back again to Xeropolis a century later. Yet, as we have seen, the area may well have been abandoned, except for funerary purposes, from 1100 until some time in the tenth century. Further, aside from the possibility that the monumental building was used as a residence, there is no evidence of settlement on Toumba Hill during the eleventh and early tenth centuries. We must describe the settlement pattern not as unstable, but as nonexistent.

Another interpretation is P. G. Calligas' view that the building was the residence of an "oikist" or head of a settlement enterprise. Early Iron Age Lefkandi, Calligas reasons, was a patriarchal society in which power was dispersed among the male heads of families. The major clans or family groupings would have established clan centers (*oikoi*) on the summits of low hills, which acted as residences, cult areas, and council houses. Such a system, Calligas believes, grew out of the unsettled conditions of the twelfth and eleventh centuries, when populations turned to a semi-nomadic, pastoral way of life. With the return of peace and stability, families or clans established permanent homes while continuing to pursue a pastoral economy. He sees the tombs on the eastern slope and at the foot of the hill as housing the remains of the members of the Toumba *oikos* over a period of several generations. When unstable conditions recurred in the late ninth and eighth centuries, fortified settlements, the direct precursors of the Archaic *poleis*, replaced the *oikoi*. The new environment proved antithetical to the old, dispersed *oikos* economy. Thus, pastoralism declined in favor of settled agriculture, with its ability to support large populations, and the power once wielded by the oikist was divided among a new rising aristocracy (Popham, Calligas, and Sackett 1993; Calligas 1988).

If this reconstruction is correct, it neglects the living members of the group. The building on Toumba Hill is large by any standards—certainly large enough to fulfill the three roles of oikist's residence, cult center, and council house. But it would be absurd to suppose that it was large enough to house the entire population of Lefkandi, even in this early period. Moreover, the chronology is flawed: why do we see the Toumba building abandoned and destroyed a century and a half before the move to fortified settlements? This thesis lacks one of the strengths of Whitley's argument, which accounts for possible divisions within the community leading to the expulsion or voluntary emigration of part of the population.

Another scenario constitutes not a model so much as a number of suggestions to bear in mind for future consideration as evidence from Lefkandi accumulates. Popham suggests a fundamental division along economic (and perhaps other) lines within Lefkandian society, manifested early in the history of the site and growing more pronounced in later periods. Landed interests—farmers and stock breeders—form one group and mercantile interests—overseas traders, cargo carriers, and adventurers—form the other. The farmers and ranchers can be considered the more conservative, while the sailors and overseas merchants should be thought of as more adventurous, more willing to take risks, and more accepting of alien ways (Popham, Sackett, and Themelis 1980). Tensions might increase between the two groups inasmuch as few pursuits could be more dissimilar than farming and overseas trade. We will find that Hesiod, in compiling his *Works and Days* (a sort of farmers' almanac) urged against this foolish endeavor of taking to the sea. Only the increased potential for profit makes the increased risk bearable.

On the other hand, one should not underestimate the long-term potential of land holders to amass wealth, power, and prestige. Land ownership at Lefkandi may have been similar to that at Corinth, which we will see was increasingly concentrated in fewer hands, possibly resulting in the beginnings of a bipartite social structure like the one Popham has suggested. As the younger sons and poor relations of the oikists became increasingly cut off from land ownership, they may have taken to seafaring, much like the younger sons of eighteenth- and nineteenth-century English nobility. Even if landed wealth was equally distributed among an oikist's sons, one could expect cycles of dispersal of land until the divided and subdivided plots could no longer support their owners, forcing small holders to abandon or exchange their unprofitable plots, and to turn to trade.

We have noticed that the usual placid development of shapes

and decorative styles of pottery was punctuated by a number of epi-sodes characterized by an acceptance of foreign motifs and experi-mentation. Of these episodes, all but the last, which represented Lef-kandi's belated entry into the Geometric period around 750, were brief and were followed by a return to severe conservatism. The first episode (ca. 1050 B.C.E.) was nearly contemporaneous with the be-ginnings of Iron Age Lefkandi; the following episodes occurred a-long with the first signs of resettlement on Xeropolis and just prior to the late ninth-century disturbances.

By superimposing Popham's bipartite structure of Lefkandian society over these episodes we can conclude that the conservative element in the community restrained innovation, but from time to time the progressive element gained the upper hand. This alterna-tive is especially noticeable in the fluctuations of Athenian influence. The first great period of Athenian influence began and ended quickly with the return to conservatism. The late ninth-century disruptions at Lefkandi occurred in the midst of a return of Athenian influence in ceramics.

The cemeteries, and specifically the burial customs, also give indications of divisions within society. In a substantial number of tombs such objects as jewelry and clothing fasteners have been found arranged as if they still adorned a body—a body made con-spicuous by its absence. P. G. Themelis, the member of Popham's team charged with analyzing the burials, has suggested that in such instances what appears to be a grave is in fact a cenotaph, that is, a memorial for one whose remains lie elsewhere. He proposes that most, if not all, of the missing bodies were cremated elsewhere (there are too few pyres to accommodate all of the missing bodies), but that the grave goods were "inhumed" in such a way as to suggest the pres-ence of a body. A seeming conflict between the older rite of inhum-ation and the more recent rite of cremation may have resulted in a unique burial practice dating back to the late twelfth century which combined elements of both (Popham, Sackett, and Themelis 1980).

"Warrior" graves provide another possible clue to societal divi-sion. Perhaps as many as three of these burials are inhumations, which suggests to Themelis that a warrior elite at Lefkandi was of the old Mycenaean stock and that its members were aware of this fact. Popham argues that the phenomenon of the "warrior" grave was

most at home in Dark Age Athens and may have been imported to
Lefkandi from there (Popham, Sackett, and Themelis 1980). The
"warrior" graves do seem to have been most common during the
periods of heightened Attic influence at Lefkandi. The traditional
account of Aiklos and Kothos, grandsons of the Athenian hero Ion,
point in this same direction. Strabo (10.1.8) remembered that after
the Trojan War they colonized both Eretria and Chalcis, and until
that time the Euboeans had been known as Abantes, an identification
also found in Homer (*Iliad* 2.536).

Another curious feature of the cemeteries at Lefkandi is the fundamental dissimilarity of evidence drawn from them. Nearly all of
the "warrior" graves have been found at Toumba: five along with
at least two, and possibly four, pyres that have yielded weaponry.
There are none at Skoubris and only one early to mid-ninth-century
example from Palia Perivolia. The concentration of such finds at
Toumba is consistent with the wealth of other high-status objects
found there.

There is a perceptible sequence in the use of the cemeteries themselves. For most of the eleventh century, Skoubris was the only cemetery. Palia Perivolia began receiving burials during the middle Protogeometric (1000–950) and was followed, presumably within a few
years, by Toumba. Their beginnings coincide with a sharp decline in
the use of Skoubris. The new popularity of Toumba seems self-evi-
dent given its proximity to the Heroön, and since Palia Perivolia is
only about 50 meters east of Toumba, its use too may be attributed to
its proximity to the Heroön. Its further distance from the Heroön
and the modesty of its tombs may reveal that Palia Perivolia was reserved for the common folk of Lefkandi, who, like the wealthier dead
buried at Toumba, accorded the great ones of the Heroön an equal
measure of reverence.

The warrior buried beneath the tumulus held such elevated status that any of the suggested epithets—king, clan chieftain, or Big
Man—might reasonably be applied. Given the small size and relative
simplicity of the community during the tenth and ninth centuries, a
leader's role was not likely to have been institutionalized either by
formal rules or cult but rather through acts of personal courage, eloquence, and generosity. During the course of the late tenth and ninth
centuries this leadership may have been formalized and passed on, as
Popham has suggested, to the descendants of the Toumba warrior

(Popham, Calligas, and Sackett 1993). If power at Lefkandi came to reside in a single family, supported perhaps by armed, dependent retainers, the outcome may have forced a division within the community which led, in the later ninth century, to the expulsion of one group by the other.

It is interesting to refer once again to the almost parallel fate of Nichoria, which, like Lefkandi, experienced a prolonged period of population decline from about the mid-ninth century. Meanwhile, the large building at the center of the settlement seems to have grown larger and more complex as the number of inhabitants shrank. Sometime in the mid-eighth century, Nichoria was destroyed by fire and abandoned—a catastrophe that may have been the result of warfare between Sparta and Messenia dating from the end of the eighth century, though it is possible that smaller scale hostilities preceded this date.

Both Lefkandi and Nichoria began experiencing difficulties during the ninth century. Why did these two sites not transform themselves into enduring *poleis?* One answer may be that they had no powerful neighbors to prompt the greater cohesion that occurred elsewhere in Greece. In the ninth century, both Nichoria and Lefkandi had room for expansion, and any civil dispute could result in the injured party simply taking up an abode elsewhere. The ensuing depopulation left the remaining community vulnerable to attack by any neighbors who were increasing their size and ambitions. Chalcis and Eretria on Euboea and Sparta in the southern Peloponnese did just this. Against their strength, small communities characteristic of the Dark Age stood little or no chance.

In summary, we believed that the disturbances of ca. 825 B.C.E. at Lefkandi can be ascribed to internal causes. Division within society may have led to civil unrest. An internal crisis may have resulted from a century and a half of the steady accumulation of land held by the few whom Calligas has identified as oikists, the leaders of transient clans who took up permanent or semi-permanent abodes in the tenth and ninth centuries. Over time, these men were able to increase their holdings through raiding, intermarriage, or purchase, while their less successful contemporaries saw their lands subdivided away, alienated for the payment of debt, or simply lost through bad luck. Those who lost their holdings will have had few choices in the struggle to gain a livelihood.

For free landless people at this time, only three alternatives to basic farming seem likely: some form of food production other than farming or stockbreeding; the production of secondary goods and services in support of the primary industry of food production; or trade and colonization. The first option entails either hunting or fishing. While various regions of Greece, notably Messenia, show evidence of increased hunting activity during the Dark Age, there is little evidence that this was the case on Euboea. As for fishing, there is no evidence that it ever counted as a significant factor in the economy of Dark Age Greece. It is instructive that Hesiod, who in *Works and Days* sang about nearly every other craft or skill, has nothing to say of either of these pursuits. The second option would be fulfilled by such tasks as pottery production, smithery, tanning, weaving, and the various construction trades. Here again Hesiod is helpful as a guide, for the society of small, independent farmers that he describes is nearly self-sufficient. Hesiod's wise farmer is also a ploughwright, a cartwright, a carpenter, and a tanner, while his long-suffering wife is a weaver and tailor. This self-sufficiency would further reduce the market for free-lance craftsmen.

Under such circumstances, the sea must have proved a powerful lure. Hesiod's own father, in order to escape poverty, took to the sea, presumably as a trader. Those adventurers with resources of their own could organize a trading venture, while those whom poverty had already caught could hire on as oarsmen. The prosperous few may also have had a hand in the new shipping ventures. It would be anachronistic to assume an aristocratic prejudice against trade at this early date. After all, Athena deigns to assume the guise of a trader in the first book of the *Odyssey*. Let us not forget that among the grave goods found beneath the tumulus on Toumba was a bronze amphora of Cypriot manufacture. The man whose remains were deposited in the amphora may have obtained it during a trading voyage to that far-away island.

Orality and Literacy in a Heroic Society

All models of Lefkandian social structure share one basic similarity: they assume what has come to be called a "heroic" society, characterized by a war-like and adventurous spirit and an obsession with honor and prestige (*time*) and fear of its opposite, shame, loss of face (*aischune*). The warrior graves, the atypical splendor of the Toumba burials, possible cults of heroes, and heroic efforts in venturing into the risky realm of Poseidon are all evocative of the heroization of life.

Display, deeds, and speech are the foundations of such a society. For the first two there is evidence in abundance, but the third by its very nature eludes us since, as we have seen, literacy appears to have vanished with the collapse of the Mycenaean palace-centered administration. However, the end-product of the oral tradition allows us to visualize inhabitants of Lefkandi gathered together to hear the remembered tradition of their community in order to deal with the present. It is easy to imagine a praise poem, a miniature epic in hexameters retelling the deeds (*ta erga*) of the great warrior buried on Toumba Hill, who made a voyage to the fabulous island of Cyprus, rich in copper, or to the land of the Phoenicians, famous for its purple cloth. It is tantalizing to think that the name of this hero might be enshrined in some familiar myth.

Somewhat ironically, we can reconstruct the nature of such oral praise poems only through the return of literacy to the late Dark Age world.[8] Where this occurred, and under what circumstances, is a matter of considerable debate. The surviving evidence dates to the eighth century but suggests steps toward adaptation of the Phoenician alphabet to the Greek language in the ninth century. Recently the case for Euboea as the place of origin has been made by Barry Powell, who argues for the confluence of several necessary factors in this island toward the end of the ninth and on into the eighth century (1991). Not only is the Euboean script close in form to the Phoenician script from which the Greek form was developed, but many of the earliest examples of Greek alphabetic writing are linked with Euboea. The traditional explanation for the purpose of the innovation is well suited to Euboea: many scholars believe that writing first served as an *aide de memoire* for traders operating in the Near East. Another possible motive—the wish to record Homeric verse— is equally at home on that island. As Powell has pointed out, the earliest extant inscriptions are poetic in nature, composed in hexameters of varying quality, and many of the surviving examples are associated with Euboea (1991, 123–29, 163–67, 185). Even the earliest

Greek inscriptions make use of a phonetic alphabet complete with vowels, consonants, and double consonants, phonetic exactness not necessary in financial and administrative documents but essential in poetry.

One of the earliest inscriptions clearly illustrates the bonds between alphabetic writing, the heroic mentality, and Euboea. A small cup (*kotyle*) found in the tomb of a twelve-year old boy at Pithekoussai in Italy has come to be known as "Nestor's Cup." Although the cup is of Rhodian manufacture, the three lines of poetry inscribed in retrograde on the cup are almost certainly Euboean. In Powell's translation they read:

> I am the delicious cup of Nestor.
> Whoever drinks this cup, straightway that man
> The desire of beautiful-crowned Aphrodite will seize.
>   (1989, 338)

Everything about this find is remarkable: the nature and early date of the inscription, the humble quality of the vessel, and the context within which the cup was found. Dated to between 735 and 720, it is the second oldest known substantial inscription. The verses reveal such familiarity with Homeric epic that the writer has been able to step from simple quotation to parody. The presence in the tomb of a number of *kraters* for wine mixing as well as the humorous, amatory nature of the verses are characteristic of the *symposion*, or a drinking-together.[9] This context, which is unusually rich, suggests that the boy may have been the son of an aristocratic family and no institution was more closely associated with the aristocracy than the *symposion*.

Although our earliest allusions to the *symposion* occur in Homer, its beginnings seem to be much earlier, perhaps well into the Bronze Age. Thus the *krater* found next to the warrior's tomb in the Heroön on Toumba could have been used as a symposiastic vessel as well as a cup for pouring libations to the deceased. The Toumba building is large enough to have served for such gatherings. As a social institution, the *symposion* suits any of the three social organizations proposed for Dark Age Lefkandi: in a society obsessed with status and prestige, the *symposion* would act as the natural context for competitive displays of wealth, eloquence, and generosity.

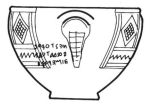

21. Nestor's Cup, with inscription. *Drawing ©Alice Alden, after K. Ruter and K. Mathiesen, in "Zum Nestorbecher von Pithekussi,"* ZPE *2 (1968) figure 1 and* CAH *2d ed., vol. 3 pt. 3, (Cambridge, 1982) p. 100. Used by permission.*

"Eikon Odusseos"

The Pithekoussan Cup of Nestor evokes the heroic nature of colonial, and by implication Euboean, society. Evidence of a cultic aspect of that society comes from the island of Ithaca, traditional home of Odysseus.[10] A series of thirteen bronze tripods of the ninth and eighth centuries B.C.E. found in the Cave of Polis overlooking the western shore of the island identifies it as a cult place at least from the ninth century and possibly as far back as the Late Bronze Age. The primary recipients of cult offerings seem to have been the Nymphs, and at times, Athena, Hera, and Artemis were also honored. But for our purposes, the greatest significance lies in the presence of the tripods and the cave's association with Odysseus. Irad Malkin argues forcefully that the hero's connection with the cave is contemporary with the tripods (1998, 94ff.). One of the tripods bears something very like the parallel ridges and running spiral motif found on castings from the molds deposit at Lefkandi dating to about 900. Even earlier, of course, is the Lefkandi Heroön, which is heroic in a quite Homeric sense of that word.

The cultic significance of the Heroön has been questioned since no evidence of cult activity has survived from the Heroön: there are no votive offerings nor are there inscribed potsherds, and no charred animal bones exist to denote burnt offerings. The date of the Heroön, around 975, would make it unique in the Hellenic world if it were indeed a hero shrine. Even the earliest hero shrines date only to the ninth century, and most date to the eighth or seventh century. Another factor to consider is that the man and woman buried beneath the tumulus were mortals, and not until the age of colonization in the eighth and seventh centuries do we find cult honors paid to the newly deceased founders of colonies. Furthermore, as Malkin has pointed out (1988), even in these cases cult honors were often not instituted until long after the death of the founder.

Could the warrior burial at Toumba be the forerunner of the later, more pervasive hero cult? While a final answer cannot be given, Toumba may represent, as Carla Antonaccio has suggested (1994), a warrior burial of truly heroic proportions consistent with the burial of Patroclus recounted in *Iliad* 23:159–296. Toumba may be an instance of archaeology preceding Homer by over two centuries.

Thus, Pithekoussai offers inscribed references to Homeric verse and the presence of Euboean colonists; the Cave of Polis presents a hero shrine dedicated in part to the Homeric hero Odysseus and containing dedications of bronze tripods, a few of which bear a striking resemblance to those crafted at Lefkandi. The cemeteries of Lefkandi provide many of the trappings of heroic society and one monumental burial, which in many respects anticipates Homer. And the Homeric corpus may have achieved something approaching its final form on Euboea. Even on the traditional view that the epics were products of the Ionian settlements of Asia Minor, who would have been better placed to spread them from Ionia to Italy than the maritime traders and adventurers of Euboea?

Lefkandi's trading contacts grew by fits and starts from as early as the mid-eleventh century, an initial impulse perhaps provided by the Aeolian and Ionian migrations to Anatolia in the eleventh and tenth centuries. Euboea was in the path of both movements. The tale of Odysseus' wandering upon the "fruitless sea" in search of home would have held special significance for the Euboean seafarers who may have been forced to take to the sea because of land subdivision or by the grasping of predatory neighbors. When the Euboeans turned their attention to the central Mediterranean in the late tenth or early ninth century, they did so as pioneers or as "proto colonists," to use Malkin's terminology. Ithaca would have singular meaning for these pioneers sailing the waters of the Ionian and Adriatic Seas, for this was the place from which the great wanderer Odysseus set out to travel to Troy and where he returned twenty years later after wandering throughout much of the Mediterranean Sea laden with a rich treasure which included a large number of tripods. Ithaca, for Greek explorers and traders, was the jumping-off point for Corcyra, the Epirote coast, and the west. Odysseus was the paradigmatic adventurer who beckoned all to follow him, with the promise of a safe, profitable return, albeit after many troubles.

It is not unreasonable to view Lefkandian activities in the Ionian Sea and central Mediterranean in such a context. Having tested the seas nearer home, as at Sindos in the northern Aegean, where a ninth-century Euboean trading station has been detected,[11] they were ready to venture further. There is evidence that they visited Ithaca during the ninth century, dedicating tripods in the Cave of Polis. They may have proceeded north to Corcyra, where a Euboean colony preceded the more enduring Corinthian settlement. Further west, a Lefkandian *skyphos* of the late ninth or early eighth century has been found at Capua, only a few miles east of the Euboean colony of Kyme. If Lefkandi sent out colonies to the central Mediterranean, we have no certain evidence of them. Yet, the earliest known colonies were Euboean foundations, and it is not inconceivable that Lefkandians took part in them. Even those great enemies Chalcis and Eretria managed to cooperate in colonizing ventures.

22. *Skyphos* (ca. 800–760). © *Deutsches Archäologishes Institut Athen; negative number ELEUSIS 512. Used by permission.*

The ninth-century trading activities of Lefkandi and the colonial foundations of Chalcis and Eretria in the eighth century had effectively brought Greece out of its Dark Age isolation. Ithaca and the Ionian Islands became for the Greeks a liminal zone, separating the Hellenic world from that of the *barbaroi*. This confrontation between Greek and non-Greek was given added force by the Odysseus tradition. Odysseus had faced the Cyclopes, who knew no law, and he had been rescued and entertained by the Phaeacians, models of heroic gentility. The Greeks viewed with a sense of wonder, mixed with a certain amount of dread, the non-Greek world newly opened to them. Undaunted, they followed in the wake of Odysseus, and in so doing established the roots of a national identity—an identity which, like so much else, had its roots in the Dark Age.

5

Corinth

The End
of the Dark Age

No matter how far the sailors from Lefkandi traveled, it is a wonder that they attracted notice from more than a handful of other communities, for the residents of Lefkandi were themselves just a "handful." The total population of the tenth-century hamlet is reckoned at fifteen people; by the ninth century, the number rose to twenty-five.[1]

But their precociousness by sea was infectious. Conditions in the Greek world had regained enough stability that many communities followed the path of the Euboean adventurers. A brisk pace of change moved across much of Greece in the eighth century. Population was increasing, in some places with breathtaking speed, with the result that some of that population had to be "exported" as far distant as southern Italy and Sicily in the west and, beginning in the next century, the Black Sea in the east. New contacts were made or earlier contacts reestablished, bringing so many fresh ideas and objects to the Greek world that the century between 750 and 650 has been dubbed "The Age of Revolution" (Starr, 1961b). While the Greeks might have been overwhelmed by the superiority of foreign technology and concepts, they managed to adapt the new forces and products to their own way of life, thereby creating a cultural identity that distinguished the Hellenic way of life from that of other peoples. No single factor is sufficient to define the Hellenic outlook, but adherence to individual small states—the descendants of earlier villages—is a conspicuous element in the end product.

In examining Lefkandi's late Dark Age conditions, we pointed to their slowness in incorporating the ceramic techniques known as Geometric. The shapes and decoration of eighth-century products clearly derive from their predecessors, but the works of the last Dark Age century show a mastery, confidence, and variety rarely encountered previously. As Susan Langdon has written, "it reveals an intimate art of minute detail, precise brush stroke, and an almost unbelievable accuracy of planning and measurement in two-dimensional enhancement of the solid vessel form" (1993, 200). This is obviously not the product of a community under constant threat.

The source of the earliest changes seems to have been Athens in its early tenth-century Protogeometric tradition, but by the ninth century, Geometric shapes and decorative elements were developing in many regions of the mainland. Two of the leaders were Athens and Corinth. However, as we have seen, the unity and strength of Athens during the early Dark Age gave way to regionalism at its end. By contrast, Corinth witnessed unification only in the later Dark Age, but with it came innovation in every aspect of life. Corinth, then, leads us—as it lead much of Greece—to the very edge of the Archaic period.

The Site

Occupation in the area of Corinth, the Corinthia, dates back to the Neolithic period.[2] The rich coastal land encouraged farming while natural springs provided water; hills and mountains offered agricultural diversity and defense in times of difficulty. Essential resources of limestone, high quality clay and, probably, timber were available in this compact region, which in the Classical period comprised roughly 900 square kilometers. The configuration of the area served

23. Artist's reconstruction of Corinth. *Drawing © Anne Lou Robkin. Used by permission.*

as a bridge between Attica and the Peloponnese as well as between the Peloponnese and central Greece. For the traveler by sea, the coastal plain and natural harbors offered protection and anchorage.

In spite of these natural resources, Corinth was not a palace center in the Late Bronze Age. Rather, the region appears to have been linked to Mycenae: remains of a road system extend northward from Mycenae into the Corinthia, and the Catalogue of Ships in the *Iliad* assigns the ships of the Corinthians to Agamemnon's command.

Though regularly settled through the Late Bronze Age, Corinth seems to have been largely deserted in the early Dark Age. Only late in the tenth century does a series of graves point to growing numbers of inhabitants and continuity of residence, a situation resembling that of Nichoria. Whether these settlers were newly arrived or remnants of the Mycenaean population cannot be learned from the surviving evidence. Tradition gives a role to the Dorians, who, it was claimed, attacked Corinth under the leadership of Aletes, a great-great-grandson of Heracles. The earlier inhabitants fled, so the account continues, allowing the new inhabitants to take possession of the site from which Aletes and his descendants ruled for five generations (Pausanias 2.3–4).

The archaeological evidence poses a serious problem to the accuracy of the tradition since there is little that is new and the long gap in settlement would set a Dorian attack more than two hundred years after the final difficulties in the Argolid, ca. 1125. The existence of several smaller groups in the area that would become the *polis* center could, but need not, indicate the coexistence of several different strands of population.

The core of Dark Age Corinth was the area around Temple Hill, a site that provided a natural source of water, protection, a vantage point, and a raised, healthy location for residence. A grouping of homes here was the earliest and largest cluster, but a second gathering of homes developed along the stream bed north of the Peirene spring. Other clusters formed on the raised terraces in the western sector of the area. We may imagine family groups or small communities resembling those of the earliest settlement at Dark Age Nichoria. And, like Nichoria, Corinth was relatively isolated until the eighth century; virtually the only influence on early Geometric pottery of Corinth came from nearby Athens (ca. 875–800).

Within the larger region, a natural growth of population, accompanied perhaps by an increase in larger estates controlled by some more fortunate families, resulted in a "filling up" of once empty spaces. This territorial synoecism seems to have been a product of the eighth century, a first step toward a sense of community in social and political respects that would develop somewhat later.

Eighth-Century Developments: The *Polis*

There is little agreement on either the time or place of origin of the form of organization that would provide the framework of Classical Greek civilization. The problem of scanty evidence is compounded by the fact that hundreds of *poleis* emerged at different times and in various forms. We have seen the results of the tenth century settlements in Asia Minor, where a need to develop and maintain secure settlements produced the conditions and attitudes of communal cohesion inherent in the *polis*. Yet the variety itself offers a clue to the development: regionalism, not cohesion, was the condition in which the *polis* form took shape. Each of these chapters has shown that the

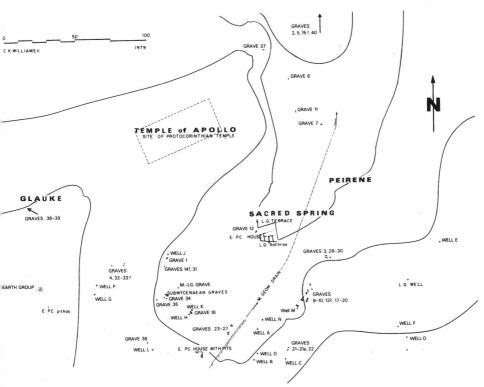

Map 10. Geometric Corinth. *J. B. Salmon (1984, figure 7). Courtesy of Oxford University Press. Used by permission.*

Dark Age is characterized by the isolated, essentially independent life of small communities. The entire process of destruction, followed by survival and then recovery, resulted eventually in the Hellenic form and conception of polity.

Destruction of the complex administrative structure of the Mycenaean Age was a first necessity for the creation of a citizen-state in which ordinary peasant farmers participated in governing themselves. The Mycenaean order was built on the exclusivity of a few, rather than the inclusion of many, members of a community. The darkest years of the Dark Age fostered a second vital element, namely a sense of adhesion to a small body of people, since during such uncertain times there could be no security without group solidarity. A third element—permanent settlement—was not initially present throughout much of Dark Age Greece. A group of people could be cohesive, yet mobile, not attached permanently to a bounded territory. We have seen indications of increased pastoral nomadism at both Nichoria and Lefkandi. A *polis*, by contrast, was equally a community of place and a community of people. So much we learn from Aristotle (*Politics* 1325b40).

But when we speak of a community of place and of people, much more is implied than the mere sharing of space and kinship. "Self-absorbed" is the term Victor Ehrenberg (1960, 94) used to describe the particular relationship of people to place and to each other in the *polis* context. Certainly they must have been self-aware—aware of themselves as a distinct people with a unique past in which remarkable things had been done, occurrences and events which had happened in the place where they now lived so that the very ground on which they stood evoked a common memory. Thus a *polis* was not simply a city, its people, and the surrounding countryside but a constellation of commonly held beliefs, aspirations, and memories concerning these things. Except for the numerous myths, legends, and genealogies which may have hearkened back to the Late Bronze Age, there is very little in the political, social, and psychological ordering of the *polis* which can be traced to Mycenaean times; a great deal was bequeathed by the Dark Age. The elements of singularity, solidarity, and self-sufficiency which ideally characterized the *polis* developed out of the forced isolation, poverty, and insecurity of the centuries following the Mycenaean collapse. Paradoxically, however, the *polis* would never have arisen had not those very conditions been altered irrevocably by population growth within the confining context of the Greek landscape. The greater numbers, relative security, and more stable communications based on the revival of trade that characterized the late Dark Age conspired with the troublesome geography of Greece to encourage the adhesion, or synoecism, of villages into larger communities.

In this respect the Corinthia was one of the most energetic regions of the Greek mainland in the eighth century. The evidence of wells and graves attests expansion from the mid-eighth century and there are signs that individual settlements, especially those around Corinth itself, were drawing closer together. While population growth seems to have occurred throughout much of the Greek

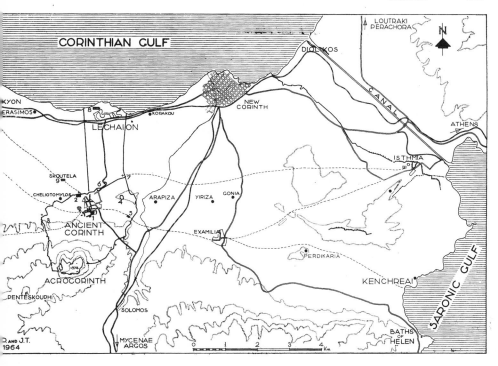

Map 11. The Corinthia. *H. S. Robinson (1965, figure 4). Courtesy of Corinth Excavations, American School of Classical Studies, Athens. Used by permission.*

world toward the end of the Dark Age, the consequences for Corinth were soon felt because of the territory's tight configuration. The region is naturally constrained: in the north and east by the Corinthian and Saronic gulfs and by mountains in the south and southwest. Though no natural barriers exist to the west, the presence of settlements expanding at much the same rate as Corinth effectively limited expansion.

The factors of high population growth and limited space led to an early political and social fusion of the Corinthia. Tradition dates the end of hereditary kingship in Corinth to 747 B.C.E. Management of communal affairs then passed into the hands of a clan known as the Bacchiadae, named for their descent from an earlier king, Bacchis.[3] The customary reckoning of their number at two hundred may indicate that the heads of two hundred families participated in the exercise of leadership, the full clan size being between eight hundred and a thousand members. Alternatively, if the full clan numbered two hundred, the family heads would have been between forty and fifty. Under the new order, control was vested in an official position called the *prytanis*, which changed hands annually. A second official position is attested, that of *polemarchos*, a title that indicates leadership in war. Even more important than these two positions was the council in which all Bacchiad heads of family sat for the rest of their lives, to deliberate matters concerning the community.

This change from the leadership of one man to control by many peers is of signal importance for on-going developments in the Archaic and Classical periods, for it marked the extension of political power to more members of the community. Its occurrence is not accompanied by spectacular stories of revolution or by the death of kings; rather it appears to have been a natural, gradual occurrence throughout the Greek world. Not surprisingly, it is apparent in the Homeric epics, especially the *Odyssey*, in which the traditional leadership of a single family (maintained at least for two generations plus the twenty years that Odysseus has been away) is being sorely tested by those best men (*aristoi*) who exercise power in the Ionian Islands.

The features inherent in the communities we have examined thus far point to the same picture of gradual transformation. Twelfth-century Mycenae showed the first necessary element: removal of the overarching central power that extended from a palace center into the surrounding region. Even had there been continuity of control at the citadel of Mycenae, its scope was severely reduced in the twelfth century. A further leveling was found at Nichoria, where homogeneity, not variety, marked almost every feature of life. If a single leader directed the affairs of his community, he did so living in the midst of others and possessing wealth of much the same order. His home was slightly larger than the dwellings of others, and most of the metal objects excavated were associated with this largest building, whose hearth may have been the scene of plan-making with other heads of families. Such a person may fit the definition of a Big Man, but it is important to remember the transitory nature of this form of control: it can quickly change hands when the prestige of another grows greater than that of the current holder. The impressive burial at Lefkandi also celebrates the status of a single man and a single woman.

Additionally, however, excavation at Lefkandi has revealed a greater quantity of material wealth distributed more widely than at Nichoria. Here, too, shifts in the focus of the settlement may reflect shifts in the locus of power.

The Corinthia during the eighth century, however, displays a level of cohesion several magnitudes greater than either Nichoria or Lefkandi. By mid-century, the Bacchiadae had brought the region under their control, thus creating a unified state, if not a "synoecized" *polis*. During the next half century, Corinth embarked on a major program of colonization, and by the end of the century a synoecism had been accomplished, uniting the various scattered villages with the urban core around Temple Hill (Roebuck, 1972). The Bacchiad clan must have gained its status through possession of land and its products. A mid-eighth century date for the clan's political ascendancy would surely reinforce this conclusion, since other forms of economic activity had only just begun. However, since landed wealth enables other forms of wealth, it is reasonable to nominate Bacchiadae as the early adventurers who traveled around the Corinthian Gulf and to the Ionian Islands. This role is not likely to have stopped with the establishment of aristocratic rule; rather it probably increased. In the words of J. B. Salmon, "Many of the foundations of Corinth's future were laid during the Bacchiad period; but they were laid by the ambition, the greed, and the skills of individuals" (1984, 74).

The words are well-chosen. Along with their enterprise, the Bacchiadae are credited with a surfeit of greed and ambition that extended to confining membership in the clan: only full members of the clan were permitted to marry. Their exclusive control lasted nearly a century, during which Corinthian enterprise grew but dissatisfaction among non-Bacchiads intensified. Bacchiad rule was forcibly brought to an end sometime around the mid-seventh century by the tyrant Kypselos, himself a Bacchiad on his mother's side. But despite their later ill-repute among the greater part of the Corinthian population, the Bacchiads did manage to organize the city as the first great commercial power in Greece: a power great enough to bully Megara over the possession of land around modern Perachora, ca. 750 B.C.E.

As the fate of Lefkandi, and possibly that of Nichoria, demonstrated, the later eighth century saw an increased frequency of warfare between neighboring communities. Boundaries between communities were flexible and, as land grew more precious, contention over border-lands became common. Indeed, the nature of Classical Greek warfare was now established as essentially war between neighboring states over the status of border territory. Gods, as well as human agents, were called upon to enforce the particular interests of individual communities. Corinth is an excellent early example of the practice of announcing territorial claims through the construction of a sanctuary. When the northern promontory of the isthmus known today as Perachora was absorbed by Corinth around the middle of the eighth century, an apsidal building was erected there in honor of Hera. Although it was soon replaced by another building, the site itself remained the location of a major sanctuary. The western end of the isthmus, too, was claimed for Corinth by sacred use in the form of a sanctuary dedicated to Poseidon, sited strategically beside a major route linking the Peloponnese to the mainland.

Corinth was by no means unique in this practice; the custom was widespread. As François de Polignac has argued, some of the cult places scattered widely through the territory of a community "manifest particularly openly the authority whose exercise over the space each city determinedly reserved to itself. These great rural sanctuaries on the edge of the plain, and small sanctuaries in mountainous or coastal areas, constitute what one might call sanctuaries of territorial sovereignty" (1994, 3f.). They were, of course, more than declarations of sovereignty. As recognized meeting places between men and gods, they were locations where genuine expressions of respect to divine authority were regularly given. Such was their value in this regard that many of the markers of territory became, paradoxically, Panhellenic centers as well.

The rise to prominence at this time by such centers was again the result of higher population, political stability, and relative ease of communications. The very forces that were transforming isolated villages into *poleis* were simultaneously creating among Greeks everywhere a recognition of those cultural elements which they held in common and which made possible the universal appeal—the Panhellenism—of Delphi or Olympia or Eleusis. The value of such centers, where people from all over the Greek world came to rub el-

24. Temple model Perachora as preserved (left), with roof restored (right). *H. Payne,* Perachora I *(Oxford, 1940) plate 9. Courtesy of Oxford University Press. Used by permission.*

bows, trade, and exchange news as well as to honor their gods cannot be overstated as a prime factor in the development of a sense of Hellenic identity. But this development was aided, also in incalculable ways, by contacts made through piracy, trade, and, increasingly, through colonization between Greek and non-Greek. Those forces which led to the rise of the *polis* also contributed to the Greek habit of sending out colonies to relieve political, social or demographic problems at home. This was a practice in which Corinth was an early and prominent adept.

Eighth-Century Developments: Colonization

As numbers of inhabitants rose, available land became inadequate: Plato defines the situation (Laws 740e) as *stenochoria*, narrowness of land. And inasmuch as the economy was almost totally reliant on the land for farming and/or herding, scarcity of land threatened the very survival of the community. Apart from the grim necessity of watching the impoverished die or wander from their home in search of livelihood elsewhere, there were two alternatives open to the community: encroaching upon the land of neighboring communities or deliberately and collectively traveling further afield to less densely populated areas. In choosing the second alternative, Corinth had a clear model in the activities of Euboean communities: Lefkandi, earlier, and now Chalcis and Eretria. They were among the first to resort to "that ancient device" discussed by Plato of "sending forth, in friendly wise from a friendly nation, of colonies consisting of such people as are deemed suitable" (*Laws* 740e; trans. Bury 1926).

In the previous chapter, we examined the role that Lefkandi (and Euboea generally) played in the re-establishment of ties between Greece and the larger Mediterranean sphere. Euboeans were actively traveling in several directions: eastward, north to the Chalcidice, and west into the Ionian and Adriatic seas. In their own search for land, the Corinthians looked westward.[4] Initially Corinthian influence is noted close to the Corinthian Gulf: north of the Gulf into central Greece, at Delphi, and in the Ionian Islands, especially Ithaca. Dedications on Ithaca suggest 780 B.C.E. as a date for the Corinthian presence there. These initial thrusts produced no colonies, but when the Corinthians extended their horizon to northwestern Greece, into the Adriatic, and to Sicily, they did establish colonies: Ambrakia, Leukas, Corcyra, Epidamnos, Apollonia, and Syracuse. The traditional date for the founding of Syracuse is 733 B.C.E., and the Corinthian settlement on Corcyra is dated to either that same year or 708 B.C.E. Irad Malkin argues strongly for the earlier date, seeing the Corinthian colonies of Corcyra and Syracuse as responses to Euboean settlements at Corcyra and Naxos (1998, 77–8). Whatever the true dates may be, it is clear that the Corinthians were preceded and guided by the Euboeans, not simply through a general model but in their choice of specific sites: the Corinthian foundation on Corcyra superseded an Eretrian colony that dates from the middle of the eighth century.

Colonization is regularly associated with land shortage in Dark Age Greece, but other factors were clearly at work as well. In fact, the initial impulse prompting Greeks to invade Poseidon's realm may have been trade rather than settlement. The Greek presence visible at the lively trade center of Al-Mina in Syria at the very start of the eighth century netted contact and trade rather than land for agricultural use. And earlier, through the darkest of the Dark Age, the limited number of Greek objects found in places like modern Taranto in southern Italy would have been carried by a handful of intrepid adventurers not groups of determined colonizers.

As we have seen in the case of Lefkandi, products that could be used for trade were now being produced in greater numbers and with higher quality. Although still in its infancy, some specialized production was returning to Greek communities in the eighth century: the tripods dedicated on Ithaca (which we discussed in connection with Lefkandi) include some of Corinthian origin. Although few in number, their size and quality reveal specialized skills, as we have noted in the case of Lefkandi. Bronze was being worked into various objects, both utilitarian and decorative. Far more gold than Dark Age Nichorians would have believed to exist has been found in eighth-century Corinth. Though the objects produced from that precious metal were often simple rings and pins, they show greater complexity than their ninth-century predecessors from Lefkandi.

Another indication of specialization is the means of transport: the construction of seafaring vessels, no matter how small they may be, demands certain skills, tools, and materials. To build his meager raft, even the hero Odysseus needed the advice of the divine nymph Calypso (*Odyssey* 5). Tradition associates improvements in shipbuilding with Corinth, maintaining that Ameinokles of Corinth built four warships for the Samians in the late eighth century. Even though many scholars would move the date to the seventh century, the assignment of the techniques to Corinth is likely to reflect reality.

At a more basic level, Corinthian pottery is an excellent gauge of diversification as it increases in quality, quantity, and distribution. Once separated from Attic influence at the start of the eighth century, Corinthian Geometric ware began to assume a character of its own, pleasing in shape and linear decoration. Abrupt change occurred about 720 B.C.E. when "orientalizing" techniques, adapted from practices of craftsmanship in the eastern Mediterranean, replaced Geometric traditions. Chester Starr's description evokes vivid images:

> First come the serene, beautifully ordered products of the Geometric stage. Here shape and decoration are integrated, in the better specimens, to form a taut, vibrant, yet disciplined unity; the motifs, almost entirely rectilinear, are severely limited; much of the vase is evenly cov-

ered with a dark coat. Then suddenly a riot of curvilinear decoration, floral, animal, even human, bursts into vision and swirls over the entire surface of the vases; on some pieces all sense of Greek logic and restraint seems to have dissolved into the wildest of experiments. The pots themselves change shape: many of the new types are smaller, more carefully studied, even dainty in effect; others are poorly proportioned and ephemeral essays in breaking away from old restraints. And finally the very technique of drawing is elaborated as outline gives way in many workshops to solid black-figure painting, picked out and enriched by the use of supplementary color and of incision to render more specific detail than Geometric potters had ever deemed necessary. (1961b, 231)

The products of individual craftsmen can be detected even earlier in the Dark Age, but now workshops are in evidence. At the site of Corinth, a settlement on a tongue of land on the western plateau of Temple Hill was converted to a work area now known as the Potters' Quarter. The area contained natural beds of good clay which had been used for pottery production since the mid-eighth century, but around 700 B.C.E. channels were cut for the flow of water into a single depression. This area would remain the center of pottery production into the Classical period.

25. Late Geometric Corinthian *Lekythos-Oinochoe* (ca. 750–720). Ceramic (ht. 21 cm., w. 23 cm., mouth diameter 5.8 cm.). *Courtesy of the Detroit Institute of Arts Founders Society. Founders Society purchase, William H. Murphy Fund (76.97). Previously Charles Seltman Collection. Photograph © 1993 The Detroit Institute of Arts.*

The products of these small workshops were not used in Corinth; rather, they were exported. It is argued that the creation of the Potters' Quarter was a "deliberate attempt to exploit the expanding market" (Salmon 1984, 111f.). Already by 750, Corinthian Geometric ware was circulating throughout the Corinthian Gulf and beyond to the Ionian islands. During the second half of the century, it reached ever more distant destinations: Messenia in the southwestern Peloponnese; Old Smyrna in Asia Minor; Corcyra and Dodona to the northwest; southern Italy and Sicily. Finds in the early colonies of others, such as Pithekoussai, a Euboean settlement, suggest that the initial impulse was trade. When Corinth founded her own colonies a bit later, Corinthian ware was dominant from the outset.

If we can assign initiative to a few adventurers carrying a small cargo of objects to trade or to offer to friendly hosts encountered in foreign parts, we must add many other sorts of participants to the actual colonizing ventures. The settlements were well sited with respect to both trade and agriculture. And while exact statistics cannot be retrieved, the emigrants must have been fairly numerous even in the last third of the eighth century, especially if the foundation of Corcyra and that of Syracuse are dated to the same year. Evidence from Syracuse alone indicates that the earliest burial area was the largest on the island.

Who were these Corinthians who were willing to leave their home with the expectation that the move would be permanent? They were people in need of land, those whose lots had been reduced by division among heirs or encroached upon by others. Also included will have been those who saw the move as offering greater opportunities for themselves—the successors of the earlier adventurers. While we have no first-hand description of a Corinthian colonial effort, we may suppose a situation akin to that facing Theraians in the seventh century: one son from each *oikos* was sent as a conscript, on pain of death for deserters, other Theraians were free to join as volunteers, and more settlers were to be admitted later—that is, if the colony survives.

> They invoked curses on those who should break these agreements and not abide by them, whether those settling in Libya or those remaining here. They fashioned wax images and burned them; and they all assembled, men, women, boys and girls, and uttered the curse. (*Supplementum Epigraphicum Graecum* IX #3, trans. Rhodes 1986, 23)[5]

If this evidence reflects the general pattern, it indicates that many levels of the community were included. Although Dark Age society was not hierarchical in the Mycenaean sense, even Nichoria shows some differentiation, and evidence for social stratification increases as the Dark Age enters its last century.

Three elements were added to this situation in the late Dark Age. Population growth is one—not necessarily the first to occur but perhaps first in importance. As Corinth shows, the region was dotted with small communities, largely independent of one another to the end of the ninth century. As population rose, it was necessary to use all available land, even though it might be marginal, to provide basic sustenance. In the process, the once separate settlements were drawn together. Postulating a Nichorian-like chief for each little settlement, the territorial coalescence would bring together, peacefully or antagonistically, a handful of such chiefs.

At the same time, it was becoming easier to accumulate greater wealth. Families situated on the best land already had an advantage, and as we suggested for Lefkandi and will see in our final example of Ascra, those families pressed their advantage to gain even more extensive estates. Others, or even some of these successful families, might be drawn by the newer possibility of gaining wealth by taking to the sea, as we have postulated for some of the inhabitants of Lefkandi. Ships and objects worthy of trade or gift-giving demonstrate a command of resources and of labor. Carl Roebuck has suggested that the production of a group of pottery known as Thapsos ware (named for the location in which it was found on Sicily) "seems to have been a deliberate response by one particular shop to an opportunity for export" (1972, 117). Ordinary folk will also have been involved both in the production and as sailors for the voyages. These less fortunate participants may well have gained wealth through their enterprise and good fortune. Those who had the most to gain, however, would have been the directors of the ventures, who possessed or procured goods for the cargo and made new alliances through guest-friend-ships.[6]

Guest-friendships, cemented by an exchange of gifts, belong to the "real" world quite as much as to the epic world where, as Moses Finley stressed, "No single detail in the life of the heroes receives so much attention" (1978, 66). Perhaps not as prevalent as it was in

26. Corinth in 1810 (looking south). *H. S. Robinson (1965, figure 9). Courtesy Corinth Excavations, American School of Classical Studies, Athens. Used by permission.*

Homeric society, exchange of gifts is clear even in the archaeological evidence of the late Dark Age. Some gifts were placed in sanctuaries, intended for the gods; others were presented to human individuals .

A Geometric wine jug made on Ithaca retains parts of its inscription: "guest-friend dear and trusted comrade," and as Kevin Robb has reconstructed its context, it was "a *xenos*-gift exchanged between host and traveling guest-friend(s), probably at a *symposion* as part of the proprieties for entertaining the *xenos*" (1994, 49). Robb continues:

> Without the institution of *xenia*—before the rise of written law and before institutionalized protections for those who are not kin or members of the clan—extensive travel would have been impossible. . . . During the Dark Ages, we may speculate, singers increasingly came to stress the proprieties of *xenia* because the social conditions of expanding trade and travel demanded it. (1994, 51f.)

The custom would continue into the Classical period with more formal conditions attached to it: an official guest-friendship was granted to a citizen of another state who was expected to represent, within his own community, the interests of the *polis* granting the honor. The recipient was chosen on the basis of strong personal ties with members of the granting state.

Population increase, diversification of occupation, and accumulation of wealth in the hands of some combined to produce the change in leadership that we are tracing for eighth-century Corinth: as more people were increasingly drawn together into a single community where specialized activities were emerging, the leadership of a single person was no longer effective or even sufficient. While even the largest community at Nichoria might conduct its business round a hearthfire, meeting whenever a need arose, a community of several thousand requires more regular direction than a single person can provide. The ambitious nature of such colonizing efforts as those of Syracuse and Corcyra assumes a large (in relative terms) and unified state with a distributed power structure. The evidence from Corinth and from other Greek communities as well indicates that responsibilities once resting on the shoulders of one were divided, their weight now distributed among several members of the community: oversight of communal justice, leadership in combat, and proper concern for the gods was a usual division. While the holders of these responsibilities might rotate, an ongoing body continued its supervisory role from year to year. Those heads of families with a greater stake in the communities were deemed to be better placed to manage the affairs of others and had the possessions and status to assert such a claim.

In this connection it is useful to consider a second definition of *stenochoria*—narrowness of land: as land ownership was narrowing by concentration in the hands of fewer people, consequences were disruptive of communal integrity (Malkin 1994). An example from the early *polis* of Sparta is instructive. The Spartan colony of Taras was peopled by the removal from Sparta of disruptive young men known as *Partheniai*, sons of unwed mothers. Thought to be born to Spartan women while their husbands were fighting the twenty-year struggle over Messenia (dated to the late eighth and early seventh centuries), they were regarded as less than full members of the community. In Malkin's words, "Sparta, in short, seems to have depended on exporting, through colonization, a significant, distinct section whose continued presence and demands threatened that community" (1994, 4). Since large estates appear to have emerged in many parts of Greece during the eighth and seventh centuries, political *stenochoria* was a probable motive behind at least some of the Corinthian emigrations.

Confirmation of this view can be found in the new settlements. The names of the leader/founders of the individual ventures identify them as aristocrats: Chersikrates headed the settlement of Corcyra, and Archias, that of Syracuse. Both were regarded as Heraclids, that is, members of the Bacchiad clan. Yet, all the settlers expected a certain plot of land in their new home. The poet Archilochus wrote of one Aethiops, who bartered his plot for a honey cake on the voyage to Syracuse (fragment 293).

Material remains at Syracuse from the first two or three generations of its existence reveal that the land was allocated with an eye to some degree of equality.[7] A model that employs the organization of funerary space to symbolize the social relationships within the living community maintains that "groups who enjoy privileged access to resources frequently bury their dead in exclusive burial grounds to preserve, reinforce and publicize their elite lineage" (Prufer 1993, 11). Non-elite will resort to lesser burial sites and practices. In the case of Syracuse, a single cemetery which served the community for its first century indicates a single corporate body with uniform access to the essential right of burial. Although there may have been an elite stratum within the community, this division was not reflected in burial practice.

Different conditions will have prevailed in other settlements, mirroring the varied developments in mainland communities. In his comparison of the evidence from the Megarian colony of Megara Hyblaea on Sicily (traditionally dated to the 720s B.C.E.), Prufer adduces signs of stratification and firm aristocratic control. A single cemetery dating to the first years of the settlement appears to have been an exclusive burial ground restricted to use by founding aristocrats. In the second generation of its history, another burial ground was established, which does not show the tangible marks of aristocratic privilege, perhaps indicating use by the ordinary members of the community.

Even when stratification existed or developed—it is a natural development in most societies, after all—the emigrants could have hoped for better opportunities in their new homes than they had in their original communities. Whether or not all were equal in land allocation, every colonizer was important to the success of the venture. Stories abound concerning the difficulties of settling; many colonies met with complete failure. The Megarians, for instance, were rebuffed in attempts to settle in two locations before being invited by a native king to occupy the land of Megara Hyblaea (Thucydides 6.2ff.). The effort required the cooperative perseverance of each member of the small band of émigrés. At home, too, a corporate identity was reinforced by the decision to send away "one son from every estate." The exodus was forced by conditions confronting the entire community and thus became a community response.

Communal ties were strengthened by the need to deal with native populations, who held greater claim to the territory than these newcomers did. A small portion of land—granted, perhaps, by a native king as in the case of Megara Hyblaea—must be guarded diligently. And, at home in the colonizing community, it was conditions of constriction created by other communities advancing their cultivation over ever more distant fields that had made emigration an option. Such circumstances sharpened an identification of a particular group of people with a particular territory, and in this sharpening we can see a defining feature of the Greek *polis*.

The Greeks and the Other

Appreciation of the expanded horizons that Lefkandi and Corinth illustrate so well helps to account for the emergence of notions of a common Hellenic culture.[8] In the case of Lefkandi, other more sophisticated travelers—probably from beyond the Aegean—were drawn to Euboea. Their own success and enterprise may well have encouraged the Euboeans to try their own hand at seafaring. Corinthians, by contrast, were driven by increasingly difficult conditions at home to venture further in the Corinthian Gulf, then beyond into the Ionian and Adriatic Seas. In both cases Greek travelers could now see that their own way of life was distinct from the cultures of non-Greeks. At the same time, Greeks were drawn into regular contact with one another through the forces of population growth, incipient trade of special commodities, and the attraction of Apollo's advice or Zeus' games so that they could appreciate features of their lives that were similar.

Differences were noted and acknowledged, but as Edith Hall and Irad Malkin have shown recently, non-Greeks were not viewed as natural enemies. Only in the fifth century, as Hall reconstructs the changing view, did foreigners become true "barbarians," "the despotic adversary of free Hellenes everywhere" (1989, 59). And as Malkin points out (1998) through numerous examples, Greek heroes were regarded as founders of non-Greek as well as Greek settlements, especially in the central Mediterranean sphere. Odysseus was accepted by non-Greek inhabitants of Italy, especially Etruscans, as their progenitor. Nestor, who, with his Pylians, was sidetracked before returning home, founded both Greek Metapontion and non-Greek Etruscan Pisa (Strabo 6.264 and 5.222). Diomedes had an early presence in non-Greek Apulia. Even less significant Trojan War heroes such as Philoktetes and Epeios were reputed to be founders of non-Greek settlements in Italy: the tools with which Epeios built the Trojan Horse were deposited in the temple of non-Greek Lagaria, while Philoktetes dedicated the bow and arrows of Heracles in non-Greek Makalla in the region of Kroton.

These contacts introduced Greeks to new skills, objects, institutions, and ideas. Whether they traveled across the Adriatic to Italy and Sicily, northward in the Aegean, or to the Levant and Egypt in the southeast, the early Greek sailors discovered notions, objects, and abilities quite unknown to their countrymen at home. Finding many of these discoveries useful or attractive or amusing, they borrowed, especially from eastern Mediterranean cultures, which by the ninth century had recovered from the time of troubles in the Late Bronze Age. The century extending from 750 to 650 B.C.E. is aptly termed by Walter Burkert the "Orientalizing Revolution." [9]

Recovery was visible in the form of monumental architecture and monumental sculpture, and it seems certain that Egypt served as instructor to the Greeks in the techniques of working massive stones. Since the same tools and techniques could be used for buildings and statues, it is likely that Egyptian artisans introduced the Greeks to the steps required for both products. Basic techniques of quarrying, lifting, clamping, and finishing heavy stone blocks were the first essentials. Moreover, many scholars accept the view that an Egyptian canon of proportions for sculpture provided the Archaic Greek formula for the refinement of the final forms.

The revolution in pottery design and decoration, by contrast, owes its inspiration to the Levant. The ordered geometric patterns of the ninth and early eighth century were quite suddenly replaced by animal and plant forms such as sphinxes and lotuses, strange and wondrous in the Greek world. Rather than a covering pattern of geometric designs, rosettes and spirals now filled the background of the vase. Colors of paint, too, suddenly changed from dark on a lighter ground to the use of multiple colors along with incision to reveal specific details of painted figures, a practice often credited to the Corinthian artists. New vase shapes, many petite in dimension, also announce foreign inspiration. Corinth was the home of the new "orientalizing" style in the last quarter of the eighth century, and that city's links with the western sphere quickly introduced the style to Greek colonies and non-Greek regions of Italy and Sicily.

The Levant was also the source of new metalworking skills and, perhaps, the production of textiles. Imported textiles have left no trace in the archaeological record, of course, but metal goods figure prominently from the eighth century on. It comes as something of a surprise that Olympia is the most significant location for finds of eastern bronzes, "richer," as Burkert states, "than all the Middle Eastern sites" (1995, 4). Imported carved ivories, together with techniques for creation of similar products, evoke Near Eastern models as well.

Other kinds of imports found their way into Greece through the expanding contacts: metals for the growing number of locally produced products had to be imported; timber for the ships that coursed the seas was scarce in the Greek mainland but far more plentiful in the northern Aegean; ivory, ebony, and cedar came from the east. And, plants and animals were carried to new locations—John Boardman suggests this time frame for the arrival of the domestic hen to Greece (1967, 75f.).

The Greek identity was founded on ideas and beliefs at least as much as on objects and skills, whether home-grown or gained through trade. Greek religion in the eighth century was an integral part of the Greek identity and seems to have been formed in much the same way as other facets of life—through contact among Greeks of different regions and between Greeks and non-Greeks. Like Greek epic poetry, Greek religion emerged from the Dark Age as a complex amalgam of ancient (perhaps pre-Hellenic) and recent, native and foreign elements. The process of borrowing and discarding practices and beliefs, gods and goddesses, was an ancient and consistent feature of Greek religion, and there is no reason to believe that Mycenaean religion was any more static than Classical religion. But that there was significant continuity between the two periods has been demonstrated by examination of the Linear B tablets. Indeed, the names of many in the Classical pantheon of great deities are attested: Zeus, Athena, Hera, Poseidon, Artemis, Dionysos, Ares, and, perhaps, Apollo. These familiar names, however, are joined with unfamiliar figures, particularly "Potnia," or Mistress, and accompanied by features unknown in post-Mycenaean times. Although certain features familiar from Classical Greek religion have roots in the Bronze Age, there is enough evidence to reveal Mycenaean religion as a combination of various strands, some quite unrecognizable from a fifth-century perspective. In other words, similarity of divine names does not signal similarity of practice and belief.

As in so many aspects of life, the Dark Age appears to have been a time of sorting and some discarding of religious practices and concepts. Elements discarded during the Dark Age would have been those practices associated with the palace centers: elaborate ceremonials like the one described on a Linear B tablet from Pylos, where offerings included gold objects and humans, perhaps as sacrificial victims; Dark Age cults show little trace of either gold or human offerings. That the pantheon of twelve had been decided by the eighth century is clear from the *Iliad* and the *Odyssey*. As William Gladstone pronounced in 1890, "Not only is the Homeric Thearchy composite as a whole, but each divinity is often composite within itself" (61f.). And since these oral epics were shaped for the audience who heard and understood them, we can assert that the Homeric conception of deity was intelligible to his Dark Age contemporaries and, in fact, reflected their own beliefs and practices.

After the Mycenaean collapse, as the elevated stratum of status, wealth, and office was stripped away, there were repercussions in the divine sphere as well as in the world of mortals. One momentous consequence is that the two spheres were brought into closer contact, a characteristic that continued into the Classical conception of deity. A change in the position of leaders from the thirteenth century to the eighth is one good illustration of this transformation. In the

Late Bronze Age, the Mycenaean kings enjoyed significant religious responsibilities and, according to some interpretations, may have held their positions on the basis of religious associations. Enjoying a special relationship to the gods, if not regarded as truly divine, this figure bridged a gap between divine and mortal. Some semblance of this role may have continued in the extraordinary burials in ninth-century Lefkandi. After this early example of heroization, however, heroic cults changed dramatically. No longer linked to a recently deceased member of the community, the practices now involved the offering of gifts at Bronze Age tombs.

Several features of the eighth- and seventh-century cults are striking. First, the anonymity of those buried centuries earlier in the tombs is notable. Since activity at the tombs had not been continuous from the Bronze Age into the late Dark Age, those buried in most cases must have been unknown. Yet, the anonymous character of the "heroes" would nicely suit the interests of the eighth-century worshippers, allowing them to trace unchallengeable ancestry to the heroic past. A second feature is the regional differences in the origin, nature, and purpose of the cults. Yet, in spite of these differences—and this is the third feature of the nature of the cults—they were linked to an assertion of status and power in certain members of each community.

It is important to stress the plural "certain members," since a number of participants joined in the activities. At the Isthmian sanctuary of Poseidon, common eating and drinking began in the late eleventh or tenth century. By the eighth century a largish terrace was defined in the sacral area to accommodate the feasters. It is possible that those partaking in the celebration were grouped according to rank. While numbers cannot be accurately counted, it is certain that the occasion had become a group activity. We have mentioned the growing sense of community in other connections; the religious association among members of settlements gaining cohesion in other respects was surely both cause and result of the sense of commonality.

The importance of the gods in the creation of the *polis* is demonstrated concretely by the emergence of grand structures honoring the gods. Prominent among the earliest examples of monumental architecture are temples, which show rapid developments in size and quality of construction in the eighth century. Corinth made significant contributions in both respects.

Just as religion played a primary part in the development of the *polis*, so also was it an important factor in efforts at colonization. Planning for emigration was not completely local; colonizers were guided by advice gained through consultation with the interpreters of Apollo at Delphi.[10] The story of Greek colonization is inseparable from the emergence of Delphi as a Panhellenic sanctuary and of Apollo as the expounder (*exegetes*) of wisdom. The designated leader of the venture, the *oikist*, consulted the oracle to learn whether there was a true need for the new foundation, specifics about the intended site, and in order to confirm his own position as leader. In providing this information, the god himself was involved in the enterprise (Malkin 1989).

Interaction between human and divine spheres is more and more prominent in Dark Age culture. While it is suggested for the hearth at the Big House at Nichoria, the joining of the two spheres is clearer at Lefkandi in the heroic individuals who towered above human counterparts so noticeably. By the eighth century, sites and activities appear that transcend individual communities and even contiguous regions. Delphi was assuming the Panhellenic character that would define it in the Classical Age.

Though evidence for cult practice in the Bronze Age exists at Delphi, activity apparently was not continuous through the Dark Age. Archaeological data provide an early ninth-century date for the Iron Age cult in the village at Delphi, and from as early as the start of the eighth century, a large collection of votives reflects origins from varied locations beyond the local community. Possible confirmation of the site's early significance occurs in the Homeric *Hymn to Pythian Apollo*, thought by some to belong to the eighth century: its bard sings of "Far-shooting Apollo, [who] searched for a spot to establish the very first shrine of oracular wisdom for men" (ll. 215f., trans. Sargent 1975).

Nor was Delphi alone in gaining an expanded role in the Dark Age: Olympia, which from the tenth century had been a local meeting place "for petty chiefs of the West" (Morgan 1993, 21) increasingly drew visitors from greater distances. Tradition firmly sets 776 as the date of the first truce declared to allow safe travel to those visiting Olympia. The early games, performed in natural surroundings, seem to date to the eighth century, perhaps to the last quarter of the century when the sanctuary site was expanded. Isthmia, too, was considerably expanded during the eighth century, having served as a local shrine for feasting since the late eleventh century. Games celebrated in honor of Poseidon also gained importance, both throughout and beyond the Greek mainland.

The increased foreign contact, whether through trade or colonization, produced further changes in Greek cult practice and in the pantheon itself. The divine sphere was enlarged and modified as certain Near Eastern gods and goddesses—for instance, the Phrygian Great Mother—were admitted to the Hellenic pantheon while others were joined to existing divine figures: the physician deity Asklepios has an Akkadian counterpart in Azugallatu. Even quintessential Hellenic heroes may have had a multicultural background. Herodotus tells that "the Egyptians have had a god named Heracles from time immemorial. They say that seventeen thousand years before the reign of Amasis, the twelve gods were produced from the eight; and of the twelve they hold Heracles to be one" (2.43). To learn as much as possible about this hero, Herodotus traveled to Tyre in Phoenicia to visit a temple of great sanctity there. The priests told him that the temple was "as ancient as Tyre itself" (2.44). Aphrodite also appears to have been a composite figure, assuming to herself features derivative of Indo-European, Semitic, and Bronze Age Cretan worship.[11] Corinth was, in fact, one of her principle centers of worship. In their conception of death, the Greeks were influenced by Egyptian beliefs in significant ways, even in the figure of the ferryman of the dead, Charon.

Homeric poetry shares features with books of the Old Testament; in fact, both were taking shape in much the same way and at the same time. In the view of some scholars, the parallels are sufficient to show that the Greek epics have antecedents in eastern Mediterranean accounts. Cyrus Gordon has persistently argued that the basis of both the Greek epics and the Hebrew biblical compositions was the earlier matrix provided through the literatures of Mesopotamia, Egypt, and the Levant. Odysseus has ordeals in common with the Egyptian sailor Sinuhe, and he wanders widely after the fashion of the Mesopotamian hero Gilgamesh. Hesiod's poetry, which will be our subject in the next chapter, testifies to similar influence in, for example, the specific tales of the gods and in the reckoning of the several Ages of Mankind. Less visible in the evidence are links to earlier conceptions of the universe, use of the seasons to create calendars, musical modes, and particular habits and customs. The Hellenic debt to Mesopotamia and Egypt is clear in astronomy and calendar-making: the very names of Phrygian and Lydian to designate two of the Greek modes of music reflect their origin, and reclining at meals may derive from the East.

More formal institutional features of eastern cultures also made an impact on the Greeks who, in their travels and trade dealings, came into contact with people living in expansive, well-structured kingdoms very unlike their own small, more homogeneous communities. Several features that began to appear in Greek communities at the end of the eighth century were in place far earlier in the eastern Mediterranean: a massed infantry force, a standard measure of wealth, and unbridled kingly power were all associated in tradition with older, non-Greek kingdoms. It is more than likely that the Greeks learned of such practices while they were gazing upon huge statues and admiring fine woven textiles. The "foreign" attribution of these innovations dovetails nicely with the other forms of influence that flooded Greece in the late Dark Age.

Finally, we must include what some regard as the greatest debt of all: alphabetic writing.[12] In looking at Lefkandi, we anticipated this eighth-century development that is regularly associated with Euboea: the adaptation of alphabetic writing from a Semitic source. From the place of first use in Greece, whether that was on the island of Euboea or elsewhere, writing spread in many directions, probably simultaneously, and Corinth is an excellent example of one of these directions. In fact, in naming Corinth we must recall the theory that links the origin of the Greek alphabet to commercial activities. When Greek traders ventured beyond familiar waters, they were first drawn eastward, in part because eastern traders had already penetrated Greek waters. At emporia such as Al-Mina they met traders who possessed special techniques as well as exotic goods. Chief among the techniques was a system for keeping records in written form—a device useful for reckoning inventories, sales, trades, and losses, or simply showing ownership of certain objects. Phoenicians, whom the

Greeks knew through commercial contacts, provided the form of writing that the Greeks now adopted, namely the alphabet.

However, once adapted to the Greek language through the addition of symbols for vowels and modification of some of the Phoenician signs, the system was employed for very different uses. Indeed, the earliest surviving inscriptions in the alphabet are not practical commercial accounts, but as we have seen in the previous chapter, they have a poetic ring. The business records may simply have perished, as has so much of the earliest written material. Nevertheless, surviving inscriptions hint at an important use of the new tool: the "earliest examples of Greek alphabetic writing show . . . that popular expressions of early Greek writing include the declaration of ownership . . . the declaration of the maker" (Powell 1991, 129). While these declarations are not of a sophisticated economic nature, they serve a practical purpose that accords well with the incipient nature of both Greek trade and literacy.

Thus we must keep well in mind the variety among both the recipients and the agents of the transmission of new ideas and objects. Alongside traders were migrant craftsmen, mainly Near Eastern in origin; singers, too, may have journeyed widely and regularly, particularly one "who has been given from the gods the skill with which he sings for delight of mortals," who "are impassioned and strain to hear it when he sings to them" (*Odyssey* 17.518ff.; trans. Lattimore 1965). Greeks of later times remembered that Homer was a great bard who journeyed from place to place. Nor must we forget the adventurers of both high and lower status who ventured their lives for the sake of something better or simply something more exciting.

All experienced these new worlds in differing ways, borrowing some skills and ideas, rejecting others, and all the while influencing non-Greeks with their own notions. For though it is true that the Greeks had much to learn from their more sophisticated eastern neighbors in the eighth century, they also had songs to sing and goods to trade. Jeffrey Hurwit has described the nature of the contact succinctly and well: "Weak cultures imitate, strong cultures steal, and like most clichés, the old adage that the Greeks always transformed what they took holds true." Greece was "not a dry sponge" (Hurwit 1985, 132, 134).

Corinth is an excellent case study of this description. On the one hand, "the full Orientalization of Greece began nowhere earlier or with greater enthusiasm than in mercantile Corinth" (Hurwit 1985, 154). Yet the huge transformation in Corinth rested on developments that had earlier occurred in the Corinthia. The proverbially rich soil of the region furnished a decent subsistence to an expanding population through most of the Dark Age. In the early eighth century, small groups of people, once living apart from one another, were forced into closer proximity as population levels continued to rise, eventually outstripping basic agrarian resources. Growing cohesion within the confined area joined with the advantage of an excellent siting on the Corinthian and Saronic gulfs to prompt an answer to the problems of land shortage. Following the example of the Euboeans, Corinthians took to the sea, probably initially in search of land as rich as their own.

Success not only solved the agrarian dilemma but also suggested other possibilities: manufacture and trade of special products and, perhaps, carrying trade for others. The effects spread through the entire culture; by the end of the eighth century, Corinthian products—perfumed oil, pottery, terra-cotta statues—declared Corinth to be the most important and wealthiest port in Greece.

6

Ascra

The End Product of the Dark Age

Our story has traced the changes in Greek culture from the collapse of the international civilization of the Bronze Age through the villages of hard-pressed survivors to the vigorous revival of the late eighth century, both at home and in distant parts of the Mediterranean. Renewal of contact with other cultures, revival of technological expertise, a dramatic rise in population, and the consolidation of a new political consciousness—all evident in the emerging *polis* of Corinth—announced the end of the Dark Age. However, the case of one expansive *polis* does not represent the force of these developments as most contemporaries would have experienced them. For this understanding, we must return to a village, since even in the full Classical period most communities had populations of a thousand people or less. Ascra in Boeotia provides a snapshot of Greece on the edge of its Classical form of civilization.

Ironically, our main informant about the way of life in Ascra

27. Artist's reconstruction of Ascra. *Drawing © Anne Lou Robkin. Used by permission.*

seems to plant it squarely in Dark Age conditions. It is "a miserable hamlet, bad in winter, sultry in summer, and good at no time," according to the poet Hesiod, Ascra's most famous son (*Works and Days* 639–40; trans. Evelyn-White 1936). The words evoke an image of eleventh century Nichoria rather than of eighth century Corinth. And, in fact, this characterization, reinforced by the obscurity of the town, has condemned Ascra in the eyes of many as an isolated pocket of backwardness in the otherwise bustling landscape of the Greek renaissance. Recent studies suggest a different conclusion: in describing his community as a *kome*, or farming village, Hesiod reflects the huge impact of the changes sweeping through Greece in small villages as well as increasingly urban centers.

The Site

It has only been within the last few years that scholars could name, with a high degree of confidence, the location of Hesiod's Ascra.[1] The members of the Cambridge/Bradford Boeotia Project have dis-

28. Valley of the Muses and Helikon from Pyrgaki. *P. W. Wallace (1974, plate 1). Courtesy of Keith Stanley, editor* Greek, Roman, and Byzantine Studies. *Used by permission.*

covered housewalls, remains of a possible circuit wall, and an extraordinarily high density of surface artefacts in a place matching the description of the Ascra site given by Strabo, who located the ruins of Ascra "to the right of Helikon" and "forty stades [about 7.5 km] distant from Thespiai" (9.2.25; trans. Jones 1927). About a century and a half after Strabo, Pausanias traveled through the region and wrote that a lone tower atop a hill was all that remained of the town (9.29.1). This tower is likely to be the fourth-century B.C.E. tower whose ruins are still visible on the summit of Pyrgaki hill at the north edge of the Valley of the Muses. If one is facing north, Pyrgaki appears at the right of Mt. Helikon some seven kilometers north of the settlement of Thespiai. The house walls and other surface evidence found by the Cambridge/Bradford team lie at the foot of the eastern slope of Pyrgaki.

Since the team conducted a survey only, the site has not been excavated. Thus, the extent of the town, its plan, and its architectural features can only be conjectured. But the settlement must have been extensive since a high density of surface finds covers an area of

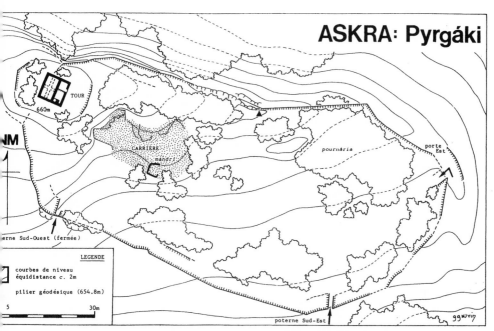

Map 12. Site plan of Ascra. *Gauvin and Morin (1992, figure 2.2).
Courtesy of John M. Fossey, editor and copyright holder of the* Boeotia
Antigua *series. All rights reserved.*

about 60 acres. To put these statistics into some perspective, the population of Ascra at its height in the late fifth through the early fourth
centuries is reckoned in the thousands. In Hesiod's time, the town
would no doubt have been considerably smaller: O. Davies estimates
two or three hundred (1928).

Although settlement evidence at Ascra does not predate the Iron
Age, Late Helladic material has been found on the upper slopes and
the summit of Pyrgaki, suggesting that a hilltop settlement existed
there during Mycenaean times. At an elevation of 650 meters, the
strategic advantages of such a height are obvious, for the hill com-
mands a wide view of the entire valley. The only practicable approach
would have been from the southeast. Pyrgaki seems to have been
abandoned in the late thirteenth or early twelfth century, and there is
no evidence of a settlement at the Ascra site until the Protogeometric
period of the late eleventh or early tenth century. The meager evidence from the tenth through the eighth centuries suggests a small
community resembling a farming village rather than a polis center.

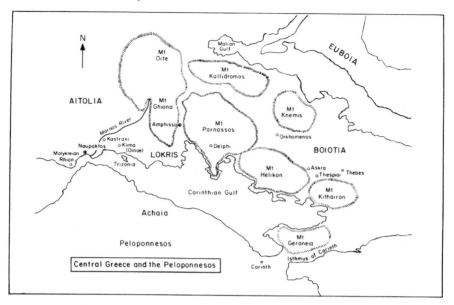

Map 13. The region of Ascra. *P. W. Wallace (1985, figure 15).*
Courtesy of John M. Fossey, editor and copyright holder of the
Boeotia Antigua series. *All rights reserved.*

As Snodgrass has pointed out, villages and towns were common in many parts of Greece that never witnessed substantial *polis* development; central Greece is one of these areas (1980a, 42–47).

Consequently, Ascra exemplifies a community midway between the simplicity of a Dark Age settlement such as Nichoria and the complexity of an Archaic *polis* of the sort that Corinth was becoming. Even so, Ascra seems to have been caught up in the consolidation that was joining villages into a single polity. For much of its history, Ascra was probably within the political sphere of the *polis* of Thespiai, a few miles to the south. Thus, its status would resemble outlying villages in Attica, such as Marathon or Eleusis, when these villages were drawn into the political orbit of Athens.

Sometime between 700 and 400 B.C.E., the Pyrgaki summit was provided with a long, elliptical ring-wall to serve as an acropolis for Ascra in times of emergency. The watch tower on the Pyrgaki summit was built during the fourth century B.C.E. Plutarch (in a possibly spurious passage in *Moralia* fragment 82) says that Ascra was destroyed by Thespiai. Since the passage names Aristotle's *Constitution of Orchomenus* as a source (also possibly spurious), this event—if it happened at all—is likely to have occurred during the first half of the fourth century (Snodgrass 1985).

Despite the reported destruction, there is no sign of an interruption of settlement, and the site appears to have continued its occupation into the third century B.C.E. There is as yet no evidence of occupation during the late Hellenistic and early Roman periods; thus it is the consensus that, like many rural and small urban sites in Boeotia at this time, Ascra was abandoned. The site enjoyed a final phase of settlement during the late Roman period from the fourth to the sixth centuries C.E. until, during the second Greek Dark Age of the sixth and seventh centuries, Ascra was abandoned for the last time.

Hesiod

Interesting for its dependent village status, Ascra is far more exciting because of the recorded poetry of one of its inhabitants, Hesiod, whose main poems are the *Theogony* and the *Works and Days*.[2] Indeed, the existence of this record renders Ascra unique with respect to the other sites considered in this book. Given the self-revelatory nature of his poems, especially the *Works and Days*, we are introduced to Hesiod himself as well as to the rural farming community within which he lived and worked. As we will see, his poetry differs from the Homeric epics, for although he uses epic form and diction, Hesiod's verse is rooted in his own time and situation.

Comparison with Homer is instructive in another respect: Homer is only a name, devoid of secure personality or biographical details, which has attached itself to two great epics. Within the *Iliad* and the *Odyssey*, the poet neither names nor characterizes himself, leading some scholars to conclude that "Homer" is a title rather than a personal name. Hesiod, on the other hand, not only refers to himself by name (*Theogony* 22), but in the *Works and Days* lets us know, or infer, where he lived, what sort of life he led, what his likes and dislikes were, whether or not he was a religious man, and whom he counted as a friend, whom an enemy. The story of early Greece is no longer anonymous.

The Ascran poet informs us that his father, whom he does not name, was originally from Aeolian Kyme on the west coast of Ana-

29. Hesiod, after a fourth-century C.E. mosaic. *Drawing © Anne Lou Robkin. Used by permission.*

tolia; in the face of unrelenting poverty, he took to trading overseas, dragging a swift ship down to the sea and putting in a cargo in order to bring home a profit (631f.). How long he continued in these activities we are not told but the assumption is that his seafaring days came to an end when he sailed westward across the Aegean Sea and settled in Ascra. We can deduce that Hesiod, and perhaps his brother Perses, was born in Ascra, for by Hesiod's own admission, the only time he set foot on shipboard was when he was ferried across the Euripus from Boeotia to Euboea.

The father's choice to settle in Boeotia makes sense if his ancestors were Aeolic speakers from Boeotia who joined in the migrations to west Anatolia during the eleventh and tenth centuries B.C.E. If this was the case, the father's move to Boeotia two hundred years later would have been like returning to the "old country." His specific selection of Ascra, however, is more difficult to explain. It was thought at one time that the area around Ascra was open territory during the eighth century and just beginning to be settled, but recent archaeological activity has demonstrated that Ascra was by this time a well-established village. Further, Hesiod's references to "gift-devouring *basileis*" imply that there were powerful land-owning nobles in the neighborhood, placing pressure on the supply of open land. Perhaps trading activities in Asia Minor allowed Hesiod's father to secure a large enough property on the Greek mainland to support himself and his family. Possibly he married an heiress with a substantial dowry. Or, having lost his ship with its cargo, he may have been forced to remain in what Richmond Lattimore translates "a hole of a village" (1959, 95: translation of line 639).

More familiar than Hesiod's father is his brother Perses, to whom the *Works and Days* is addressed. Throughout the 828 lines of poetry, Hesiod recalls, for Perses' edification, the "true" way of life, constantly reminding Perses that he does not understand what that life is. Following their father's death, Hesiod and Perses entered into a dispute over the division of their patrimony, a dispute which Perses apparently won (34–41), for Hesiod in this passage appeals to the more perfect justice of Zeus to counteract the corrupt justice of the judges. While Hesiod appears to have come away with the lesser portion of his father's property, with hard work and proper management it seems to have been more than sufficient for his needs. And in spite of the fact that Perses has won the larger share of the estate, it is he who comes begging at his brother's door. *Works and Days*, then, is partly an admonishment of Perses for his greedy and lazy behavior, and partly a bestowal of advice on the benefits of hard work and the efficient management of a farm.

Unless Hesiod's advice was entirely empty, we must assume that he practiced what he preached and that his household, his *oikos*, bore some resemblance to the well-managed farm described in the poem.[3] The picture Hesiod renders of the efficient farm is one which, while

30. Boeotian Late Geometric pedestalled *krater* (ht. 33.5 cm.). *J. N. Coldstream (1968, figure 44j).*

it requires hard work, is nevertheless a prosperous enterprise. This household consists of the farmer, his wife, and preferably one son (Hesiod has nothing to say of daughters). In addition to this nuclear family, whose size is a concern due to limited land, there are an unspecified number of slaves, both male and female, who are engaged mainly in field work. The farmer just getting established needs first of all to secure a house, a slave woman, and an ox (405–406). Later on it is wise to have a second ox, two plows in case the first one breaks in the furrow, and a plowman who is steady and of an age not to be easily distracted from his work (432–45). We are not told whether the plowman should be a slave or a hired hand. It is possible that during plowing and harvesting when the farm was at its busiest, the farmer would bring in temporary hired help from among those inhabitants of the area who were free but landless. Another slave is mentioned, whose job is to cover the seed at sowing time to frustrate the birds. In addition to the two plows and various small tools such as rakes, sickles, and hoes, the well-run farm needs a wagon—an item Hesiod claims requires a hundred timbers. Besides the two oxen, other animals mentioned are dogs, goats, and sheep; in Greece there were as yet no cats to keep down rodent infestations. If chickens had been imported to Greece by Hesiod's time, they apparently were not yet known to the Ascrans. We have no way of knowing whether the farm described in the poem was typical or ideal, but if, as seems likely, it reflects Hesiod's own circumstances, then he must have been master of a fairly substantial property.

A farmer's life was not entirely limited to the land. Though no avid seafarer, Hesiod announces that he will present the rules of the "loud-roaring sea" (648): when it is somewhat safe to sail, when it is not, and how much cargo to carry. The occasion for Hesiod's seafaring was funeral games for an obviously important person, Amphidamas of Chalcis, who is reported to have been killed in a battle during the war between Chalcis and Eretria. Hesiod says simply that he won the contest with his song, bearing off the prize of a handled amphora, which he set up in honor of the Helikonian Muses, who had given him the gift of "glorious song" (*Theogony* 22).

As we have said repeatedly, the Dark Age was a time of nonliteracy and thus effective speech was necessary at all levels of society. His success at the games for Amphidamas demonstrates that Hes-

iod had the exceptional powers of a bard in the tradition of Homer.
He may have been different, however, in joining his poetic gift to a
knowledge of the new skill of alphabetic writing, a skill that marks
the end of the Dark Age in several ways. Perhaps more than any
other cultural trait, writing and literacy announce complexity, contact with other cultures, and the return of specialization.

Ascra had room for specialists of several sorts: in addition to
bards, the poem mentions potters, builders, and a blacksmith. Some
diversification, though minimal, is discernible in the poem. Since
Hesiod does talk about the importance of nearby neighbors coming
to one's aid (342ff.), it may be that he lived somewhat removed from
Ascra and even farther from the larger Thespiai where more specialists practiced their crafts. Even in the Classical period, central
Greece had fewer urban centers than the southern regions of the
mainland·

The attitudes and prejudices displayed by Hesiod in the poem
have often been cited as typical of those entertained by peasants of all
periods and locales. As Dorothea Wender remarks in the introduction to her translation of *Works and Days*, Hesiod's "ethical advice is
narrow, joyless and old-fashioned, but there is nothing laughable a-
bout it; it is a remarkably consistent and well-articulated prescrip-
tion for how to be a well-adjusted and successful peasant" (1973, 20).

Paul Millett (1984) has argued persuasively that Hesiod's narrowness, his surly conservatism, as well as his fabled misogyny, are all
typical of peasant attitudes.[4] Citing the anthropologist George M.
Foster's studies of the peasants of Central Mexico, he adds that they
are all attributable to what Foster calls the "image of the limited
good," a phrase describing the tendency among peasants the world
over to assume that all things necessary for the maintenance of life
occur in limited quantities. Thus if one man's household prospers, it
does so only at the expense of another. Early in the poem (20–26)
where we find neighbor vying with neighbor, potter angered with
potter, craftsman with craftsman, the individual potter or craftsman
engages in such competition solely to gain a larger share of a limited
good, not to increase the supply of goods in any absolute sense. The
successful potter, by his very success, dooms his competitor. The
image of the limited good applies to such abstract concepts as health,
fertility, and honor, as well as to tangible goods.

Another attitude that seems to fit hand-in-glove with this image is that of individualism. Hesiod's individualism is so pronounced that even his blood relatives are affected by it. In financial dealings, he counsels "even with your brother smile—and get a witness" (371–72). In Hesiod's world, the individual is expected to survive on his own with as little outside help as possible. In the matter of lending and borrowing, for instance, Hesiod is particularly anxious to avoid the lending of what we might call capital goods—seed for sowing, heavy equipment, or draft animals. Even the temporary loss of such items would decrease the efficiency of the farm for the duration of a loan, further limiting an already limited good. Thus, "It is better to leave your stuff at home for whatever is abroad may mean loss" (365). As for the would-be borrower, such transactions are to be avoided because they entail a heavy burden of repayment, restraining the borrower's self-sufficiency—also a limited good.

Hoarding can be overcome in Hesiod's world by the reciprocal borrowing of small items; as he instructs Perses, "take fair measure from your neighbor and pay him back fairly with the same measure, or better, if you can" (349–51; trans. Evelyn-White 1936). In better-documented peasant societies, such borrowing goes on all the time and acts to establish a web of alliances founded on the mutual obligations such loans create. The loan of a rake, for instance, creates an obligation on the part of the borrower, who is expected to return not only the rake, but something extra besides—perhaps something that was raked with the borrowed tool—thereby creating a counter-obligation on the part of the original lender. An alliance is maintained through a reciprocity of obligations. Trouble would arise between lender and borrower only if the former gave something which could not easily be repaid, establishing a patron/client relationship, or if the borrower repaid the lender exactly what the former was given, in which case the "alliance" would be concluded (Foster 1967a).

The phenomenon of reciprocal borrowing is reminiscent of a practice we have examined in earlier chapters—that of ritual or competitive gift exchange. As we remarked in our discussion of Nichoria, competitive gift exchange was a practice characteristic of Big Man societies. In both cases, one result is the creation of a network of alliances. However, the alliances created through competitive gift exchange are not between equals, for there can be only one Big Man;

rather they are between the Big Man and a clientele of lesser men. Reciprocal borrowing, on the other hand, occurs between equals, its purpose being to create alliances of mutual support between households of a similar status. Such reciprocities also create an informal market for peasants who might have difficulty gaining access to a more formal arena of exchange. It is a paradox of reciprocal borrowing that it establishes a firm foundation upon which a peasant's self-sufficiency can be maintained.

In another significant respect, the peasant cannot control his own fate: "Often," Hesiod warns, "a whole *polis* suffers for one bad man" (240). Hesiod is much concerned with justice, which in Ascra has become an issue for the entire community.

> There is an outcry when justice is dragged perforce,
>   when bribe-eating
> men pull her about, and judge their cases
>   with crooked decisions.
> She follows perforce, weeping, to the city
>   and gatherings of people. . . .
> But when men issue straight decisions
>   to their own people
> and to strangers, and do not step at all
>   off the road of rightness,
> their city flourishes, and the people
>   blossom inside it. (220–22, 225–27; trans. Lattimore 1959)

Hesiod has no ready solution for the injustice he sees and indeed feels he has suffered. He can predict, however, that Zeus, who witnesses everything, will exact punishment for evil acts.

The gaze of Zeus must fall frequently upon those "gift-devouring *basileis*," who make crooked decisions when judging cases—as Hesiod knows from his own experience over the division of his father's estate. The presence of several such conspicuous men in the midst of a community points to another aspect of the late eighth century: no longer was a single Big Man sufficient to the tasks of maintaining communal order. While Hesiod's gift-devourers gained their status through the personal qualities available to the chieftain of Nichoria and the hero of Lefkandi, they have acquired more permanent status as well as rights and responsibilities attendant on their status. The "gifts" that these judges "devour" may be an incipient "tax" for their services to the community akin to the "gifts" that the

Phaeacian king Alcinoos describes in the *Odyssey* 13.13–15. Not yet *polis* officials, the *basileis* of the *Works and Days* are moving toward that position.

Even more structure is evident in the world of the gods, as it is defined by Hesiod in his second long poem, the *Theogony*. Twenty percent longer than the *Works and Days*, the *Theogony* traces the history of the universe through the genealogy of the gods. After praising the Muses who taught him glorious song, he entreats them to come to his aid on this occasion to celebrate the holy *genos*, or race, of immortals who live forever (104–105). Having secured this gift, he recounts that initially there was Chaos but then came Earth, "dwelling place of all things" (117). From them sprang, first, Day and Night, then Heaven and the Sea, even the long hills, and later the first generation of gods, the Titans and Cyclopes, who bore offspring of their own. Rhea and Kronos, the leaders of the elder gods, were parents of Hestia, Demeter, Hera, Hades, Poseidon, and finally, Zeus, who alone of the infants escaped being swallowed by his father, who was protecting himself from the prediction that he would be vanquished by one of his own sons. Through the trickery of his mother, Zeus lived to fulfill that very prediction, causing Kronos to disgorge his brothers and sisters in the process. This younger divine generation bore the remaining figures of the Pantheon, as Zeus sired Athena, the twins Apollo and Artemis, and Hermes; Hera bore Hephaistos; and Poseidon fathered Ares. The listing continues through offspring of mixed divine and human parentage: Heracles, the son of Zeus and human Alcmene, for example, and Achilles, son of Thetis and mortal Peleus.

Just as *Works and Days* complements the Homeric corpus by introducing the reader to the non-heroic, non-aristocratic life of the peasant farmer, so does the *Theogony* complement the image of the Classical Greek pantheon already present in the *Iliad*. While the pantheon springs fully formed from the verses of Homer, the *Theogony* delves deep into the past—into the time before time—to provide the gods with a beginning and a genealogy. Homer depicts the gods in present action; Hesiod gives them a history and a legitimacy. Between the two poets, a social and religious edifice was constructed which had profound implications for Greeks of subsequent ages.

It has been common practice among historians to characterize

Greek religion as non-canonical. The Greeks produced no collection of writings equivalent to the Judaeo-Christian Bible or the Islamic Koran, documents which not only governed the behavior of believers, but at different times even carried the force of law. The fact that the Homeric and Hesiodic poems embodied something less than a legal code or a covenant between man and God does not mean that this poetry was devoid of influence in matters of social, political, or religious import; just the opposite is true. It would be difficult for us to imagine Greek society of the seventh and subsequent centuries without some reference to the works of both poets. The Greeks themselves, with few exceptions, considered the events of the *Iliad* and *Odyssey* to be real, and their conception of the gods was formed in large part by their knowledge of the *Theogony*. Modes of behavior and standards of morality were also heavily influenced by the exemplary models of Achilles and Odysseus on the one hand, and by the thrift and piety of Hesiod's wise farmer, on the other.

Like the siege of Troy and the wanderings of Odysseus, the creation of the world and the genealogy of the gods recounted in the *Theogony* did not originate with the poet whose name is associated with the poem. It is quite likely that substantial parts of the *Theogony* can be traced back to Bronze Age Hittite and Semitic models. In particular, the tale of the rebellion of the younger gods, led by Zeus, against Kronos and the Titans, is very close to the Hittite myth of Kumarbi, itself probably based on an old Babylonian or Sumerian original.

We are reminded that Hesiod's father came from Kyme in Asia Minor, an area where such tales may have been current during much of the Dark Age. We must also bear in mind Hesiod's connection with Euboea, a possible port of entry for such tales along with travelers and goods from beyond the Aegean. However, the existence of Bronze Age analogues to the events recounted in the *Theogony* does not necessarily mean that these stories had a similar antiquity in Greece. They could have become current among the Greeks during the Bronze Age or just as easily, during the Euboean and Corinthian commercial expansion of the later Dark Age.

While some of the events retold in the *Theogony* and even the epic style itself may owe a debt to Near Eastern sources, most of the deities who appear in the poem, with a few important exceptions, were ancient inhabitants of the Aegean area even in the time of Hesiod. In fact, as we have noted, the majority of Olympians are attested in the Mycenaean Linear B records. In those records, Zeus and Hera appear to be paired in a way suggesting that they were regarded as consorts. Offerings are made to individual deities but also to "all the gods," a practice that again evokes a Classical parallel. At the same time, however, there are names and situations that do not accord with later Greek religion. "Potnia," "the Mistress," has a prominent role in the tablets, possessing at least five different qualifying adjectives. And the palace administration plays a conspicuous part in cult activity from the *wanax* down to special priests, priestesses, and slaves of a particular god.

Thus, while the tablets show a certain continuity with the Archaic and Classical pantheon, in the conception and honoring of divinity, we must agree with Chester Starr that "Mycenaean civilization is not a system from which historical Greek culture emerged on a straight line" (1961b, 56).

Ascra: Product of the Dark Age

In blending older and, presumably, newer conceptions of divinity, Hesiod's *Theogony* reveals the long, slow transformation accomplished between 1200 and 700 B.C.E. Details of his own life in Ascra that appear almost between the lines of the *Works and Days* show the full transfiguration of Greek society during those centuries.

First, Mycenae and all that it represented had to disappear for Ascra to become an independent community and for a peasant/bard to enjoy a significant role in that community. Ascra demonstrates the disappearance of the power of Bronze Age citadels particularly well inasmuch as settlement at Ascra begins only in the Iron Age. Although there are Bronze Age remains on the summit of Pyrgaki, Ascra itself does not have Bronze Age roots. No hints of a redistributive economy, complex administrative titles, elaborate palace architecture, or international links appear in Hesiod's poetry. Sailing across the narrow straits from the mainland to Euboea to join in funeral games for a local hero comprised Hesiod's sole seafaring experience.

Ascra matched Dark Age Nichoria far more closely than it re-

sembled Mycenae, even in its weakened twelfth century form. Especially in its earliest Iron Age form, Nichoria was small, compact, isolated, and self-sufficient. Its population of some forty people gave
Nichoria the character of an extended family managed by its head-
man. By comparison, the *Works and Days* constantly stresses the importance of the individual *oikos* under its own head, the desired goal
of which is self-sufficiency based on the land. But, even though Hesiod would not admit it, there has been progress since the early days
of Nichoria: the community no longer shelters on the heights of
Pyrgaki its members coming down the slopes by day to till the soil as
did the residents of early Nichoria. Residences seem to be dispersed
rather than clustered near a slightly larger home, suggesting a greater
sense of security than the residents of Nichoria's ridge had felt. In
fact, since each of the "gift-devouring *basileis*" is likely to possess a
larger residence along with more extensive lands, the territory of
Ascra must have supported several larger homes. Economic specialization accompanied this political distinction in Ascra: potter vies
with potter, builder contends with builder, and a blacksmith has a
known location for his work. Even for one who fears the sea, seafaring is a possibility for an inhabitant of late eighth-century Ascra.

Developments in Dark Age Athens were shared by other communities and it is very probable that Athens contributed directly
to the lives of Ascrans and possibly to Hesiod's family in particular.
Most evident is the migration of small groups to Asia Minor around
1000 B.C.E. tied by tradition, as we have seen, to Athens and its unusual circumstances in the earlier Dark Age. Hesiod's father moved
in reverse—from Asia Minor back to the mainland when the Aegean
had become almost, if not entirely, a Greek-bounded sea. Circumstances also made Athens a center for such developments as the Protogeometric style of pottery and, perhaps, greater proficiency in iron
manufacture. Though no picture survives of the pots Hesiod describes to mark them as Geometric, he leaves no doubt that his generation is of the hateful Age of Iron (174 ff.).

While Athenian initiative may have taken Hesiod's ancestors to
Asia Minor, the return of his father to mainland Greece owed more
to the spirit of Lefkandian sailors. Like them, Hesiod's father took to
the sea to make a livelihood, returning to the land when he failed to
prosper by trade. Both options were increasingly available in the later

Dark Age: we have noted that there is evidence of a division in Lef-kandi between those attached to the land and others willing to risk sea travel as traders or adventurers.

Euboea may have been the source of yet another innovation in Ascra: this island was instrumental in the return of literacy to Greece in the form of alphabetic writing. That this new means of storing information took its place alongside the medium of oral transmis-sion—not replacing but standing rather like a handmaiden to the more traditional means—is clearly evidenced in the creativity of Hes-iod. Instructed by the Helikonian Muses, he became adept in weav-ing sweet song from inherited lore and formulaic language—so adept that he won a prize at the funeral games for Amphidamas of Chalcis. But he may well have also recorded his song in more permanent form through the newly discovered alphabet.

Nearest in time to Ascra was eighth-century Corinth, even more active in Poseidon's realm than Lefkandi had been in the previous century. Much of the impetus behind Corinthian seafaring came from growing pressure on the limited territory of the fledgling *polis*. As numbers rose, a few families flourished, but most were disadvantaged as each generation divided the inherited estate into smaller parcels, as Hesiod and Perses did. The situation had political as well as eco-nomic ramifications as the wealthy few took on management of com-munal affairs. In the case of Corinth, a safety valve was discovered in colonization. Apparently this mechanism was not part of Ascran de-velopment. Anyone whose share of the inheritance was meager could only rail at the "gift-devouring *basileis*" whose decisions were crooked.

In Sum

Ascra is more than the sum of developments symbolized by Mycenae, Nichoria, Athens, Lefkandi, and Corinth. Much of its character de-rives from its particular location and its individual local history. In fact, this rather insignificant village is remembered because of one person whose imprint on future centuries was so deep that his home has become part of the record. In our attempt to uncover the process of change that transformed Mycenae into Ascra, we have sought to emphasize the individuality of settlements along with the common tendencies running across the larger Greek world. Such duality marks the very nature of Classical Greece: the assertive autonomy of hundreds of *poleis* will not destroy the recognition that Greeks of very different *polis* societies shared a common language and blood, religious ritual, indeed a whole way of life (Herodotus 8.144). The slow, difficult reworking of society on the heels of the collapse of the Bronze Age world produced both results.

GLOSSARY

Aipytos: Legendary king of Messenia; son of Kresphontes, one of the Sons of Heracles (see under *Heraclidae*).

Ahhiyawa: The name of a people or place referred to in Hittite records of the fourteenth and thirteenth centuries B.C.E. It, or they, have often been identified as Mycenaeans, or Homer's Achaeans (Ahhiyawa = Akhaia). The location of Ahhiyawa has been variously proposed as coastal Thrace, west or southwest coastal Anatolia, the islands of the eastern Aegean, particularly Rhodes, and mainland Greece itself. The records also mention a settlement named Millawanda, which some scholars have identified as Miletus. If Ahhiyawa was centered at Millawanda, and if Millawanda was indeed Bronze Age Miletus, that would provide powerful evidence that the Ahhiyawans were in fact Mycenaeans.

Apollodorus: Mythographer of the first or second century C.E. Author of the *Bibliotheca*, or *Library*.

apse, apsidal: In architecture, a semicircular termination of a building. Such terminations are common among buildings dating from the Dark Age and early Archaic period.

Bacchiadae: Dominant clan in eighth-century Corinth, reputedly descended from a legendary King Bacchis. The Bacchiads were known for their greed and arrogance, going so far as to forbid clan members from marrying outside the clan, but it was also during their ascendancy that Corinth began its commercial and colonial expansion.

***basileus* (pl., *basileis; qa-si-re-u*):** A title of great antiquity, the term first appears on Linear B tablets as *qa-si-re-u* and seems to refer to a rather minor functionary found in rural areas. He may have been the equivalent of a village head man or overseer. We next meet the term in Homer in its modern form, *basileus*. In the epics, *basileus* can refer to any leader of the warrior class, and in the *Iliad* such heroes as Achilles, Odysseus, and Ajax are all bearers of this title even though Agamemnon, also a *basileus*, is their commander and chief. Clearly in Homer's time the term did not mean "king" in quite the sense we have come to expect. *Basileus*, in the sense of "monarch," was used by the Greeks primarily in reference to legendary Greek kings such as Cecrops of Athens or Eurystheus of Mycenae. Among contemporaries, the term was often used in reference to the kings of Persia.

Big Man: The term *Big Man* first appeared in the 1960s in the scholarly literature dealing with the anthropology of the Melanesian islanders of the southwest Pacific. The term *Big Man* refers to no formal office, but instead indicates a type, much like such terms as *captain of industry* or its negative counterpart, *robber baron*. These are not offices to which people may be appointed or elected, but rather they are a state of being which people attain through their own deeds. The term *Big Man* carries some of the same informal, *ad hoc* quality in its meaning. Any man, if he is energetic enough and has a few valuable connections, can be a *Big Man*. The motive that drives ordinary men to become *Big Men* is the attainment of status, and the means of attaining it is through the competitive display and distribution of wealth. Such men commonly have large groups of followers whose devotion is repaid by the *Big Man* with gifts and food.

cist grave: A simple pit burial used for the interment of one, or at most two individuals. Such burials were often lined and covered with stone slabs. Although cist graves were common during the Dark Age, they were not unique to that period, nor did they necessarily signify the presence of an alien population, as was thought by many adherents of the invasion/migration model explaining the collapse of Mycenaean civilization. Cist graves were also used both before and during the Late Bronze Age.

Close Style: A style of pottery found in late Mycenaean contexts of the twelfth century B.C.E. The term *Close Style* refers to habit of filling all available space with either natural figures or geometric designs.

cyclopean: In Mycenaean architecture, the term refers specifically to a type of wall construction using large undressed stones. According to legend, Perseus built the walls of Tiryns and Mycenae employing Cyclopes from Lycia who alone were capable of lifting such large stones.

Dorian: An inhabitant of the central Greek region of Doris. A speaker of the Doric Greek dialect common in Classical times to much of the Peloponnese, Crete, the southern Cyclades, and the Greek cities of the southwest coast of Asia Minor. One who claims descent from the Dorian followers of the Sons of Heracles, who, according to legend, conquered much of southern Greece in the eightieth year after the fall of Troy.

Dorian Invasion: A legendary invasion of the Peloponnese led by the Sons of Heracles and beginning eighty years after the fall of Troy. For many years the preponderance of scholarly opinion favored this explanation for the destruction of the Mycenaean citadels, but lack of evidence for the subsequent settlement of southern Greece by northern Greeks or an alien population has led most scholars in recent decades to doubt the reality of such an invasion.

Geometric: In Greek archaeology, a style of ceramic decoration common during the Middle and Late Dark Age consisting for the most part, or entirely, of geometric shapes. Long thought to have originated in Athens. The term nowadays refers to any artefact deriving from the period ca. 900–750 B.C.E.

Granary Style: So named because it was first found in association with the building thought to be a granary at Mycenae, this twelfth-century pottery style was in many ways the antithesis of the *Close Style*, of which it was a contemporary. Whereas the *Close Style* is characterized by the decoration of all available space on the outside of the pot, the *Granary Style* is noted for the absence of decoration. Such pots tend to be decorated with one or two straight or wavy lines running around the belly. These lines are usually of a light color to add contrast with the dark background commonly applied to the entire outside surface, and often the inside as well.

Handmade Burnished (Barbarian) Ware: Dating from the early decades of the twelfth century and found at several sites in the Peloponnese, this pottery, with its rough fabric and crude decoration, is thought by some to be the product of local people forced to make their own pottery following the collapse of the citadels (and with them the market in fine pottery). Other scholars believe that this ware, unlike either the *Close Style* or *Granary Style* ware, is intrusive, deriving from the north, particularly Bulgaria, where similar ware has been found.

Helladic (Early/Middle/Late): In archaeology, the three major subdivisions of Bronze Age Greece. In absolute terms, the Early Helladic lasted from ca. 3000–2100/2000 B.C.E.; the Middle Helladic from ca. 2100/2000–1550 B.C.E.; and the Late Helladic, which corresponded with the Mycenaean period, lasted from 1580–ca. 1100 B.C.E., or until 1050 B.C.E., if one includes the Submycenaean period.

Heraclidae (Sons of Heracles): According to legend, following the death of Heracles, his sons, led by Hyllus, were banished from the Peloponnese by Heracles' sworn enemy, King Eurystheus of Mycenae. Attempting to re-enter the Peloponnese from their base at Marathon, they were repulsed and Hyllus was slain. Bowing to the oracle of Delphi, which said that they were not to enter the Peloponnese until the "third crop" (meaning the third generation), they took to wandering and were eventually given asylum by Aigimios of Doris. In the third generation after the death of Hyllus, the Heraclidae, led by Temenos, Kresphontes, and the twins Prokles and Eurysthenes and aided by a large contingent of Dorians, again invaded the Peloponnese. This invasion was successful, taking Mycenae and slaying Tisamenes (the son of Orestes) in the process. They then went on to occupy the entire Peloponnese, establishing a kingdom in Laconia and forcing into exile the last of the Neleids of Messenian Pylos.

Herodotus (484–425 B.C.E.): Called "the father of history," his subject was the Persian Wars of 490–479, although much else is included as background material. He was born at Halicarnassus in southwest Asia Minor, then a subject of the Persian Empire, and emigrated to Athens in 447. His *History* is wide-ranging both in time and space, and to this day is considered one of greatest works of historiography, not only for its style (which owes much to oral folktale), but also for his interest in and documentation of the traditions of the Greeks, Persians, Egyptians, and the many peoples of Asia Minor.

heroön: A shrine dedicated to a local hero, who may or may not have been an actual personage. Many heroes, such as Hyakinthos of Amyklai, are extremely ancient, their cult dating back well into the Bronze Age, and are the stuff of mythology. Others, such as Battos of Cyrene, are historical persons who were granted cult rites as founders of colonies.

Hesiod (fl. ca. 700 B.C.E.): After Homer, the earliest of Greek poets. It is a matter of debate whether he was the poet of both the *Theogony* and *Works and Days*, for the one is in the epic style while the other has been classified as *wisdom literature*, a genre common to Egypt and Syria-Palestine. It is also not known whether he recited or wrote his poetry. While the poet refers to himself in both poems, he actually names himself only in the *Theogony*. In *Works and Days* we learn that he was a native of Ascra in Boeotia and that he won a prize for poetry at the funeral games of Amphidamas of Chalcis on the island of Euboea.

hoplite (hoplites): A term denoting a heavily armed infantryman, from the Greek *hoplon* (a heavy, round shield). Such soldiers formed the backbone of Greek offensive forces from the mid-seventh century until the end of the Peloponnesian War (404 B.C.E.). They differed from the old mounted infantry of the later Dark Age in that they were drawn from the large group of free, non-aristocratic landowners, who, while unable to afford the upkeep of a horse, were wealthy enough to get themselves the weapons and armor requisite for close order combat. Hoplites were equipped with a bronze helmet, corselet, and greaves, and their primary weapon was a short thrusting spear. They also carried a short sword for hand-to-hand fighting. The development of hoplite units had profound political implications for the larger Greek *poleis* for the simple reason that warfare was no longer an exclusively aristocratic activity, and since the citizen soldiers forming the ranks of hoplite units ran the same risks as their aristocratic superiors, they could, and did, claim the same rights.

hydria **(from** *hydor,* **"water"):** a water pot, bucket, or pitcher.

koine **(meaning common, shared in common, public):** In archaeology this term refers to a commonality of cultural and artistic traits held by a wide variety of Greek communities during the Late Bronze Age, particularly during the period ca. 1350–1250 B.C.E. This *koine* is most evident in the ceramic material. V. R. d'A. Desborough posits the existence of a later *koine* during the tenth and ninth centuries centered around the Dark Age settlement of Lefkandi on Euboea. In linguistics, the term refers to a common dialect of Greek spoken throughout the Near East during Hellenistic, Roman, and early Byzantine times. The New Testament was written in *koine* Greek.

kotyle: a small cup or vessel.

krater: a mixing bowl, especially for mixing wine with water.

Kresphontes: In Greek mythology, one of the Heraclidae (*q.v.*). After the conquest of the Peloponnese, he was allotted Messenia, but because he favored the people rather than the aristocracy, he was assassinated. His son, Aipytos, was smuggled out of the country and lived to avenge his father's death and resume control of Messenia.

kylix **(pl.,** *kylikes***):** A drinking cup. Shaped rather like a champagne glass, it was a popular vessel during late Mycenaean times.

Linear B: The most highly developed of a number of syllabic scripts current in different areas of the Aegean during the Bronze Age. These other scripts include the so-called Cretan hieroglyphic (or more accurately, pictographic) script, which is found in northern Crete; Linear A, found throughout Crete and elsewhere among the southern Cyclades; and Cypro-Minoan, which has been found on Cyprus and at Ugarit in north Syria. Just how Linear B is related to these scripts is yet to be worked out, but it is generally agreed that it is a later development of Linear A. Examples of Linear B have been found in large quantities at Knossos in Crete and at Pylos in Messenia. Bronze Age Thebes and Mycenae have also yielded smaller numbers of Linear B tablets. The vast majority of Linear B samples are from clay tablets, which were initially sun-dried, but survived fortuitously by being baked in the destruction fires of the sites where they were found. The surviving evidence indicates that the script was used almost exclusively as a means of keeping administrative records and was unsuitable for the writing of long documents, whether of prose or poetry. The script itself consists of nearly seventy basic signs, each of which represents an entire syllable. There are also a number of special signs representing numerals, weights, and measures and about thirty ideograms, or pictographs, representing agricultural commodities, weapons, and other artefacts. Although Sir Arthur Evans, the excavator of Knossos, began collecting and describing examples of the Linear B script as early as 1900, he made little progress in its decipherment. It was not until 1952, following the publication of both Evans' collection and the large find of tablets at Pylos, that Michael Ventris succeeded in deciphering the script, determining that it was an archaic form of Greek.

megaron: A large oblong room featuring a central hearth open to the sky and a porch on the short side. Such rooms are often centrally located within the Bronze Age palace complexes and are sometimes quite large. Megarons may have served ceremonial functions, although the precise nature of the ceremonies, whether cultic or political, cannot be determined. Mycenae had two such rooms—the great hall on the summit and the Hall of Columns—a phenomenon which complicates the identification of the megaron with the throne room.

Neleus, Neleids: In mythology Neleus was the twin brother of Pelias, king of Iolkos, and son of Poseidon. Driven out of Iolkos by his brother, Neleus conquered Pylos and founded the Neleid dynasty. The most famous of the Neleids was Nestor, son of Neleus, who, though an old man, took part in the fighting against Troy. The Neleids were expelled from Pylos by the Heraclidae. Some were able to escape to Athens, where they helped in the defense of the city against the Heraclidae, while others fled overseas to found cities in Ionia.

oikos: A word which in its broadest sense may be translated as "household" and which denotes the simplest and most basic unit of early Greek social organization. Although cognate with Latin *vicus* and Germanic *wic* (English *wick*), *oikos* does not denote a township or settlement, but the land, buildings, and movable property of an individual family.

orientalizing: The process of acquiring cultural influences from Anatolia, the Semitic Near East, and Egypt. While periods of strong Near Eastern influence occurred during the Bronze Age and the Classical and Hellenistic periods, the term *orientalizing period* or *orientalizing revolution* has come increasingly to pertain to the late Dark Age and early Archaic periods of about 750 to 650 B.C.E. Although such influences were initially thought to have affected artistic styles primarily (particularly in statuary, metal working and pottery decoration), Near Eastern traits are now seen to have significantly influenced Homeric and Hesiodic poetry and the philosophic systems of the pre-Socratics.

Partheniai: In Sparta, the sons of unwed mothers. During the long struggle over Messenia during the late eighth and early seventh centuries, such men grew in numbers and presented, at least to the full citizens of the Spartiate class, a threat to public peace. Sparta solved this problem by sending out a colony composed largely of Partheniai to Taras in Italy.

Pausanias (ca. 110–ca. 180 c.e.): The author of a travel guide to Greece. Little is known about him except that he lived for a time in Magnesia in Ionia and may have been a native of the town. His guide, written between the late 150s and 170s c.e., was intended for the benefit of wealthy Romans traveling in Greece. Besides providing an invaluable description of the cities and monuments of the Classical, Hellenistic, and early Roman periods before the neglect of the third century and the Christian vandalism of the fourth, the guide also recounts much in the way of local legend and history not found elsewhere. Of particular value are his description and history of the Olympic games and an account of the First and Second Messenian Wars.

penteconter: A fifty-oared ship. Often denoting a warship, the term is sometimes used to denote merchantmen.

Pherekydes: A sixth century B.C.E. writer known through fragments and attributions in later sources. The birth of the gods and the creation of the world were his subjects. He was considered the first Athenian prose writer.

pithos: An earthenware wine-jar. Large *pithoi* were often used for purposes other than the storage of wine. Pits in the floor of the apse in the *Heroön* at Lefkandi indicate the likely presence of large *pithoi* for the storage not only of wine but also of grain or other agricultural products. During the Bronze Age, particularly on Crete, such vessels were sometimes placed in pits below house floors for the burial of children.

Plutarch (ca. 45–ca. 120 C.E.): Greek biographer and essayist and the author of the *Parallel Lives* and the *Moralia*. He is said to have written a biography of his fellow-Boeotian Hesiod, which unfortunately is lost.

polemarchos: At Corinth, Athens, and possibly Thebes, a war leader. At Sparta, the leader of a division, or *mora*.

polis: In the simplest sense, a community situated around an *agora*, or marketplace. By the Classical period, the term had come to stand for the state generally, including the city itself along with the lands and lesser towns controlled by the city. The term denotes the citizen body of the state or city, while another term, *astu*, refers to their dwellings.

Potnia (*po-ti-ni-ja*): A very ancient term found both in Mycenaean Linear B and later Greek contexts. The word in its Bronze Age context is very likely an honorific meaning "lady" or "mistress," and as such it cannot yet be determined whether it was applied to a goddess, a queen, or both. Once the term is coupled with the name Athena, as in *a-ta-na po-ti-ni-ja*, but this does not mean that the term *potnia* always, or even usually, referred to the goddess Athena. In later contexts, the plural, *potniai*, is used in reference to the goddesses Demeter and Persephone. Whether this association can be traced back to the Bronze Age cannot now be determined. A variant of the term, *potniades*, was used in later times to refer to the *maenads*, the wild female devotees of Dionysos.

propylon: An area before an entryway or gate. A portico or vestibule.

Protogeometric: This term refers both to a pottery style and a chronological subdivision of the Dark Age, lasting from about 1050 to 900 B.C.E. It succeeds the Submycenaean period and precedes the Geometric. As a pottery style, the Protogeometric begins at Athens, but is soon followed at Argos and Lefkandi on Euboea, which develop their own Protogeometric styles. Protogeometric pottery is characterized by a greater discipline in pottery production both in form and in decoration. Decoration is simple and features the use of bands of paint to separate pottery surfaces into distinct regions. A new development of the period is the use of multiple brushes attached to a compass to create concentric circles and semicircles on the shoulder and belly of the vase.

Wavy lines are retained from the late Mycenaean and Submycenaean periods. The style is overwhelmingly, though not totally, devoid of pictorial representation.

prytanis: In Corinth under the Bacchiadae, the president of the council. At Athens a member of the *prytaneis*, or a committee of fifty selected from among the council of 500 (*boule*).

pyxis: A box or small jar usually for the storage of unguents.

ra-wa-qe-ta (lawagetas): "leader of the people." At first, this Linear B term was thought to indicate a war leader, as in *leader of the host*, but the context of the tablets in which the term appears seems to refer to a religious function. Whatever the duties of the *lawagetas*, he seems to have been an official of some importance, for aside from the *wanax*, he is the only one to receive a parcel of land, or *temenos*. Given the religious connotations associated with *temenos* in later contexts, it is possible that this land given to the *lawagetas* was to be used for religious purposes.

Sea Peoples: A confederation of peoples mentioned in Egyptian texts of the late thirteenth and early twelfth centuries B.C.E. They are said to have unsuccessfully attacked Egypt twice, the first time, around 1230, from the west in the company of Libyans. The second time, around 1190, they attacked the Delta by sea and simultaneously over land from Sinai. The first group is said to have been composed of the Lukka, Meshwesh, Sheklesh, Sherden, Akawasha, and the Tursha, all in addition to the Libyan tribesmen from the Western Desert. Except for the unknown Meshwesh, these peoples may be identified with the Lycians, Sicels of Sicily, Sardinians, Achaeans, and Tyrrhenians. The second group was again composed of the Sheklesh and Sherden, and in addition the Peleset, or Philistines, the Danuna (perhaps Greek Danaoi), and another unknown group, the Weshesh. This second group is said to have previously overrun Hatti (the Hittites), Carchemish in north Syria, Arzawa (possibly somewhere in western Anatolia), and Alasiya, or Cyprus. There is also solid archaeological reason to believe that they destroyed the Syrian city of Ugarit. Having been implicated in the destruction of the Hittites and possibly the Bronze Age cities of Cyprus, there has been much speculation that some configuration of these peoples may also have had a hand in the downfall of the Mycenaean citadels as well. See Sandars 1978 and Drews 1993.

skyphos: a cup, beaker, or flagon. A popular shape during the Protogeometric period. At Lefkandi the term *psc skyphos* refers to the habit of decorating the surfaces of such cups with pendant semicircles.

stenochoria: narrowness of space, want of room. Population increases in the eighth century, exacerbated by the rise of powerful landed interests and the simultaneous division of smaller freeholds among the sons of the landowner, produced a lack of arable land which was alleviated in many places by colonization. This situated is alluded to by Plato in *Laws* (740e).

stirrup jar: A large jar with handles shaped like stirrups.

Strabo (ca. 60 B.C.E.–ca. 10 C.E.): The author of a multi-volume geography, which, like Pausanias' Guide to Greece, is valuable for its recounting of local legends and history.

Submycenaean: The term refers both to a pottery style and a chronological period (ca. 1125–ca. 1050 B.C.E.). This is the darkest period of the Dark Age. In terms of pottery, the style is largely derivative of decorative traits and shapes already present in the latest Mycenaean period, LHIIIC, ca. 1200–1125 B.C.E. Decoration features crudely drawn bands of paint separating regions of the pottery surface, inexact concentric circles, and indifferently executed wavy lines on the shoulders and belly. Handles are often inexpertly shaped and often seem not to match or fit the vessels to which they are attached. Aside from pottery, the one new element in this period is the increasing use of iron. The development of an iron industry, however, may have been less a matter of technological innovation than a hard necessity as the sources of copper and tin needed for the production of bronze may have been disrupted during the period of Mycenaean collapse.

symposion **(or in Latin, *symposium*):** Literally, a drinking together, or drinking party. Far more than the literal translation of the term implies, the *symposion* was an aristocratic institution of great antiquity and social importance. Although there are a few indications that the *symposion* may have had a Bronze Age analogue, our earliest evidence comes from the late Dark Age and early Archaic. The institution seems to have grown out of feasts of a semi-ritual nature held by local *basileis*, or chieftains, and to which his band of warrior followers, or *hetairoi*, were invited. Aside from feasting and drinking, the proceedings may have included the distribution by the *basileus* of gifts, a not so subtle method of maintaining the loyalty of the *hetairoi*. Thus the *symposion* was different in spirit from the more democratic *poluxeinos daitos*, or common feast, referred to by Hesiod (*Works and Days* 722), where each guest brought something to eat and drink. While the *symposion* resembled the *potlatch*, Hesiod's feast was more like the *potluck*. The *symposion* also featured games and competitive bouts of eloquence or extemporaneous poetry. Most of our earliest examples of written poetry, dating perhaps from the eighth century, are of a symposiastic nature, and often deal with sexual feats and amorous desire. The *symposion* of the later Archaic and Classical periods provided a context for philosophical and political discussion.

synoecism (*synoikismos*): to make to dwell together, or to join in one city. The joining together, whether by force or mutual consent, of disparate villages to form a single community, or *polis*. The legends concerning Theseus' achievement of Athenian domination of the Attic hinterland is often held to reflect the process of synoecism which formed the Athenian state during the Dark Age.

te-re-ta **(possibly equivalent to Classical *telestas*):** If Linear B *te-re-ta* is the Mycenaean equivalent to *telestas*, then a case could be made that the term referred to a high magistrate of some sort within the citadel administration. Even then, however, there would be some debate as to what sort of functionary the term referred to. He may be a religious magistrate or priest whose title might be related to the word *telei*, "religious obligations"; or it might be related to *telos*, "service, obligation," in which case he may have fulfilled some feudal capacity. Whatever the function of the *te-re-ta*, he seems to have been the owner of land, or the recipient of land grants.

temenos: A piece of land cut off and allotted for any purpose; a portion of land, particularly arable land. Land sacred to, or dedicated to a god, such as the precincts of a temple. The term appears in Linear B as *te-me-no* and refers to lands given to, or owned by, a god, the *wanax* (as in *wa-na-ke-te-ro te-me-no*), or the *lawagetas* (as in *ra-wa-ke-si-jo te-me-no*).

tholos, tholoi: A dome or circular vault; any round or vaulted building. Large, circular, stone-lined underground tombs used for series of burials during the Bronze Age. The most magnificent examples are to be found at Mycenae and date from the late fourteenth and thirteenth centuries. They were built into the side of a hill, and the roofs usually project above ground level. In addition, such tombs usually feature a long processional entryway called a *dromos*, or "race course."

Thucydides (ca. 455–ca. 400 B.C.E.): With his older contemporary Herodotus and Polybius (ca. 205–125 B.C.E.), Thucydides was one of the three greatest historians of antiquity. His subject was the Peloponnesian War, fought between Athens and Sparta and their various allies from 431 to 404. Thucydides was appointed *strategos*, or general, in 424, and was sent out to hold the allied city of Amphipolis in Thrace against the Spartan general Brasidas. He was too late to save the city, and although he was able to secure the nearby port of Eion against Brasidas, the Athenians punished him for the loss of Amphipolis with exile. His exile gave him the opportunity to compile his history of the war; the account breaks off before the end of the war. Refusing to take seriously any of the myth or folk-tale elements to be found in Herodotus or Homer, Thucydides set to write a rational account of the war, its causes, and the motives of the two great combatants. The success of this venture can be measured by the fact that Thucydides is still considered to be the model of the historian who is at once unsentimental and passionate about his subject.

transhumance: The seasonal movement of livestock and herders from one location to another as a means of securing adequate pasturage. In the geographic and seasonal pattern of movement, transhumance displays a greater social cohesion and stability than nomadism.

votive: Anything dedicated or consecrated, as in votive offering, an offering dedicated to a deity.

***wanax* (in Linear B, *wa-na-ka*, later *anax*):** A lord or king. As a title, the term is applied to any of the gods. The term may also refer to an earthly king or prince, which is how the word is used in the Linear B tablets.

***xenia* (from *xenos*, stranger):** The state of guest-friendship, often between strangers. In aristocratic Greece from the Dark Age down to Classical times, *xenia* was the formal exchange of gifts between strangers. With the bride-price and *symposion*, *xenia* was used to establish or strengthen alliances between families. *Xenia* also implied the protection of the guest by the host so long as the guest, or *xenos*, remained with the host. On the part of the *xenos*, the arrangement also implied, at the least, good behavior toward the host, his family, and property. Thus the *casus belli* of the Trojan War was a gross breach of hospitality on the part of Paris, who was staying at Sparta as a guest-friend of Menelaus when he abducted Helen, Menelaus' wife.

ABBREVIATIONS

AA	Archäologischer Anzeiger
AJA	American Journal of Archaeology
AR	Archaeological Reports (supplement to Journal of Hellenic Studies)
BAR	British Archaeological Reports
BSA	Annual of the British School at Athens
CA	Classical Antiquity
CP	Classical Philology
CR	Classical Review
GRBS	Greek, Roman and Byzantine Studies
JFA	Journal of Field Archaeology
JHS	Journal of Hellenic Studies
JIES	Journal of Indo-European Studies
JMA	Journal of Mediterranean Archaeology
OJA	Oxford Journal of Archaeology
PCPS	Proceedings of the Cambridge Philological Society
SMEA	Studi Micenei ed Egeo-anatolici
ZPE	Zeitschrift für Papyrologie und Epigraphik

NOTES

Introduction

1. On the emerging definition of the Greek Dark Age, see I. Morris 1995.

2. A recent retelling of the recognition of the earliest culture of Greece is Fitton 1996.

3. While his subject is the Bronze Age, Oliver Dickinson (1994) treats the period of collapse and regularly points to changes that will occur in the succeeding Dark Age.

4. General studies include: Coldstream 1977; Desborough 1964 and 1972; Hurwit 1985; Robin Osborne 1996 (whose emphasis is on the eighth century); Snodgrass 1971; Vanschoonwinkel 1991; Langdon 1993 and 1997.

5. Davis 1992; Rutter 1993; Watrous 1994; Shelmerdine 1997.

6. James et al. 1993. For a review see Leonard 1993.

Chapter 1: Mycenae

1. The phrase is that of Robert J. Buck (1969).

2. It is striking to compare figures 4.24 and 4.28 in Oliver Dickinson (1994): the first—a map of the Mycenaean mainland—is crowded with sites; on the second—a map of the post-palatial Aegean sphere—the number has shrunk to thirty-five. Jacques Vanschoonwinkel (1991, 519–525), provides a useful table of sites from the thirteenth into the tenth century.

3. Major sources describing the site of Mycenae include Schliemann 1878; Tsountas and Manatt 1897; Wace 1949; Taylour 1983; Mylonas 1966 and 1983; Hope Simpson and Dickinson 1979; Desborough 1964; Kilian 1988. Truly fine illustrations, maps, and photographs may be found in the museum guide by Nicos Papachatzis (1978).

4. On the process of nucleation, see Branigan 1987; Donlan and Thomas 1993; and Halstead 1988.

5. Vincent Desborough was one of the most outspoken advocates for placing Mycenae in a special position (1964, 218ff.) . For one reappraisal, see C. G. Thomas 1970b. On the special position of Mycenae vis-à-vis other palace centers, see French 1989; Wright 1987; C. G. Thomas 1995; and Cline 1987.

6. E. S. Sherratt (1980) argues against the view that the *koine* began in LHIIIA2 and lasted through LHIIIB2 (ca. 1350–1200 B.C.E.) by demonstrating that this uniformity of style began fraying during LHIIIB2 rather than in LHIIIC. On pottery shapes and styles, see Mountjoy 1986, 93–133.

7. On the date of the destruction at Pylos, see Hope Simpson and Dickinson 1979 (128–29) and Popham 1991.

8. The "Hand Burnished Ware" was first brought to scholarly atten-

tion by Elizabeth Wace French (1969). The argument for the intrusive nature of the ware is delineated by Jeremy B. Rutter (1975). Critiques of Rutter's argument and rebuttals by him and others can be found in Gisela Walberg, "Northern Intruders in Mycenae IIIC?" *AJA* 80 (1976) 186-87; J.
Rutter, "'Non-Mycenaean' Pottery: A Reply to Gisela Walberg," *AJA* 80
(1976) 187–88; E. French and J. Rutter, "The Handmade Burnished Ware
of the Late Helladic IIIC Period: Its Modern Historical Context," *AJA* 81
(1977) 111–12; H. W. and E. A. Catling, "'Barbarian Pottery From the Mycenaean Settlement at the Menelaion, Sparta," *BSA* 76 (1981) 71–82; B. P.
Hallager, "A New Social Class in Late Bronze Age Crete: Foreign Traders
in Khania," in O. Krzyszkowska and L. Nixon (eds.), *Minoan Society: Proceedings of the Cambridge Colloquium 1981* (Bristol: Bristol Classical Press,
1983) 111-19; N. K. Sandars, "North and South at the End of the Mycenaean Age," *OJA* 2.1 (1983) 43–68; A. M. Snodgrass 1983 (quote from
78–79); H. A. Bankoff and F. A. Winter, "Northern Intruders in LH IIIC
Greece: A View from the North," *JIES* 12.1&2 (1984) 1–30; D. B. Small,
"Handmade Burnished Ware and Prehistoric Aegean Economics: An Argument for Indigenous Appearance," *JMA* 3.1 (1990) 3–25; and in the same
volume, J. Rutter, "Some Comments on Interpreting the Dark/Surfaced
Handmade Burnished Pottery of the 13th and 12th Century BC Aegean,"
29–49. For an examination of the Trojan aspect of this discussion, see Sandars 1971. Small 1997 urges closure to the debate.

   9. In the words of Emily Vermeule (1964, 258): "From the end of the
Middle Bronze Age, militarism was so congenial to the mainland tempera-
ment that both its aesthetics and its technology focused on the trained sol-
dier with his equipment and this is also the aspect of the Mycenaean world
most striking to outsiders in their rare comments about Achaians." See also
Doxey 1987; Barber 1981 and 1987 (33); and Mee 1984 (50). The sea peoples are treated by Sandars (1978). The argument for new military tactics
introduced by peoples from the central Mediterranean is presented by Robert Drews (1993). On natural causes, see Bintliff 1977 (49f., 74 f.); Wright et
al. 1990 (esp. 585–93); and Carpenter 1966. Although supported by clima-
tologists such as R. A. Bryson, H. H. Lamb and David L. Donley (1974),
evidence for the "triggering" effect of drought is minimal. See also Henri
van Effenterre (1974) on "la colère de Poséidon." For the case of "systems
collapse," see Betancourt 1976; Renfrew 1979; and Tainter 1988.

   10. Jean-Nicolas Corvisier (1991) provides an excellent accounting of
movement into and out of northern Greece.

Chapter 2: Nichoria

   1. On the site, see Rapp and Aschenbrenner 1978; McDonald and Wilkie 1992; McDonald, Coulson, and Rosser 1983; Loy 1970; and periodic
Pylos Regional Archaeological Reports, e.g. *Archaeological News* 19 (1994)
24–27.

   2. Consideration of the various tempos of centralization (especially per-
taining to Pylos) include Bennett 1995; C. G. Thomas 1995; Shelmerdine
1973; Chadwick 1976; Hooker 1987; and Carlier 1984.

   3. That stone working continued even with the increase of iron technology is convincingly argued by Runnels (1982).

   4. Snodgrass 1987 (193–209). See also Halstead and O'Shea 1982, and
Sherratt 1982.

5. Eric Havelock transformed our understanding of the role of the spoken word in early Greece, beginning with his *Preface to Plato* (1963) and continuing through a host of articles and books to his last book, *The Muse Learns to Write* (1986).

6. A general overview of the debate with excerpts representing the several conclusions can be found in C. G. Thomas 1970a. A new image is offered in C. G. Thomas 1993. See also Raaflaub 1991; Morris 1986; and Manning 1992. On the nature of oral transmission, see Vansina 1965; Ong 1967 and 1982; and R. Thomas 1989 and 1992. Our position on the "Homeric Question" is akin to that of Kurt Raaflaub and Walter Donlan.

7. Even the Mycenaean base of the "Catalogue" of Greek forces at Troy has recently been examined by J. K. Anderson (1995). While not attempting to disprove the Bronze Age reality of certain sites named in the catalogue, Anderson suggests how the catalogue itself changed over time. It is a fine demonstration of the manner in which remembered knowledge evolved over the centuries of the Dark Age.

8. The term seems to have been coined by Marshall Sahlins in an important paper, "Poor Man, Rich Man, Big Man, Chief" (1963). See also Lewis R. Binford (1983), who disagrees with Sahlins on several points. Binford believes that the model is flawed in that it argues for a motiveless altruism on the part of the Big Man for which there is no evidence and, in so doing, seems to misinterpret the meaning of *generosity* as at root altruistic. He also takes issue with the supposed role of the Big Man as an agent of redistribution. In rejecting the notion that the Big Man gains status through competitive generosity or, as he defines them, acts of altruism, he can hardly accept economic redistribution as a by-product of such activities.

9. A sampling of views on social and political organization in Dark Age society includes: Qviller 1981; Donlan 1982, 1985, and 1989; Murray 1983; and Whitley 1991a.

Chapter 3: Athens

1. Pottery evidence is presented by Stubbings 1947; Kopcke 1977; and Desborough 1952.

2. The long-term cycle of regionalism/unification is shown for the Argolid in van Andel and Runnels 1987.

3. A strong case for the late emergence of the Mycenaean citadel center was made by J. A. Bundgaard (1976). S. A. Immerwahr has concluded that "one cannot claim Athenian synoicism or even domination of Attica in early Mycenaean times" (1971, 151). For a possible reconstruction, see C. G. Thomas (1982).

4. On the Mycenaean acropolis, see Iakovidis 1983 (73–90); Mylonas 1966 (35–43). The population estimate is that of Richard Hope Simpson (1981, 21, 43).

5. See Snodgrass 1980b and Astrom et al. 1986.

6. For early Ionia, see Emlyn-Jones 1980; Huxley1966; Roebuck 1955 and 1959.

7. The settlement patterns of Dark Age Athens are presented by James Whitley (1991b, esp. chapter 3, 54–74).

8. For comparative evidence from France, see Ladurie 1974.

9. On the role of Ionia in the emergence of the *polis*, see Ehrenberg 1960. For the description of Old Smyrna, see Nicholls 1958–59.

10. Probable political and social developments are treated in the accounts of early Ionia. See also C. G. Thomas 1976.

11. Ian Morris (1987) discusses the evidence from burial. Later regionalism in Attica is treated by R. Sealey (1960).

Chapter 4: Lefkandi

1. Substantial excavation has taken place in the northeast sector of Xeropolis Hill and in the several cemetery areas to the northwest of the hill. In addition, three series of test trenches have been opened on several areas of the hill.

2. The essential reports are Popham and Sackett 1968; Popham, Sackett, and Themelis 1980; Popham, Calligas, and Sackett 1993; Popham, Touloupa, and Sackett 1982; Popham, Calligas, and Sackett 1988–89. On the LHIIIC intramural burials, see Musgrave 1991.

3. Negbi 1992 (esp. 606–607); Aubet 1996; Kopcke 1992.

4. Some years later, the skeletons of two more horses were found among the tombs excavated on the north edge of the cemetery (Popham, Calligas, and Sackett 1988–89, esp. 118 and 123). Because they were found in no obvious association with a datable tomb, the skeletons cannot be securely dated.

5. This apparent "sexual dimorphism" of Iron Age Greek ceramics was first noticed by Desborough (1952). More recently, see Whitley 1991b (105 ff.).

6. Archaeologists making note of the long retention at Lefkandi of Protogeometric shapes and decorative styles have established a three phase Subprotogeometric period sandwiched between Protogeometric and Geometric. SPGI (ca. 900–875), SPGI II (ca. 875–850), which is roughly analogous to Attic Early Geometric, and SPG III (ca. 850–750), which coincides with Attic Middle Geometric.

Only three new pottery shapes were introduced during the period Subprotogeometric I-II: a tray, or *kanoun*, with three loop handles, a shallow bowl with rolled handles at the rim, and a shallow bowl with flat base and horizontal handles. A conservatism marked by retention of shapes and decorative schemes, and in a few instances reversion to older schemes, particularly when coupled by a paucity of new shapes introduced during the period, poses real problems for archaeologists studying Euboean exports. An inability to narrow the chronological field makes it equally difficult to narrow the provenance of the *skyphos* within the Euboean domain. If, for example, we were confident that such a find belonged to the earlier ninth century, the likelihood that it derived specifically from Lefkandi would increase. Later in the century, however, particularly after ca. 825, the possibility arises that the vase might have been of Chalcidian or Eretrian derivation since the rise to prominence of Chalcis and Eretria is usually dated to the late ninth and eighth centuries, a period which coincides with the abandonment of the cemeteries at Lefkandi and a contraction of the settlement on Xeropolis.

7. For the centaur, Desborough, Nicholls, and Popham 1970; West 1988 (esp. 166f.). Another possible influence is a series of late Minoan sphinxes which use the same technique of attaching solid arms, legs, and heads onto a hollow wheel-made cylindrical body.

8. The introduction of writing is a subject of huge scope. The following references represent a tiny fraction of fairly recent studies: Davison 1962;

Heubeck 1962. On the return of literacy, see Jeffery 1976 (25f.); Harris 1989; Robb 1994; Powell 1989 and 1991.

Since an alphabet was in use in the Near East in the second millennium, many Near Eastern specialists argue that it was introduced into the Aegean in the late second or early first millennium: see Naveh 1982. A summary of the issue is Cross 1989. However, the actual inscriptional evidence from Greece dates only from the eighth century B.C.E.

9. For the *symposion*, see Murray 1983 and 1994.

10. Benton 1934–35; Malkin 1998; Coldstream 1976; Polignac 1995; Antonaccio 1994.

11. The discussion of Euboean activity in the north Aegean is from "Secrets of Sindos" by Michalis A. Tiverios, Professor of Classical Archaeology, Aristotelian University of Thessaloniki, in excerpts and summaries of translations of articles on archaeological topics in daily Greek newspapers by Carol Zerner of the American School of Classical Studies for the electronic list *Aegeanet*; week of 26.ix.95–2.x.95.

Chapter 5: Corinth

1. The figures are those of A. M. Snodgrass (1980a, 18).

2. Basic discussions of early Corinth include: Roebuck 1972; Will 1955; H. S. Robinson 1965; Salmon 1984.

3. On political developments, see Starr 1957 and 1986; Raaflaub 1993; Donlan 1985 and 1989; Polignac 1995.

4. See Malkin 1994 and 1998; Graham 1964; and Morgan 1988.

5. Some scholars believe that the inscription may be a late invention: see Jeffery 1961. But even if it is an invention, the straitened circumstances faced by the communities that colonized are likely to have been like those described.

6. On gift exchange, see Finley 1978; Coldstream 1983; and Robb 1994.

7. For discussion of the significance of burial evidence, see Morris 1987; Sax 1970; Goldstein 1976; and Prufer 1993.

8. Perception of "otherness" and common Hellenism is treated by Edith Hall (1989) and Robin Osborne (1987). On the role of religion in the growth of Hellenic identity, see Polignac 1994 and 1995. See also Gebhard 1994 and, more generally, Tomlinson 1976.

9. For the Orientalizing period, see Burkert 1992; S. Morris 1992; Iverson 1957; Vermeule 1979; and Gordon 1955.

10. On Delphi's role in colonization, see Malkin 1989; Forrest 1957; and Morgan 1993.

11. See Friedrich 1978, 9–54.

12. On the economic function of early writing, see Lombardo 1988.

Chapter 6: Ascra

1. On the site of Ascra, see Bintliff 1985 and 1989; Bintliff and Snodgrass 1985; Snodgrass 1985 and 1987 (121–28); Fossey 1988; Gauvin and Morin 1992; Davies 1928; Wallace 1974.

2. For Hesiod, a fine translation is that of Richmond Lattimore (1959), with evocative line drawings by Richard Wilt. See also Wender 1973; West 1966, 1978, and 1988; R. M. Cook 1989; and Wade-Gery 1958.

3. On aspects of Hesiod's world, Joseph Fontenrose (1974) presents a well-reasoned argument that *Works and Days* is one long exhortation to work, and thereby to create a just society and win the blessings of the gods. See also Starr 1977.

4. Understanding of Hesiod's world is assisted by comparative examples such as that provided by P. Millett (1984). See also Diaz 1967 and Foster 1967a, 1967b, and 1967c.

REFERENCES

Alden, M. J. 1981. *Bronze Age Population Fluctuations in the Argolid from the Evidence of Mycenaean Tombs*. Göteborg: Paul Astrom.

Anderson, J. K. 1995. "The Geometric Catalogue of Ships." In *The Ages of Homer*, ed. J. Carter and S. Morris, 181–91. Austin: University of Texas Press.

Antonaccio, C. M. 1994. *An Archaeology of Ancestors: Tomb Cult and Hero Cult in Early Greece*. Boston: Rowman and Littlefield.

Arendt, Hannah. 1958. *The Human Condition*. Chicago: University of Chicago Press.

Astrom, P., R. Maddin, J. D. Muhly, and T. Stech. 1986. "Iron Artifacts from Swedish Excavations in Cyprus." *Opuscula Atheniensia* 16:27–41.

Aubet, Maria E. 1996. *The Phoenicians and the West: Politics, Colonies and Trade*. Cambridge: Cambridge University Press.

Barber, R. L. N. 1981. "The Late Cycladic Period: A Review." *BSA* 76:1–21.

———. 1987. *The Cyclades in the Bronze Age*. Iowa City: University of Iowa Press.

Bennett, John. 1995. "Space through Time: Diachronic Perspectives on the Spatial Organization of the Pylian State." In *Politeia: Society and State in the Aegean Bronze Age*. Fifth International Aegean Conference, vol. 2, ed. Wolf-Dietrich Niemeier and Robert Laffineur. *Aegaeum* 12:587–602.

Benton, Sylvia. 1934–35. "Excavations at Ithaca III." *BSA* 35:45–73.

Benzi, Mario. 1975. *Ceramica Micenea in Attica*. Milan: Istituto editoriale Cisalpino-La Goliardica.

Bernal, Martin. 1990. *Cadmean Letters: The Transmission of the Alphabet to the Aegean and Further West before 1400 B.C.* Winona Lake, Ind.: Eisenbrauns.

Betancourt, Philip P. 1976. "The End of the Greek Bronze Age." *Antiquity* 50:40–47.

Binford, Lewis R. 1983. *In Pursuit of the Past: Decoding the Archaeological Record*. London: Thames and Hudson.

Bintliff, J. L. 1977. *Natural Environment and Human Settlement in Prehistoric Greece*, Pt. 1, *BAR* Supplementary Series 28(i). Oxford: British Archaeological Reports.

———. 1985. "The Development of Settlement in South-west Boeotia." In *La Beotie Antique*, ed. G. Argoud and P. Roesch, 49–70. Paris: Editions du Centre national de la recherche scientifique.

———. 1989. "Reflections on Nine Years with the Bradford-Cambridge Boeotia Project." *Boiotika Antiqua* 8:13–21.

———, and A. M. Snodgrass. 1985. "The Cambridge/Bradford Boeotian Expedition: The First Four Years." *JFA* 12:123–61.

Boardman, John. 1967. *Pre-Classical: From Crete to Archaic Greece*. Harmondsworth: Penguin.

Branigan, Keith. 1987. "The Economic Role of the First Palaces." In *The

Function of the Minoan Palaces, ed. R. Hägg and N. Marinatos, 245–49. Stockholm: Swedish Institute in Athens.

Bryson, R. A., H. H. Lamb, and David L. Donley. 1974. "Drought and the Decline of Mycenae." *Antiquity* 48:46-50.

Buck, Robert J. 1969. "The Mycenaean Time of Troubles." *Historia* 18:276–98.

Bundgaard, J. A. 1976. *Parthenon and the Mycenaean City on the Heights*. Publications of the National Museum of Denmark: Archaeological-Historical Series, vol. 18. Copenhagen: The National Museum of Denmark.

Burkert, Walter. 1992. *The Orientalizing Revolution: Near Eastern Influences on Greek Culture in the Early Archaic Age*. Cambridge: Harvard University Press.

Bury, R. G., tr. 1926. *Plato: The Laws*. Cambridge, Mass.: Harvard University Press.

Calligas, P. G. 1988. "Hero-cult in Early Iron Age Greece." In *Early Greek Cult Practice*, ed. R. Hägg, N. Marinatos, and G. C. Nordquist, 229–34. Stockholm: Swedish Institute in Athens.

Carlier, Pierre. 1984. *La royauté en Grèce avant Alexandre*. Strasbourg: Association pour l'étude de la civilisation romaine.

Carpenter, Rhys. 1966. *Discontinuity in Greek Civilization*. Cambridge: Cambridge University Press.

Chadwick, John. 1976a. *The Mycenaean World*. Cambridge: Cambridge University Press.

———. 1976b. "Who Were the Dorians?" *La Parola de Passato* 31:103–17.

Cline, Eric. 1987. "Amenhotep III and the Aegean: A Reassessment of Egypto-Aegean Relations in the 14th Century B.C." *Orientalia* 56:1–36.

Coldstream, J. N. 1968. *Greek Geometric Pottery: A Survey of Ten Local Styles and Their Chronology*. London: Methuen.

———. 1976. "Hero-Cults in the Age of Homer." *JHS* 86:8–17.

———. 1977. *Geometric Greece*. London: Ernest Benn.

———. 1983. "Gift Exchange in the Eighth Century." In *The Greek Renaissance of the Eighth Century B.C.: Tradition and Innovation*. Proceedings of the Second International Symposium at the Swedish Institute in Athens (1–5 June 1981), ed. R. Hägg, 201–206. Stockholm: Swedish Institute in Athens.

Cook, J. M. 1958–59. "Old Smyrna, 1948–1951." *BSA* 53–54:1–34.

Cook, R. M. 1989. "Hesiod's Father." *JHS* 109:170f.

Corvisier, Jean-Nicolas. 1991. *Aux Origines du Miracle Grec*. Paris: Presses Universitaires de France.

Cross, F. M. 1989. "The Invention and Development of the Alphabet." In *The Origins of Writing*, ed. W. Senner, 77–90. Lincoln: University of Nebraska Press.

Davies, O. 1928. "Askra." *CR* 42:62.

Davis, Jack L. 1992. "Review of Aegean Prehistory I: The Islands of the Aegean." *AJA* 96:699–755.

Davison, J.A. 1962. "The Homeric Question." In *Companion to Homer*, ed. A. J. B. Wace and F. H. Stubbings, 215–233. London: MacMillan.

Desborough, V. R. d'A. 1952. *Protogeometric Pottery*. Oxford: Clarendon Press.

———. 1964. *The Last Mycenaeans and Their Successors: An Archaeological Survey, c. 1200–c. 1000 B.C.* Oxford: Clarendon Press.

———. 1972. *The Greek Dark Ages*. London: Ernest Benn.

————, R. V. Nicholls, and M. R. Popham. 1970. "A Euboean Centaur." *BSA* 65:21–30.

Diaz, May N. 1967. "Economic Relations in Peasant Society." In *Peasant Society: A Reader,* ed. J. M. Potter, M. N. Diaz, and G. M. Foster, 50–56. Boston: Little Brown.

Dickinson, Oliver. 1994. *The Aegean Bronze Age.* Cambridge: Cambridge University Press.

Donlan, Walter. 1982. "The Politics of Generosity in Homer." *Helios* 9:1–15.

————. 1985. "Social Groups of Dark Age Greece." *CP* 80:293–308.

————. 1989. "The Pre-State Community in Greece." *Symbolae Osloensis* 64:5–29.

————, and Carol G. Thomas. 1993. "The Village Community of Ancient Greece: Neolithic, Bronze and Dark Ages." *SMEA* 31:61-71.

Doxey, Denise. 1987. "Causes and Effects of the Fall of Knossos 1375 BC." *OJA* 6.3:301-23.

Drews, Robert. 1993. *The End of the Bronze Age: Changes in Warfare and the Catastrophe ca. 1200 B.C.* Princeton: Princeton University Press.

Dryden, John, tr. 1932. *Plutarch: The Lives of the Noble Grecians and Romans.* New York: Modern Library.

Ehrenberg, Victor. 1960. *The Greek State.* Oxford: Blackwell.

Emlyn-Jones, C. J. 1980. *The Ionians and Hellenism: A Study of the Cultural Achievement of the Early Greek Inhabitants of Asia Minor.* London: Routledge and K. Paul.

Evelyn-White, H. G., tr. 1936. *Hesiod: The Homeric Hymns and Homerica.* Cambridge, Mass.: Harvard University Press.

Finley, M. I. 1978. *The World of Odysseus,* 2d ed. New York: Viking.

Fitton, J. Lesley. 1996. *The Discovery of the Greek Bronze Age.* Cambridge: Harvard University Press.

Fontenrose, Joseph. 1974. "Work, Justice, and Hesiod's Five Ages." *CP* 69:1–16.

Forrest, W. G. 1957. "Colonisation and the Rise of Delphi." *Historia* 6:160–75.

Fossey, John M. 1988. *Topography and Population of Ancient Boiotia,* vol. 1. Chicago: Ares.

Foster, G. M. 1967a. "The Dyadic Contract: A Model for the Social Structure of a Mexican Peasant Village." In *Peasant Society: A Reader,* ed. J. M. Potter, M. N. Diaz, and G. M. Foster, 213–30. Boston: Little Brown.

————. 1967b. "Peasant Society and the Image of Limited Good." In *Peasant Society: A Reader,* ed. J. M. Potter, M. N. Diaz, and G. M. Foster, 300–23. Boston: Little Brown.

————. 1967c. "What Is a Peasant?" In *Peasant Society: A Reader,* ed. J. M. Potter, M. N. Diaz, and G. M. Foster, 2–14. Boston: Little Brown.

French, E. B. 1969. "The First Phase of LHIIIC." *AA* 84.2:133-36.

————. 1989. "'Dynamis' in the Archaeological Record at Mycenae." In *Images of Authority: Papers Presented to Joyce Reynolds on the Occasion of her Seventieth Birthday,* ed. M. M. MacKenzie and C. Roueche. Cambridge Philological Society Supplementary Volume, no. 16:122–30.

Friedrich, Paul. 1978. *The Meaning of Aphrodite.* Chicago: University of Chicago Press.

Gauvin, G. and J. Morin. 1992. "Le Site d'Askra et ses carrières." *Boeotia Antigua* 2:7–15.

Gebhard, Elizabeth R. 1994. "The Evolution of a Pan-Hellenic Sanctuary." In *Placing the Gods: Sanctuaries and the Sacred Space in Ancient Greece*, ed. Susan E. Alcock and Robin Osborne, 154–77. Oxford: Clarendon Press.

Gladstone, Sir William. 1890. *Landmarks of Homeric Study*. London: Mac-Millan.

Goldstein, L. 1976. "Spatial Structure and Social Organization." Ph.D. Thesis, Northwestern University.

Gordon, Cyrus. 1955. "Homer and Bible." *Hebrew Union College Annual* 26:43–108.

Graham, A. J. 1964. *Colony and Mother City in Ancient Greece*. Manchester: Manchester University Press.

Hall, Edith. 1989. *Inventing the Barbarian*. Oxford: Clarendon Press.

Halstead, Paul. 1988. "On Redistribution and the Origin of Minoan-Mycenaean Palatial Economies." In *Problems in Greek Prehistory*, ed. E. B. French and K. A. Wardle, 519–530. Bristol: Bristol Classical Press.

———, and J. O'Shea. 1982. "A Friend in Need is a Friend Indeed: Social Storage and the Origins of Social Ranking." In *Ranking, Resources and Exchange*, ed. C. Renfrew and S. Shennan, 92–99. Cambridge: Cambridge University Press.

Harris, William. 1989. *Ancient Literacy*. Cambridge: Harvard University Press.

Havelock, Eric. 1963. *Preface to Plato*. Cambridge: Harvard University Press.

———. 1986. *The Muse Learns to Write*. New Haven: Yale University Press.

Heubeck, A. 1982. "L'origine della lineare B." *SMEA* 23:195–207.

Hooker, James. 1987. "Titles and Functions in the Pylian State." *Studies in Mycenaean and Classical Greek Presented to John Chadwick, Minos* 20–22:257–67.

Hope Simpson, Richard. 1981. *Mycenaean Greece*. Park Ridge, N.J.: Noyes Press.

———, and O. T. P. K. Dickinson. 1979. *A Gazeteer of Aegean Civilisation in the Bronze Age*. Göteborg: Paul Astrom.

Hurwit, Jeffrey M. 1985. *The Art and Culture of Early Greece, 1100–480 B.C.* Ithaca: Cornell University Press.

Huxley, G. L. 1966. *The Early Ionians*. London: Faber.

Iakovidis, Spiros E. 1983. *Late Helladic Citadels on Mainland Greece*. Monumenta Graeca et Romana, vol. 4. Leiden: Brill.

Immerwahr, S. A. 1971. *The Neolithic and Bronze Ages*. The Athenian Agora, vol. 13. Princeton: American School of Classical Studies at Athens.

Iverson, Erik. 1957. "The Egyptian Origin of the Archaic Greek Canon." *Mitteilungen des deutschen archaeologischen Instituts, Abt. Kairo* 15:134–47.

James, Peter, I. J. Thorpe, Nikos Kokkinos, Robert Morkot, and John Frankish. 1993. *Centuries of Darkness: A Challenge to the Conventional Chronology of Old World Archaeology*. London: Jonathan Cape.

Jansen, Anton. 1997. "Bronze Age Highways at Mycenae." *Echos du Monde Classique* n.s. 16.1:1–16.

Jeffery, L. H. 1961. "The Pact of the First Settlers at Cyrene." *Historia* 10:139–47.

———. 1976. *Archaic Greece: The City States c. 700–500 B.C.* London: Ernest Benn.

Jones, H. L., tr. 1917–1932. *The Geography of Strabo*. 8 vols. Cambridge, Mass.: Harvard University Press.

Jowett, Benjamin, tr. 1900. *Thucydides.* 2d ed., rev. Oxford: Clarendon Press.

Karageorghis, Vassos. 1990. *The End of the Late Bronze Age in Cyprus.* Nicosia: The Pieridis Foundation.

———. 1992. "The Crisis Years: Cyprus." In *The Crisis Years: The 12th Century B.C.*, ed. W. Ward and M. Joukowsky, 79–86. Dubuque, Iowa: Kendall/Hunt.

Kilian, Klaus. 1988. "Mycenaeans Up to Date, Trends and Changes in Recent Research." In *Problems in Greek Prehistory*, ed. E. B. French and K. A. Wardle, 115–52. Bristol: Bristol Classical Press.

Kopcke, Günther. 1977. "Figures in Pot-Painting Before, During and After the Dark Age." In *Symposium on the Dark Ages in Greece*, ed. Ellen N. Davis, 32–50. New York: Archaeological Institute of America.

———. 1992. "What Role for Phoenicians?" In *Greece between East and West: 10th–8th Centuries B.C.*, ed. G. Kopcke and I. Tokumaru, 103–13. Mainz: Philipp von Zabern.

———, and I. Tokumaru, eds. 1992. *Greece between East and West: 10th–8th Centuries B.C.* Mainz, Philipp von Zabern.

Ladurie, Emmanuel Le Roy. 1974. *The Peasants of Languedoc*, tr. John Day. Urbana: University of Illinois Press.

Langdon, Susan, ed. 1993. *From Pasture to Polis: Art in the Age of Homer.* Columbia: University of Missouri Press.

———, ed. 1997. *New Light on a Dark Age: Exploring the Culture of Geometric Greece.* Columbia: University of Missouri Press.

Lattimore, Richmond, tr. 1959. *Hesiod.* Chicago: University of Chicago Press.

———, tr. 1965. *The Odyssey of Homer.* New York: Harper and Row.

Leonard, Albert, Jr., ed. 1993. *Colloquenda Mediterranea: A Review of Peter James et al.* December 1991. Bradford, Eng.: Loid Publishing.

Levi, Peter, tr. 1971. *Pausanias: Guide to Greece.* 2 vol. Harmondsworth: Penguin.

Lombardo, Mario. 1988. "Marchands, transactions économiques, écriture." In *Les Savoirs de l'écriture en Grèce ancienne*, ed. Marcel Detienne, 159–87. Lille: Presses Universitaires de Lille.

Loy, William G. 1970. *The Land of Nestor: A Physical Geography of the Southwest Peloponnese.* Foreign Field Research Program, report no. 34, Washington, D.C.: National Academy of Sciences.

Malkin, Irad. 1989. "Delphoi and the Founding of Social Order in Archaic Greece." *Metis* 4:129–53.

———. 1994. "Inside and Outside: Colonization and the Formation of the Mother City." *Annali di Archeologia e Storia Antica* n.s. 1:1–9.

———. 1998. *The Returns of Odysseus: Colonization and Ethnicity.* Berkeley: University of California Press.

Manning, Sturt W. 1992. "Archaeology and the World of Homer: Introduction to a Past and Present Discipline." In *Homer: Readings and Images*, ed. C. Emlyn-Jones, L. Hardwick and J. Purkis, 117–142. London: Duckworth in association with the Open University.

McDonald, William A., and George R. Rapp, Jr., eds. 1972. *Minnesota Messenia Expedition: Reconstructing a Bronze Age Regional Environment.* Minneapolis: University of Minnesota Press.

———, D. E. Coulson, and John Rosser, eds. 1983. *Excavations at Nichoria in Southwest Greece, vol. 3: Dark Age and Byzantine Occupation.* Minneapolis: University of Minnesota Press.

———, and Nancy C. Wilkie, eds. 1992. *Excavations at Nichoria in Southwest*

Greece, vol. 2: The Bronze Age Occupation. Minneapolis: University of Minnesota Press.

Mee, C. B. 1984. "The Mycenaeans and Troy." In *The Trojan War: Its Historicity and Context,* ed. Lin Foxhall and J. K. Davies, 45–56. Bristol: Bristol Classical Press.

Millett, P. 1984. "Hesiod and His World." *PCPS* 30:84–115.

Morgan, Catherine. 1988. "Corinth, The Corinthian Gulf and Western Greece during the Eighth Century B.C." *BSA* 83:313–38.

———. 1993. "The Origins of Pan-Hellenism." In *Greek Sanctuaries: New Approaches,* ed. N. Marinatos and R. Hägg, 18–44. London: Routledge.

Morris, Ian. 1986. "The Use and Abuse of Homer." *CA* 5:81–138.

———. 1987. *Burial and Ancient Society: The Rise of the Greek City-State.* Cambridge: Cambridge University Press.

———. 1995. "Periodization and the Heroes: Inventing a Dark Age." In *Inventing Ancient Culture: Historicism, Periodization, and the Ancient World,* ed. M. Golden and P. Toohey, 96–131. London: Routledge.

Morris, Sarah. 1992. *Daidalos and the Origins of Greek Art.* Princeton: Princeton University Press.

Mountjoy, P. A. 1986. *Mycenaean Decorated Pottery: A Guide to Identification.* Göteberg: Paul Astrom.

Murray, Oswyn. 1983. "The Symposium as Social Organisation." In *The Greek Renaissance of the Eighth Century B.C.: Tradition and Innovation,* ed. Robin Hägg, 195–99. Stockholm: Swedish Institute in Athens.

———, ed. 1994. *Sympotica: A Symposium on the Symposion,* rev. ed. Oxford: Clarendon Press.

Musgrave, Jonathan H. 1991. "The Late Helladic IIIC Intramural Burials at Lefkandi, Euboea." *BSA* 86:273–96.

Mylonas, George E. 1966. *Mycenae and the Mycenaean Age.* Princeton: Princeton University Press.

———. 1983. *Mycenae Rich in Gold.* Athens: Ekdotike Athenon.

Naveh, Joseph. 1982. *The Early History of the Alphabet.* Leiden: Brill.

Negbi, Ora. 1992. "Early Phoenician Presence in the Mediterranean Islands: A Reappraisal." *AJA* 96:599–615.

Nicholls, R. V. 1958–59. "Old Smyrna: The Iron Age Fortifications and Associated Remains on the City Perimeter." *BSA* 53–54:36–137.

Ong, W. J. 1967. *The Presence of the Word.* New Haven: Yale University Press.

———. 1982. *Orality and Literacy: The Technologizing of the Word.* London: Methuen.

Osborne, Robin. 1987. *Classical Landscape with Figures.* London: George Philip.

———. 1996. *Greece in the Making, 1200–479 B.C.* London: Routledge.

Papachatzis, Nicos. 1978. *Mycenae-Epidaurus-Tiryns-Nauplion.* Athens: Ekdotike Athenon.

Polignac, François de. 1994. "Mediation, Competition, and Sovereignty: The Evolution of Rural Sanctuaries in Geometric Greece." In *Placing the Gods: Sanctuaries and the Sacred Space in Ancient Greece,* ed. Susan E. Alcock and Robin Osborne, 3–18. Oxford: Clarendon Press.

———. 1995. *Cults, Territory, and the Origins of the Greek City-State,* tr. J. Lloyd. Chicago: University of Chicago Press.

Popham, M. R. 1991. "Pylos: Reflections on the Date of Its Destruction and on Its Iron Age Reoccupation." *OJA* 10.3:315–24.

———, and L. H. Sackett. 1968. *Excavations at Lefkandi, Euboea, 1964–66: A Preliminary Report.* London: British School at Athens.

———, M. R., E. Touloupa, and L. H. Sackett. 1982. "Further Excavations of the Toumba Cemetery at Lefkandi, 1981." *BSA* 77:213–48.

———, P. G. Calligas, and L. H. Sackett. 1988–89. "Further Excavations of the Toumba Cemetery at Lefkandi, 1984 and 1986: A Preliminary Report." *AR* 35:117–29.

———, M. R., L. H. Sackett, and P. G. Themelis, eds. 1980. *Lefkandi I: The Iron Age.* London: British School at Athens.

———, P. G. Calligas, and L. H. Sackett, eds. 1993. *Lefkandi II: The Proto-geometric Building at Toumba.* London: British School at Athens.

Powell, Barry. 1989. "Why Was the Greek Alphabet Invented? The Epigraphical Evidence." *CA* 8:321–50.

———. 1991. *Homer and the Origin of the Greek Alphabet.* Cambridge: Cambridge University Press.

Prufer, Rob. 1993. "The Birth of Colonial Communities and the Death of Their Denizens: The Organization of Funerary Space and the Evolution of Social Structure in Archaic Syracuse and Megara Hyblaea." M.A. Thesis, University of Washington.

Qviller, Bjorn. 1981. "The Dynamics of the Homeric Society." *Symbolae Osloenses* 56:109–55.

Raaflaub, Kurt. 1991. "Homer und die Geschichte des 8.Jh.s v.Chr." In *Zweihundert Jahre Homer-Forschung*, ed. J. Latacz, 205–56. Stuttgart und Leipzig: B. G. Teubner.

———. 1993. "Homer to Solon: The Rise of the Polis." In *The Ancient Greek City-State*, ed. M. Herman Hansen. Copenhagen: Royal Danish Academy of Arts and Sciences.

Rapp, George, Jr., and S. Aschenbrenner, eds. 1978. *Excavations at Nichoria in Southwest Greece, vol. 1: Site, Environs, and Techniques.* Minneapolis: University of Minnesota Press.

Renfrew, Colin. 1972. *The Emergence of Civilisation: The Cyclades and the Aegean in the Third Millennium B.C.* London: Methuen.

———. 1979. "Systems Collapse as Social Transformation." In *Transformations: Mathematical Approaches to Culture Changes*, ed. C. Renfrew and K. L. Cooke, 481–506. New York: Academic Press.

———. 1987. *Archaeology and Language: The Puzzle of Indo-European Origins.* Cambridge: Cambridge University Press.

Rhodes, P. J. 1986. *The Greek City States: A Source Book.* London: Croom Helm.

Robb, Kevin. 1994. *Literacy and Paideia in Ancient Greece.* New York: Oxford University Press.

Robinson, H. S. 1965. *The Urban Development of Ancient Corinth.* Athens: American School of Classical Studies at Athens.

Roebuck, Carl. 1955. "The Early Ionian League." *CP* 50:26–40.

———. 1959. *Ionian Trade and Colonization.* New York: Archaeological Institute of America.

———. 1972. "Some Aspects of Urbanization in Corinth." *Hesperia* 41:96–127.

Runnels, C. 1982. "Flaked-Stone Artifacts in Greece during the Historical Period." *JFA* 9:363–73.

Rutter, Jeremy B. 1975. "Ceramic Evidence for Northern Intruders in Southern Greece at the Beginning of the Late Helladic IIIC Period." *AJA* 79:17-32.

———. 1993. "Review of Aegean Prehistory II: The Prepalatial Bronze Age of the Southern and Central Greek Mainland." *AJA* 97:745–97.

Sahlins, Marshall. 1963. "Poor Man, Rich Man, Big Man, Chief: Political Types in Melanesia and Polynesia." *Comparative Studies in Society and History* 5:285–303.

Salmon, J. B. 1984. *Wealthy Corinth: A History of the City to 338 B.C.* Oxford: Clarendon Press.

Sandars, N. K. 1971. "From Bronze to Iron Age: A Sequel to a Sequel." In *The European Community in Later Prehistory: Studies in Honour of C. F. C. Hawkes*, ed. J. Boardman, M. A. Brown, and T. G. E. Powell, 3–29. Totowa, N.J: Rowman and Littlefield.

———. 1978. *The Sea Peoples: Warriors of the Ancient Mediterranean, 1250–1150 B.C.* London: Thames and Hudson.

———. 1983. "North and South at the End of the Mycenaean Age: Aspects of an Old Problem." *OJA* 2.1:43–68.

Sargent, Thelma, tr. 1975. *The Homeric Hymns.* New York: Norton.

Sax, A. 1970. "The Social Dimensions of Mortuary Practice." Ph.D. Thesis, University of Michigan.

Schliemann, Heinrich. 1878. *Mycenae: A Narrative of Researches and Discoveries at Mycenae and Tiryns.* New York: Scribner, Armstrong and Co.

Sealey, R. 1960. "Regionalism in Archaic Athens." *Historia* 9:155–80.

Shelmerdine, Cynthia. 1973. "The Pylos Ma Tablets Reconsidered." *AJA* 77:261–75.

———. 1997. "Review of Aegean Prehistory VI: The Palatial Bronze Age of the Southern and Central Greek Mainland." *AJA* 101:537–85.

Sherratt, A. 1982. "Mobile Resources: Settlement and Exchange in Early Agricultural Europe." In *Ranking, Resources and Exchange*, ed. C. Renfrew and S. Shennan, 13–26. Cambridge: Cambridge University Press.

Sherratt, E. S. 1980. "Regional Variations in the Pottery of Late Helladic IIIB." *BSA* 75:175–202.

Sinclair, T. A. 1966. *Hesiod: Works and Days.* Hildesheim: Georg Olms.

Small, David B. 1997. "Can We Move Forward? Comments on the Current Debate over Handmade Burnished Ware." *JMA* 10: 223–228.

Snodgrass, Anthony M. 1971. *The Dark Age of Greece.* Edinburgh: Edinburgh University Press.

———. 1980a. *Archaic Greece: The Age of Experiment.* London: J. M. Dent and Sons.

———. 1980b. "Iron and Early Metallurgy in the Mediterranean." In *The Coming of the Age of Iron*, ed. T. A. Wertime and J. D. Muhly, 335–74. New Haven: Yale University Press.

———. 1983. "The Greek Early Iron Age: A Reappraisal." *Dialogues d'Histoire ancienne* 9:73-86.

———. 1985. "The Site of Askra." In *La Beotie Antique*, ed. G. Argoud and P. Roesch, 87–95. Paris: Editions du Centre national de la recherche scientifique.

———. 1987. *An Archaeology of Greece: The Present State and Future Scope of a Discipline.* Berkeley: University of California Press.

———. 1988. "The Archaeology of the Hero." *Annali dei Seminario di studi del mondo classico e del Mediterraneo antico* 10:19–26.

Starr, C. G. 1957. "The Early Greek City-State." *La Parola del Passato* 12:97–108.

———. 1961a. "The Decline of the Early Greek Kings." *Historia* 10:129–38.

———. 1961b. *The Origins of Greek Civilization, 1100–650 B.C.* New York: Knopf.

————. 1977. *The Economic and Social Growth of Early Greece, 800–500 B.C.* New York: Oxford University Press.

————. 1986. *Individual and Community: The Rise of the Polis, 800–500 B.C.* New York: Oxford University Press.

————. 1992. "History and Archaeology in the Early First Millennium B.C." In *Greece between East and West: 10th–8th Centuries B.C.*, ed. G. Kopke and I. Tokumaru, 1–6. Mainz: Philipp von Zabern.

Stubbings, F. H. 1947. "The Mycenaean Pottery of Attica." *BSA* 42:1–75.

Tainter, Joseph. 1988. *The Collapse of Complex Societies.* Cambridge: Cambridge University Press.

Taylour, Lord William. 1983. *The Mycenaeans*, rev. ed. London: Thames and Hudson.

Thomas, C. G. 1970a. *Homer's History: Mycenaean or Dark Age?* New York: Holt, Rinehard and Winston.

————. 1970b. "A Mycenaean Hegemony? A Reconsideration." *JHS* 90: 184–90.

————. 1976. "From Wanax to Basileus: Kingship in the Greek Dark Age." *Hispania Antigua* 6:187–206.

————. 1982. "Theseus and Synoicism." *SMEA* 23:337–49.

————. 1993. "The Homeric Epics: Strata or a Spectrum?" *Colby Quarterly* 29:273–82.

————. 1995. "The Components of Political Identity in Mycenaean Greece." In *Politeia: Society and State in the Aegean Bronze Age.* Fifth International Aegean Conference, vol. 2, ed. Wolf-Dietrich Niemeier and Robert Laffineur. *Aegaeum* 12:349–54.

————, and K. Webb. 1993. "From Orality to Rhetoric: An Intellectual Transformation." In *Persuasion: Greek Rhetoric in Action*, ed. I. Worthington, 3–25. London: Routledge.

Thomas, Rosalind. 1989. *Oral Tradition and Written Record in Classical Athens.* Cambridge: Cambridge University Press.

————. 1992. *Literacy and Orality in Ancient Greece.* Cambridge: Cambridge University Press.

Tiverios, Michalis A. 1995. "Secrets of Sindos," in articles on archaeological topics in daily Greek newspapers by Carol Zerner of the American School of Classical Studies for the electronic list *Aegeanet*; week of 26.ix.95–2.x.95.

Tomlinson, R. A. 1976. *Greek Sanctuaries.* New York: St. Martins Press.

Tsountas, Ch. and J. Irving Manatt. 1897. *The Mycenaean Age: A Study of the Monuments and Culture of Pre-Homeric Greece.* Boston: Houghton Mifflin and Co.

van Andel, T. H. and C. Runnels. 1987. *Beyond the Acropolis: A Rural Greek Past.* Stanford: Stanford University Press.

van Effenterre, Henri. 1974. *La Seconde Fin du Monde.* Toulouse: Editions des Hesperides.

Vanschoonwinkel, Jacques. 1991. *l'Égée et la Méditerranée orientale à la fin du IIe millénaire.* Louvain-la-Neuve: Département d'archéologie et d'histoire de l'art, Collège Érasme and Brown University: Center for Old World Archaeology and Art.

Vansina, Jan. 1965. *Oral Tradition: A Study in Historical Methodology*, tr. H. M. Wright. Chicago: Aldine.

Vermeule, Emily. 1964. *Greece in the Bronze Age.* Chicago: University of Chicago Press.

————. 1979. *Aspects of Death in Early Greek Art and Poetry*. Berkeley: University of California Press.

Wace, A. J. B. 1949. *Mycenae: An Archaeological History and Guide*. Princeton: Princeton University Press.

Wade-Gery, H. T. 1958. "Hesiod." In *Essays in Greek History*, 1–16. Oxford: Blackwell.

Wallace, P. W. 1974. "Hesiod and the Valley of the Muses." *GRBS* 15: 5–24.

————. 1985. "The Tomb of Hesiod and the Treasury of Minyas at Orkhomenos." In *Proceedings of the Third International Conference on Boiotian Antiquities*, ed. J. M. Fossey and H. Giroux, 165–79. Amsterdam: J. C. Gieben.

Wardle, K. A. 1980. "Excavations at Assiros, 1975–9." *BSA* 75:229–265.

Watrous, L. Vance. 1994. "Review of Aegean Prehistory III: Crete from Earliest Prehistory through the Protopalatial Period." *AJA* 98:695–753.

Wender, D., tr. 1973. *Hesiod: Theogony, Works and Days; Theognis: Elegies*. Harmondsworth: Penguin.

West, M. L. 1966. *Hesiod: Theogony*. Oxford: Clarendon Press.

————. 1978. *Works and Days*. Oxford: Clarendon Press.

————. 1988. "The Rise of the Greek Epic." *JHS* 108:151–72.

Whitley, James. 1991a. "Social Diversity in Dark Age Greece." *BSA* 86:341–65.

————. 1991b. *Style and Society in Dark Age Greece: The Changing Face of a Pre-Literate Society, 1100–700 B.C.* Cambridge: Cambridge University Press.

Will, Édouard. 1955. *Korinthiaka*. Paris: E. de Boccard.

Wright, James. 1987. "Death and Power at Mycenae." In *Thanatos: Les Coutumes Funéraires en Egée à l'âge du Bronze*, ed. Laffineur. *Aegaeum* 1:171–84.

————, et al. 1990. "The Nemea Valley Archaeological Project: A Preliminary Report." *Hesperia* 59.4:579–659.

INDEX

Achaea: haven for refugees, 19–20, 32; expulsion of the Ionians, 72

Achaeans: militarism of, 176n9; among the Sea Peoples, 169

Adriatic Sea: 113, 126, 134

Aegean: xv, xxv, xxxi, 14, 17, 23, 67–70, 72, 86, 134–36, 166; seismic activity, 23; spread of iron technology, 70–71; Greek lake, 79–81, 159

agriculture: 10–11, 24–26, 108; village nucleation, 10; systems collapse, 24–26; land tenure in post-plague France, 76–77; use of slaves, 78, 152; land shortage or stenochoria, 125; hired help, 152; peasant farmer's outlook, 153–55

Ahhiyawa, Ahhiyawans: 79, 163

alphabet: xx–xxi, xxv, 89, 109–10, 141–42, 160; epic poetry, xxxi, 109–10, 142, 153, 160; Phoenician origin, 109, 178n8, 141–42; Nestor's Cup, 110–11

Amenhotep III (Egyptian Pharaoh): 6, 14

Amphidamas of Chalcis: 152, 160, 165

Anatolia (Asia Minor): xv, xxiii, xxvi, xxx–xxxi, 1, 23, 71, 72–84, 86, 91, 112, 118, 129, 149–50, 157, 159, 163, 164, 165, 167, 169; Phrygia and Lydia, 80, 140–41

Androclus (leader of Ionian Migration and founder of Ephesus): 72, 82, 84

Apollo: 134, 156; Linear B evidence, 137; Oracle at Delphi, 139

Arcadia: 3, 19–20; haven for refugees, 20, 55

archaeology: xxii–xxviii, 8, 88

Ares: 156; Linear B evidence, 137

Argolid, Argive Plain: xxv–xxvi, 2, 16, 19, 30, 65, 66; dominated by Mycenae, 13, 26, 33–34, 61; late-thirteenth-century destructions, 16–17, 30; population, 16; Heraclidae banished from, 20; twelfth-century conditions, 25–31; twelfth-century depopulation, 27; Athenian contacts, 65, 68, 72; Argive refugees in Attica, 78

Argos: xxiii, 15, 16, 32, 168; dominated by Mycenae, 15

aristocracy: 81–83, 97, 103, 110, 166, 171; Athens, 81, 83; Ionian Migration, 81; decline of kingship, 83; Ionian towns, 83; Lefkandi, 103; trade, 108; symposion, 110, 170; Corinth, 123; colonization, 133

Aristotle: 81, 120, 148–49

Artemis: 111, 156; Linear B evidence, 137

Ascra: xxxii, 130, 144–61; kome, 145; Hesiod, 145–58, 165; location of, 145–46; site, 145–49; Protogeometric settlement of, 147; settlement on Pyrgaki, 147; dominated by Thespiai, 148–49; fortifications on Pyrgaki, 148; farm village life, 151–56; craft specialization, 153, 159; peasant society, 153–55

Asia Minor. *See* Anatolia

Athena: 108, 111; Linear B evidence, 137, 168

Athens: xviii, xxiii, xxxi, 1, 17, 32, 54, 56, 60–84, 86, 92, 99, 105, 116, 118, 148, 159, 160, 163–71 passim; survivor of twelfth-century destructions, 17, 32,

CAROL G. THOMAS
is Professor of Ancient Greek History
at the University of Washington. Her books include
*Decoding Ancient History: A Toolkit for the Historian
as Detective* (with D. Wick); *Myth Becomes History;
Progress into the Past,* 2nd edition (with William A.
McDonald); and *Paths from Ancient Greece.*
She is two-time president of the
Association of Ancient
Historians.

CRAIG CONANT
is a long-time student of ancient
Greek history and works as a records
manager for the Environmental
Protection Agency in Seattle,
Washington.